John W. Elrod teaches philosophy
at Iowa State University.

BEING AND EXISTENCE IN
KIERKEGAARD'S PSEUDONYMOUS WORKS

John W. Elrod

Being and Existence in
Kierkegaard's Pseudonymous Works

PRINCETON UNIVERSITY PRESS, NEW JERSEY

Library of Congress Cataloging in Publication Data will
be found on the last printed page of this book.

Publication of this book has been aided by a grant from the
Andrew W. Mellon Foundation.

This book has been composed in Linotype Baskerville.

Printed in the United States of America
by Princeton University Press,
Princeton, New Jersey

To Mimi

Contents

Acknowledgments

I WOULD like to express my sincere appreciation to Professor John Macquarrie, Oxford University, and Professor Paul Lehman, Union Theological Seminary, Richmond, for their helpful criticisms of the first half of the book.

I would also like to express my great indebtedness to Professor James A. Martin, Jr., Columbia University, and the late Professor Daniel D. Williams, Union Theological Seminary, New York, for their guidance and support in the writing of the book, and also to Professor Williams for bringing the book to the attention of Princeton University Press.

I also want to thank my editor at Princeton University Press, Ms. Carol Orr, for her most generous assistance in the editing of this book.

And to Professor Richard Van Iten, Iowa State University, I am also grateful for his interest in the book and for his criticisms of the last chapter. I must also express my thanks to Iowa State University for defraying the typing costs in preparing the manuscript for publication.

And, finally, to my wife, Mimi, without whose patience and encouragement I could never have completed this work, I am most grateful of all.

John W. Elrod

Abbreviations

THE following abbreviations designate works by Søren Kierkegaard from which more than one passage is quoted.

CD	*The Concept of Dread*
CUP	*Concluding Unscientific Postscript to the Philosophical Fragments*
DODE	*De Omnibus Dubitandum Est* or *Johannes Climacus*
E/O, I, II	*Either/Or*, volumes I and II
FT	*Fear and Trembling*
PF	*Philosophical Fragments*
R	*Repetition*
SKJ	*The Journals of Søren Kierkegaard*
SKJP	*Søren Kierkegaard's Journals and Papers*
SKP	*Søren Kierkegaards Papirer*
SLW	*Stages on Life's Way*
SUD	*Sickness Unto Death*

BEING AND EXISTENCE IN
KIERKEGAARD'S PSEUDONYMOUS WORKS

Introduction

MORE often than not, passing remarks are just that and no more. However, they sometimes serve as important clues or hints to a man's thought. There are obvious risks involved in paying them close attention, for it is all too easy a matter to make too much of such remarks. Those coming from the pen of Søren Kierkegaard are no exception. Indeed, given Kierkegaard's flair for the ironic, one must be especially cautious in assaying the significance of his passing remarks. On at least two occasions, Kierkegaard suggests that ontology should be the main task of those who propose to understand man and his existence. In both cases, we are left without amplification or justification. Two possibilities occurred to me. Either Kierkegaard was challenging his reader to discover the ontology already at work in his writings, or he was suggesting a priority for future philosophical investigation. It also occurred to me that these passing remarks concerning ontology were just that and nothing more. But after a long study of the pseudonymous writings, I was led to conclude that these were not simply casual, off-hand remarks but that they reflected one of Kierkegaard's fundamental interests. Indeed, I became convinced that Kierkegaard was not only interested in the ontological question but in fact that he developed an ontology in the pseudonyms in his writings on the self. I further was convinced that this ontology functions as the unifying principle of his many descriptions of the three stages of existence in the pseudonyms. The essay which follows is an argument in support of these three points. In the following introductory remarks, I would like briefly to amplify them.

First, my study of the pseudonyms led me to conclude

that they contain an ontology which is not accidentally present but essential to the overall project of the pseudonymous works. Initially, I was fascinated by the imaginative descriptions of the various possibilities open to human existence appearing in the character sketches and essays in *Either/Or, Fear and Trembling, Repetition,* and *Stages on Life's Way.* I was only subsequently struck by what appeared to be the quite different task in *The Concept of Dread* and *Sickness Unto Death* of ontologically accounting for these different existence possibilities which he had aesthetically described. These latter two books, while concerned with the task of description, seemed more preoccupied with answering the question: How is it possible for human existence to be the way that it is? In these two books, in particular, Kierkegaard seems not so concerned to say, "My dear reader, these are the existence possibilities open to you; take your choice." Rather, he was struggling with the more fundamental problem of discovering the ontological structures which make these different modes of existing possible at all. Only later did it occur to me that Kierkegaard was trying to carry out two tasks simultaneously in the pseudonyms. On the one hand, he was attempting simply to point out to his reader the different types of existence possibilities open to man. And, on the other hand, he was concerned with carrying out the more fundamental philosophical task of ontologically accounting for human existence which he was also trying accurately to describe. In short, Kierkegaard was developing philosophically an ontology which would account for the occurrence and relations of the stages of existence described in the pseudonyms.

Kierkegaard's stages of existence are familiar to the most casual reader of his books. One of the chief objectives of the pseudonyms seems to be an in-depth investigation and description of these three existence possibilities. And time and again, we have been led through discussions of these stages by students of Kierkegaard who are content to limit themselves to this sort of uncritical analysis. But such an

4

approach leaves perplexing questions unturned. We may ask, for example, how it is possible for these to be human possibilities at all. And why are there three rather than four, five, or fifteen such possibilities? Further, the issue of how these possibilities are related to each other remains problematic. Are they mutually exclusive options? That is, must an individual choose either pleasure, duty, or faith as his fundamental life orientation? Or can they be conceived as a unity? Is the individual who attains an *eternal happiness* one whose pursuit of pleasure is enriched by duty and one whose duty is fulfilled in faith? This seems to be the position Kierkegaard himself advocates. But then the following question appears: How is it possible for the realization of these three possibilities to be unified in a single man? And, finally, is the description of these possibilities of existence carried through from a philosophical or theological point of view? Is Kierkegaard working in the pseudonyms as a philosopher or a theologian? Or is he trying to combine the two in the manner of Augustine in order to create his own version of a Christian Philosophy? My argument is that it is precisely these issues with which Kierkegaard is struggling in the development of his ontology.

As I have indicated, Kierkegaard himself states in his journal that one of the most important tasks before modern philosophy is the construction of an ontology. Given the relative isolation of this remark along with his failure programmatically to set forth this ontology, many interpreters have concluded that no such ontology exists in his writings. This remark, along with another in *Stages on Life's Way*, is likely to be regarded as a casual hint of an appropriate undertaking for a later philosopher. And, indeed, it has been argued by some that what Kierkegaard had in mind was in fact taken up by philosophers like Heidegger, Sartre, and Jaspers. But it would not be unlike Kierkegaard to make such a suggestion and then cryptically follow it up himself, leaving his unwary reader to conclude that this task must be done later by someone other than himself. This is precisely what I think Kierkegaard has done. These casual remarks reflect not a directive for future philosophical inquiry but a task which Kierkegaard himself undertook. My reading of the pseudonyms has convinced me that, in spite of his polemics against philosophical speculation, he has intentionally developed and submerged in his pseudonyms an ontology which philosophically accounts for the vast topography of human existence described in the major portions of his pseudonyms.

Anyone who has seriously studied the pseudonyms is familiar with Kierkegaard's demonic delight in confusing his reader. He deliberately goes out of his way to make it difficult to understand him, and he has warned us that the most obvious routes into his writings are most likely not the correct ones. So, following his own warning not always to take him literally or at face value, I have embarked upon an interpretation of the pseudonyms which requires that we take this enigmatic Dane at his word and expect the unexpected—in this case, the presence of an ontology in his writings. In the opening chapter, I argue that there are sound philosophical reasons for including an ontology in his writings and, from Kierkegaard's point of view, sound reasons for obscuring its presence in these same writings.

The second conclusion which I reached in my study of the pseudonyms is that Kierkegaard's ontology is developed in his writings on the self. Kierkegaard never refers to the self as the ontological foundation of human existence. Further, he does not formally show how human existence is constituted and determined by the self. He is cryptic, if not deceptive, about all this for reasons which I shall explore in the opening chapter of the essay. But it is nevertheless the case that Kierkegaard understood human existence as formally and substantively constituted by the self.

Initially, my attention was directed to the importance of the self by the work of Helmut Fahrenbach[1] and Johannes

---

[1] Helmut Fahrenbach, *Kierkegaards existenzdialektische Ethik* (Frankfort: V. Klostermann, 1968).

Sløk.[2] Both recognized that Kierkegaard was attempting not only to describe the different possibilities open to existence but also to develop formally a philosophical theory of man, which they saw in Kierkegaard's writings on the self and which they called an anthropology. Fahrenbach was also helpful in alerting me to the dynamic character of the self which involved a dialectical relation between freedom and consciousness. My own position that the self constitutes an ontology which is determinative of Kierkegaard's concept and description of existence reflects a strong departure from Fahrenbach, and especially from Sløk who argues that Kierkegaard's self is useful only with respect to understanding the man who does not exist before God. I will strongly disagree with Sløk's claim that the self is not useful in understanding the Christian who exists before God. A major portion of the second part of the essay attempts to disclose how the self as an ontological structure is a necessary condition for the emergence and realization of Christianity as a human possibility.

It should also be noted that my claim that there is an ontology in the pseudonyms is not entirely original. Both Michael Wyschogrod and Calvin Schrag have already advanced this argument. Through comparative studies of Kierkegaard and the early Heidegger, both have attempted to expose an ontology in the pseudonyms. Wyschogrod[3] correctly argues that Kierkegaard's basic existential interests do not allow him to assume an open and objective interest in ontological problems, but that it is mistaken to overlook the basic ontological position which underlies and unifies the shifting points of view represented by the various periods and pseudonymous authors. He has also pointed out that every existential situation described by Kierkegaard has at its basis an ontological structure generating the very

[2] Johannes Sløk, "Das existenzphilosophische Motiv im Denken von Kierkegaard," *Studia Theologica*, IX (1956), 116-130.

[3] Michael Wyschogrod, *Kierkegaard and Heidegger* (New York: Humanities Press, 1954).

7

situation being described. But Wyschogrod is mistaken, however, in assuming that Kierkegaard's ontology includes a concept of Pure Being which, when opposed to its opposite, temporal being, generates the existential situations and possibilities described. As I will show in my discussion of Kierkegaard's philosophical method in the opening chapter, no such concept is permissible in his ontology because it would require a kind of reasoning capacity unavailable to finite human beings who are submerged in existence.

Calvin Schrag[4] has attempted to show that the methodology of *Being and Time* as well as its phenomenological ontology are both implicitly present in the pseudonymous writings. He approaches Kierkegaard explicitly from the point of view of *Being and Time*, allowing it to determine the ontological structure of Kierkegaard's writings. Therefore, the concepts of anxiety, finitude, time, history, guilt, choice, death, conscience, authenticity, and inauthenticity are extracted from Kierkegaard's pseudonyms and arranged in such a way as to give the appearance that Kierkegaard is best understood as an anticipation of the early Heidegger. While these themes occupy important roles in the pseudonyms, and while it is possible to arrange them so as to present the appearance that Kierkegaard is a forerunner of Heideggerian ontology, it is my view that by orienting Kierkegaard toward Heidegger, Schrag, along with Wyschogrod, fails to perceive the self-structure as that which really constitutes the ontological foundation of the pseudonyms. Moreover, both completely overlook the dialectically developing character of human existence which is exclusively grounded in Kierkegaard's notion of the self.

The final conclusion emerging from my study of the pseudonyms is that Kierkegaard as a thinker continues to elude us. Over a century after his death, we are still in search of a unified interpretation of his books, journals, and papers. No one has yet succeeded in writing an interpretation

---

[4] Calvin Schrag, *Existence and Freedom* (Chicago: Northwestern University Press, 1961).

which does justice to the rich diversity of philosophical and theological themes and issues in Kierkegaard's work. There is first the problem of the unity of the pseudonyms. Is there a unifying thread binding them all into a coherent and intelligible unity? This problem is surpassed in complexity by the question concerning the relation of the pseudonymous writings to those published under his own name. How are the *Edifying Discourses* and the later more straightforward theological works related to the pseudonyms? Are they so different that we cannot speak of a relation at all? Must we limit ourselves to speaking of *earlier* and *later* Kierkegaards? Or is it possible to discover a key which will unlock the mystery of the unity of these two Kierkegaards?

In the following essay, I do not attempt to resolve the latter problem of the relation of the pseudonymous and non-pseudonymous Kierkegaards. My undertaking is considerably more modest. I concentrate exclusively on the pseudonyms and argue that the concept of the self in the pseudonyms provides a philosophical principle of unity which enabled Kierkegaard to develop a coherent, systematic, and unified view of human existence.

The book is divided into two parts. Part One is concerned to elucidate the ontology present in Kierkegaard's pseudonyms, and Part Two attempts to show how this ontology makes possible and unifies the aesthetic, moral, and religious modes of existence. In the opening chapter, I argue that Kierkegaard was fully aware of the importance of grounding his concept and description of existence ontologically and that he provides his ontology in the pseudonyms. But at the same time Kierkegaard's recognition of man's vocation as the discovery and appropriation of his being prevented him from engaging in a straightforward analysis of the ontological question. Kierkegaard's desire to lure his reader into a practical rather than abstract or theoretical involvement with philosophical problems prevented him from writing a book with a title like *The Ontological Foundation of Human Existence*. But at the same time Kierkegaard recognized that his shifting of the style of philosophical reflection from the theoretical to the practical did not preclude the possibility, indeed the necessity, of developing an ontology.

The second and third chapters are devoted to a reconstruction of this ontology by drawing it together from the various corners of his pseudonymous writings on the self. In Chapter II, I discuss Kierkegaard's conception of the self as a synthesis of opposites and in Chapter III his conception of the self as spirit. My argument is that, taken together, these two aspects of the self constitute an ontology of human being.

In the second part of the essay, I argue that the self and existence are not synonymous. The self is the being of the individual, and the stages of existence are constituted by the individual's ethical responsibility for understanding and actualizing his being. The ethical task of understanding and actualizing one's self (being) leads the individual on a long journey over the vast topography of human existence. Chapter IV attempts to show how ethics, thus understood, is grounded in Kierkegaard's ontology and how it assumes the task of achieving self-understanding. Chapters V and VI engage in an analysis of how Kierkegaard's ontology makes ethico-religious existence in both its forms possible. And the final thrust of my argument in the essay is that religious existence is the deepening and fulfillment of the ethical task of understanding and actualizing one's self (being) and not a contravention of it.

PART ONE

KIERKEGAARD'S ONTOLOGY

CHAPTER I

Methodological Foundations

THE SYSTEMATIC FOUNDATION IN KIERKEGAARD'S THOUGHT

THE last decade witnessed the waning of both Neo-orthodox Theology and Existentialist Philosophy. The fortunes of Søren Kierkegaard's thought were deeply embedded in the dissipation of these two movements. Barth's identification of his notion of the wholly otherness of God with the thought of Kierkegaard, on the one hand, and Heidegger and Sartre's designation of Kierkegaard's concepts of anxiety and existence as the proper subject matter for philosophical reflection, on the other, unfortunately pulled the Kierkegaardian corpus in two opposing directions. These theological and philosophical investments in Kierkegaard's thought molded the two major interpretive approaches to his thought, which were followed in both Continental and English Kierkegaard scholarship from 1930 to 1960.[1] With respect to the pseudonymous corpus, this meant that one was forced into *choosing either a theological or a philosophical Kierkegaard.* The choice involved not only accept-

[1] The autobiographical-psychological approach should also be mentioned. It attempts to understand Kierkegaard's thought in terms of his personal history and psychology. One of the earliest examples of this approach is Walter Lowrie's *Kierkegaard* (Harper Torchbook, New York: Harper and Row, 1962). A more recent example is Josiah Thompson's *The Lonely Labyrinth: Kierkegaard's Pseudonymous Works* (Carbondale, Ill.: Southern Illinois University Press, 1967). While this approach is interesting because of Kierkegaard's bizarre personal history and neurotic personality, it is not particularly helpful in understanding and resolving the complex issues and problems in his thought.

ing an already established interpretive perspective but also concentrating on certain of the books and dismissing others. The theologians, for example, turned to *Philosophical Fragments* and *Training in Christianity*, the philosophers to *Either/Or* and *The Concept of Dread*, while both worked on *The Sickness Unto Death* and Kierkegaard's greatest work, *Concluding Unscientific Postscript*.

The philosophers and theologians are not to be faulted for this double interpretation of Kierkegaard, because the structure of the total Kierkegaardian corpus itself suggests this duality. First, there is the sharp division between the aesthetic-philosophical pseudonymous corpus and the more religiously and theologically oriented books, which Kierkegaard, with the major exception of *Training in Christianity*, published under his own name. Second, the subject matter of the pseudonymous corpus can also be divided along theological and philosophical lines. Theologians naturally gravitated toward Kierkegaard's discussions of subjects like God, Christ, faith, sin, and repentance; and philosophers moved toward his analyses of subjects like existence, self, anxiety, freedom, consciousness, and ethics. Unfortunately, Kierkegaard is less than explicit about the relations between these two subject matters, and, therefore, the division of interest and research in subsequent scholarship was a natural development.

It should not be denied that this division of interest produced two extremely rich and resourceful traditions of thought. But to the extent that Kierkegaard is identified with either of these traditions their dissipation has meant the subsiding of interest in, and the importance of, Kierkegaard himself for contemporary thought. The loss of the momentum of these two movements, then, has produced an unfortunate loss of interest in Kierkegaard as well. But the exhaustion of these two movements has also provided the opportunity for attempting to see him in a new light, and to this end, two new, and not irreconcilable, fronts are developing in Kierkegaard scholarship. The first one is historically oriented and seeks to understand Kierkegaard's relation to German and Danish Idealism.[2]

The second one is attempting to transcend the philosophical-theological division in Kierkegaard's writings in order to see them as unified by an underlying system of some sort within the writings themselves. Until now Kierkegaardians have reacted in horror to the claim that some sort of system is present in Kierkegaard's writings and that it can be disclosed by a discerning and unprejudiced eye. Some still wince at the thought but the idea that a Christology,[3] an ontology,[4] or an anthropology[5] of some sort lies hidden in and unifies this massive corpus is finding increasing acceptance among Kierkegaard scholars. Ultimately those committed to this approach to Kierkegaard argue for either a theological or a philosophical interpretation of his thought, but they are all in agreement that his corpus is characterized fundamentally by a systematic understanding of human existence.

To speak of a system in Kierkegaard's authorship is not to suggest either that the writings themselves have a systematic structure or that Kierkegaard's style has a systematic character. His ideas do not possess a logical and necessary inter-relatedness such that the outcome of his work appears as a massive rational edifice in which each book and each thought finds its appropriate place. On the contrary,

[2] See Robert L. Horn, "Positivity and Dialectic: A Study of the Theological Method of Hans Lassen Martensen" (Diss., Union Theological Seminary, New York, 1969); and Niels Thulstrup, *Kierkegaards Forhold til Hegel og til den spekulative Idealisme indtil 1846* (Copenhagen: Gyldendal, 1967).

[3] Paul Sponheim, *Kierkegaard on Christ and Christian Coherence* (New York: Harper and Row, 1968).

[4] Calvin Schrag, *Existence and Freedom* (Chicago: Northwestern University Press, 1961); Michael Wyschogrod, *Kierkegaard and Heidegger* (New York: Humanities Press, 1954).

[5] Gregor Malantschuk, *Kierkegaard's Thought* (Princeton University Press, 1971); Helmut Fahrenbach, *Kierkegaards existenzdialektische Ethik* (Frankfort: V. Klostermann, 1968).

15

his books contain an almost countless number of poetical and imaginative descriptions of the topography of human existence. In open rebellion against the systematizing mindset of the nineteenth century, Kierkegaard flooded Denmark with a wealth of existential reflection which in quantity and in its expression of psychological depth and insight contemptuously defied the systematizer to work his logical sleight of hand on his writings. It seems that Kierkegaard with calculated deliberateness went out of his way to make it impossible to understand his authorship, much less to systematize it. The use of pseudonyms; the maieutic method of communication; the explicit avowal of logically contradictory notions; the attempt to work simultaneously on both theological and philosophical problems; the abrupt abandonment of the pseudonyms and the indirect method of communication for a direct method of communication, only to pick them up and abandon them once again—all this conspires to create a subtle and complex authorship in which there seems to be no final and authoritative pattern or system.

But should we be surprised at this apparent absence of a system in Kierkegaard's writings? Doesn't he argue that it is both inappropriate and impossible to reduce existence to a system?[6] It is true that his original and subtle descriptions of different existential phenomena cannot be conceptually grasped or known. But it is possible, nevertheless, to discover and explain the occurrence and relations of these phenomena. While it is not possible, for example, to grasp conceptually such phenomena as guilt, sin, suffering, choice, faith, repentance, and anxiety, it is possible to explain why they appear when and where they do in the life of the existing individual and to clarify conceptually the structure of existence which makes them possible. Thus, in speaking of a system in Kierkegaard's thought I mean at best only the

[6] "An existential system is impossible." Søren Kierkegaard, *Concluding Unscientific Postscript*, trans. David Swenson and Walter Lowrie (Princeton University Press, 1941), p. 107.

conceptual clarification of these structures which, on the one hand, makes these existential phenomena possible and, on the other, binds them into an explicit unity of relations.[7]

One of the most explicit references to the presence and importance of such a structure in human existence appears in *Stages on Life's Way*.

> There are three existence-spheres: the aesthetic, the ethical, the religious. The metaphysical is abstraction; there is no man who exists metaphysically. The metaphysical, ontology, *is* but does not *exist*; for when it exists it is in the aesthetic, in the ethical, in the religious, and when it *is* it is the abstraction of or the *prius* for the aesthetic, the ethical, the religious.[8]

It is true that Kierkegaard is less concerned to delineate this ontological structure than he is to describe the various existential ways of being which it makes possible, but it is, nevertheless, present in his writings and essential to his total project.

It appears that his lack of emphasis on the ontological question can be attributed to his reaction to what he regarded as an overemphasis on the question of being to the exclusion of the question of human existence in Hegelian

---

[7] It should be noted here that those scholars who have broken free of the bias against discussing the inter-relations of the stages of existence, instead of viewing them as autonomous spheres of existence which are not dialectically related, still have not gotten to the heart of the problem. The question remains as to why there are only three major stages and not six or twelve. Any attempt to grasp the systematic pulse governing the authorship must also account for the stages themselves. It is not enough to explain each existential phenomenon in terms of its presence in one of the stages, nor it is sufficient to demonstrate the dialectical relations of the stages. One must go a step further and disclose the ontological foundation of the stages themselves. For an excellent analysis of the developmental character of the three stages, see Regis Jolivet, *Introduction to Kierkegaard* (London: Frederick Muller, 1950).

[8] Søren Kierkegaard, *Stages on Life's Way*, trans. Walter Lowrie (Princeton University Press, 1940), p. 430.

metaphysics.[9] Kierkegaard reminds us over and again that his writings have primarily an edifying intention. He addresses his books to the existing individual in order to help him to come to terms with his own existence. His writings have an openly therapeutic quality about them in that they are intended to assist his reader to overcome the spiritual sickness of despair, which he refers to as *the sickness unto death*. Kierkegaard's preeminent concern is not to lead his reader through an ontological maze like Hegel's *Logic* but to lead him out of despair into the light of a spiritually healthy existence. For this reason alone, then, ontology has a low priority in his writings.

This strategic disagreement with the Hegelians over the relative importance of ontology is supplemented also by a substantive disagreement. Kierkegaard wrote that Hegel's metaphysics would have been one of the most brilliant pieces of philosophical speculation in the history of western philosophy if he had supplemented it with one single footnote claiming that it had nothing to do with human existence. Kierkegaard believed that the individual's pathos and suffering, the ineluctable *ought* permeating his existence, and the *ought's* accompanying freedom simply could not be accounted for by Hegel's ontology. In Kierkegaard's mind, Hegelian ontology positively contravened that which essentially characterizes human existence, and he therefore replaces it with an ontology of his own.

Finally, in opposition to the systematizing *spirit of the age*, Kierkegaard diffuses his ontology throughout his discussion of the three major modes of human existence, which he describes as pleasure, duty, and faith. He chooses to emphasize the issues of how one discovers one's being in these three modes of existing and how this process of discovering and appropriating one's being is constitutive of individual existence. He is more concerned with the ethical

9 The Hegelians whom Kierkegaard knew best and opposed most vigorously were Heiberg, Denmark's poet laureate, and Martensen, one of its leading theologians. Both were Kierkegaard's contemporaries.

task of existing, *understood as knowing and actualizing one's being*, than he is in abandoning this existential problem for a more detached and objective investigation of the ontological structure which makes human existence possible. Ethics and ontology are inextricably linked in Kierkegaard's thought, and we can therefore speak of his ethico-ontological outlook on the problem of human existence.

It may be objected at this point that Kierkegaard is pre-eminently a religious or Christian thinker and writer and that if there is an ontology in Kierkegaard's pseudonyms it must be regarded as religious, Christian, or theological in nature. By maintaining that Kierkegaard's ontology is philosophical, I do not wish to deny that he is fundamentally concerned with religion. One cannot seriously question Kierkegaard's assertion in *A First and Last Declaration* that the pseudonymous writings attempt to explore afresh human existence in order to rediscover the meaning of being religious.[10] I shall argue that this exploration of existence gives rise to an ontology, because Kierkegaard is attempting to establish the priority of the self quite apart from any religious beliefs with respect to what the self is *qua* self. He says that the self is a synthesis of the finite and the infinite which freedom is responsible for actualizing in human existence. This definition emerges simply in the process of trying to take existence seriously apart from any divine revelation concerning the nature and purpose of human existence. We shall see how the individual's attempts to actualize himself as a synthesis gives rise to the possibility of religious existence.

One of Kierkegaard's central questions is: "How is it possible to be religious in any sense, Christian or otherwise?" His doctrine of the self lays the ontological foundation for the possibility of a variety of modes of existence, including Christianity. I do not mean to imply here that given his interest in ontology Kierkegaard is not a thinker who is vitally interested in Christianity. He most certainly is. The only

[10] *CUP*, p. 554.

claim which I wish to make here is that his understanding of Christianity and his ontology are formally distinct.

This ontology is most consistently discussed in *The Concept of Dread, The Sickness Unto Death, De Omnibus Dubitandum Est*, and in parts of *Either/Or, Stages on Life's Way, Philosophical Fragments*, and *Concluding Unscientific Postscript*. In the following chapters, I shall attempt to analyze this doctrine of the self and to demonstrate its consequences for Kierkegaard's existential descriptions of the ethical and religious modes of existing as they are described in the pseudonymous writings.

EXISTENCE: THE DOMAIN OF HUMAN BEING AND THINKING

Kierkegaard says that the individual is an "existing infinite spirit."[11] This is one of Kierkegaard's expressions for the ontological structure by which human existence is constituted. Within this fundamental structure, existence has three different meanings. In the first instance, *existence* (*Tilvaerelse*) designates the real, concrete, temporal, contingent being of human existence. In the second sense, *existence* (*Eksistens*) refers to the abstract concept of existence. That is to say the idea of existence itself exists but as necessary and ideal.

> But the *concept*, existence, is an ideality, and the difficulty is precisely whether existence is absorbed in the concept. . . . In all the relationships of ideality it holds true that *essentia* is *existentia*. . . . But existence corresponds to the individual as Aristotle has already taught; however, the individual lies outside and is not absorbed in the concept.[12]

11 *CUP*, p. 75.

12 *Søren Kierkegaard's Journals and Papers*, ed. and trans. Howard V. Hong and Edna H. Hong, 2 vols. (Bloomington, Ind.: Indiana University Press, 1967-1970), I, 1057.

This last sentence leads us to the third meaning of the term in Kierkegaard's thought. The individual can be said to exist (*eksistere*) in the moment that he becomes determinate in the decisive actualization of the idea of existence in the contingent realm of becoming.[13] In this third sense, existence refers to the act by which the ideal is realized in the realm of becoming, thereby producing an existential content which defies conceptual or even aesthetic description. The act of existing is not subject to demonstration, because reason inevitably proceeds away from and not toward existence. The moment existence is defined, it is converted into possibility, essence. A possibility or essence which actually exists is qualitatively different from that same possibility which exists as thought or reflected.

Kierkegaard, then, uses the notion of existence to apply to the nature of man's total being, including his contingency, necessity, and decisive self-determination. The authorization for this general usage lies in the fact that existence is for man his fundamental mode of reality to which all the determinants of his being must be related. In this sense, existence, as Fahrenbach has pointed out, is the scene, the place, of human reality in its entirety, and it can, consequently, stand for the whole of man's being.[14]

Now the third meaning of the term expresses the most frequent sense in which Kierkegaard uses it. His most philosophically cogent discussion of the nature of human existence in the "Interlude" of the *Philosophical Fragments* exclusively confines the use of the term to its third meaning.[15] Thus, the concept of existence in Kierkegaard's ontology does not primarily refer to the dialectically opposing poles of the self; i.e., to the existence-essence distinction, but to

---

[13] *CUP*, pp. 293-295.

[14] Fahrenbach, *Kierkegaards Ethik*, p. 8.

[15] Søren Kierkegaard, *Philosophical Fragments*, David Swenson translation revised and Niels Thulstrup introduction and commentary trans. Howard V. Hong (2nd ed. rev., Princeton University Press, 1962), pp. 89-111.

the decisive act by which the existing individual actualizes possibility in the contingent and becoming realm of being. Kierkegaard can say, then, that the single problem confronting the existing individual is to exist.

The existence-essence distinction is more commonly discussed by Kierkegaard in terms of his formal category of the self as a synthesis of dialectically opposing moments which are united by a *postive third* element which he identifies as spirit. I shall argue that it is this triadic self-structure in Kierkegaard's thought which is the constitutive structure, the ontological principle, of all the successes and failures of the individual's struggle to accept and to realize the challenge to exist.

However, before discussing this triadic definition of the self, it is necessary to analyze the method of thought by which Kierkegaard arrives at this definition of the self as the most cogent expression for this ontology.

THE EXISTENTIAL THINKER AND
THE PROBLEM OF COMMUNICATION

Kierkegaard has often been the whipping boy for those who accuse existentialism of being anti-rational. But Kierkegaard never denies the validity of thought. What he denies is that all thought should be confined to an objectifying activity. Kierkegaard is anxious to draw a sharp distinction between pure and existential thought. Pure thought is a theoretical and detached kind of thinking which characterizes the spectator of existence. Existential thinking reflectively examines and describes existence while maintaining a relationship with it.[16] Kierkegaard says in defense of existential thinking that

to express existentially what one has understood about oneself, and in this manner to understand oneself, is in

[16] *CUP*, pp. 277-278.

no way comical. But to understand everything except one's self is very comical.[17]

The task of the existential thinker is to understand himself, and he accomplishes this not by understanding the concrete abstractly, but, on the contrary, by understanding the abstract concretely. Kierkegaard never attacks the pure thinker for thinking abstractly but only for thinking abstractly about the wrong subject matter and in the wrong manner. The pure thinker is comical, in Kierkegaard's view, not because he thinks abstractly and systematically, but because he fails to footnote his system with the warning that it has no relation to existence. The first task of the thinker is not to turn away from the particular in order to understand man in general; on the contrary, "the subjective thinker seeks to understand the abstract determination of being human in terms of this particular existing human being."[18] Consequently, the speculative thinker is philosophically wrong and ethically dangerous, because he does not provide the individual with categories within which the individual can both exist and understand himself as an existing individual.

The pure thinker cannot provide the individual with categories for existential understanding and accentuation, because his thought is directed away from and not toward existence. Kierkegaard's ontological categories are, however, universals which are derived from existence and serve conceptually to clarify the nature and purpose of one's own existence. The categories of Kierkegaard's ontology are universals, but not in the rationalist or essentialist sense of the word. They are not *a priori* conditions of thought which are logically necessary; they are universals which are read off from man's concrete, lived experience. These universals are peculiar determinants of human existence and arise only in the process of historical self-actualization. The existentialist

[17] *CUP*, pp. 315-316.   [18] *CUP*, p. 315.

analysis of the structure of existence is worked out by a thinker who is himself engulfed in the process of existing, and he first becomes aware of himself in this living concreteness. This is the single theme permeating Kierkegaard's notion of the existential thinker. The existential thinker is always involved in the process of becoming, and his universal categories both arise from and return to his own concrete existence. Kierkegaard says that every human being must be in possession of what is essentially human,[19] but the disclosure of this universal self-structure must begin and end with the existing thinker himself.[20]

Two other points emerge in Kierkegaard's opposition to speculative thinking as adequate for understanding individual existence. The first point concerns the ethical posture of all existential thinking. In defense of this form of thought, Kierkegaard asserts that

> the only reality that exists for an existing individual is his own ethical reality. To every other reality he stands in a cognitive relation; but true knowledge consists in translating the real into the possible.

> The real subject is not the cognitive subject; since in knowing he moves in the sphere of the possible; the real subject is the ethically existing subject.[21]

The only reality which exists for an existing individual is his own ethical reality, and true knowledge consists in translating that reality, one's own reality, into an abstraction to which one can be ethically related. That is to say, the existential thinker cannot be indifferently related to his abstractions. True knowledge is ethically qualified insofar as it stands in relation to the individual as possibility and not as a neutral concept. Kierkegaard uses the terms *possibility* and *ideality* to refer to true knowledge in order to emphasize the ethical character of the relation between thinking

---

[19] *CUP*, p. 317.   [20] *CUP*, p. 314.   [21] *CUP*, pp. 280, 281.

and what is thought. The existential thinker proposes to abolish neutral abstractions through the projection of abstractions which can shape and direct and make understandable one's existence.

The second point stresses the fact that the ethical posture of the existential thinker is motivated by the thinker's infinite interest in himself. Kierkegaard argues that existence constitutes the highest interest for the existential thinker, and that as soon as thought attempts to break free of existence in order to impose a necessary teleology on itself and reality upon its abstractions,[22] self-interest intervenes by disclosing the existential irrelevance of such pure and speculative system building. Kierkegaard is fond of reminding the Hegelians of Socrates, whose thought is reflection stimulated by passion and interest. Socrates is the existential thinker *par excellence*, because he concentrates upon accentuating rather than avoiding one's own individual existence.[23] With Socrates, Kierkegaard agrees that the abstractions of the existential thinker are motivated by the thinker's interest in himself, and that they serve ethically to accentuate one's existence since one must initially be related to his existence abstractly.[24]

Now in Kierkegaard's view the existential thinker has not only the task of understanding himself in existence but also the task of communicating this understanding to others. But the manner of communicating this knowledge constitutes a special problem for Kierkegaard, because of the objectively unknowable nature of that which is to be communicated.[25] We remember that the true subject is not the cogni-

[22] Hegel's *Logic* was Kierkegaard's prime target of criticism with respect to this point.

[23] *CUP*, pp. 279-280. Cf. Kierkegaard, *De Omnibus Dubitandum Est*, trans. T. H. Croxall (Stanford, Cal.: Stanford University Press, 1958), pp. 151-152.

[24] *CUP*, pp. 183-186.

[25] See the following studies on Kierkegaard's theory of communication: Hermann Diem, *Kierkegaard's Dialectic of Existence*, trans. Harold Knight (New York: Frederick Ungar, 1965). Paul Holmer, "Kierke-

tive subject but the ethically existing subject. And the truth of existence cannot be known objectively, i.e., by thought, but only by existing in the truth itself. Consequently, Kierkegaard denies that the truth of existence is objective as are the truths of mathematics and science, and affirms that the method of communicating it must be indirect rather than direct. Indirect communication of the truth of existence means communicating it in the form of possibility.

> But existential reality is incommunicable. . . . Everyone who makes a communication, in so far as he becomes conscious of this fact, will therefore be careful to give his existential communication the form of possibility, precisely in order that it may have a relationship to existence.[26]

Not only must existence be communicated indirectly, but also it must be communicated as an ethical requirement.

> Whatever is great in the sphere of the universally human must therefore not be communicated as a subject for admiration, but as an ethical requirement. In the form of possibility it becomes a requirement.[27]

Through reflection on his own existence, Kierkegaard conceptually clarifies the *universally human* which he discovers underlying his own existential topography. But the task of communicating the universally human cannot be as simple as passing on this reflected conceptual structure as hard, objective information. On the contrary, the existential thinker is responsible for transforming himself into an "instrument that clearly and definitely expresses in existence whatever is essentially human."[28] So the communication really operates on two levels. On one level, the existential

---

gaard and Religious Propositions," *Journal of Religion*, xxxv, no. 3 (July 1955), 135-146. Robert Cumming, "Existence and Communication," *International Journal of Ethics*, lxv, no. 1 (1954-1955), 79-98.
26 *CUP*, p. 320.   27 *Ibid.*
28 *CUP*, p. 318; cf. *SKJP*, i, 649.

thinker who seeks to express in existence the universally human provides a graphic and detailed description of his own struggle to realize the universally human. He elucidates through description his own immediate experience, and he challenges his reader to investigate his own experience to see if he discovers a similar existential topography. On the other level, the existential thinker communicates explicitly what he has discovered to be the universally human. Fahrenbach argues that the success of Kierkegaard's existential communication depends in part upon the transmission of an ontology along with his descriptions of existence. He maintains that Kierkegaard combines scientific rigour with his edifying intentions in order to make his communication of existence complete.[29] I am inclined to accept this notion, for someone as rational as Kierkegaard could not have been unconcerned about rationally defending his presentation of the problem of existence. But it is also clear that Kierkegaard was trying to communicate explicitly a conceptual clarification of the nature of individual existence for an ethical reason. Without the conceptual and structural underpinning, the wealth of description would have been only a vast, uncharted sea on which the reader would haplessly wander without direction and understanding. Unless man has some conceptual grasp of his nature, he cannot be held responsible for himself. That is to say, unless man abstractly knows who or what he is, he cannot in existence become what he is. The challenge, says Kierkegaard, is to exist, and one accomplishes this only by realizing in existence what he has abstractly understood to be the case about his existence. Consequently, Kierkegaard can say that "concreteness is attained through bringing the existential categories into relation with one another."[30] And he continues that, unlike the categories which in themselves have no existence, but make existence possible, historical existence constitutes a reality whose depth and breadth defy

29 Fahrenbach, *Kierkegaard's Ethik*, p. 2.
30 *CUP*, p. 320.

description and direct communication. As we have already noted, Kierkegaard would say that the existential experience of guilt cannot be described or directly communicated, but the ontological conditions of its possibility, viz., that man is a synthesis of the infinite and the finite which is united by spirit, can be described and even directly communicated. But it should be noted that the direct communication of what man *is* also takes the form of possibility so as to express the ethical requirement which confronts each man with the challenge to exist in what he is.

One final word needs to be said with respect to the nature of the content of the communication. We have already seen that the existential thinker's ontology can make no claim to final certainty. This is the case simply because the individual is eternally bound to existence and the process of becoming. He cannot transcend existence and comprehend it as a whole because he is irrevocably immersed in the process of becoming.[31] The existential thinker can at best hypothetically reflect the truth of existence as possibility for the purpose of organizing, interpreting, and accentuating his own individual existence. This kind of conceptual clarification is not only possible for human beings but also is ethically required. The next step in this analysis is to delineate this ontological structure of human existence.

[31] "It is perfectly true, as philosophers say, that life must be understood backwards. But they forget the other presupposition, that it must be lived forwards. And if one thinks over that proposition it becomes more and more evident that life can never really be understood in time simply because at no particular moment can I find the necessary resting place from which to understand it—backwards." *The Journals of Søren Kierkegaard*, ed. and trans. Alexander Dru (Oxford: Oxford University Press, 1938), #465.

CHAPTER II

The Dialectical Self

THE structural principle to which I have been referring is the self. The purpose of this chapter is to reveal the onto-logical dimensions of Kierkegaard's understanding of the self. I hope to accomplish this goal, first, by providing a definition of the self, and second, by examining in detail the five ways in which Kierkegaard discusses the self.

A DEFINITION

Kierkegaard's formal definition of the self (*Selv*) has three aspects. First, he says that the self is spirit (*aand*). Second, he says that the self is a relation (*Forhold*) which relates itself to its own self. Then he modifies this aspect of the definition. "The self is not the relation but consists in the fact that the relation relates itself to its own self." And when the relation relates itself to its own self, "the relation doubt-less is the third term," which constitutes this relation. And this constituting positive third term is the self (spirit). And third, Kierkegaard says that "this relation (the third term) is in turn a relation relating itself to that which constituted the whole relation."[1]

The first part of the definition designates the becoming character of the self. The second part of the definition indi-cates the givenness of the self's being. Fahrenbach refers to these parts respectively as *Wie-Sein* and *Was-Sein*.[2] Hence,

[1] Kierkegaard, *The Sickness Unto Death*, trans. Walter Lowrie (Princeton University Press, 1954), p. 146.

[2] Fahrenbach, *Kierkegaards Ethik*, p. 12.

this triadic structure of the self is developed by Kierkegaard in order to include both the *what* and the *how* of its being. Spirit refers to the dynamic, becoming character of the self's being. The different expressions of the self as a synthesis *(Synthese)*[3] refer to the formal structure of the self's being to which the spirit is bound in its development. The third part of the definition implies that the structural whole is related to an *other* as its ground. This formal definition of the self is Kierkegaard's most cogent expression of the ontology which permeates his thought.

The self is spirit. By this designation, Kierkegaard is not implying that spirit is the highest level or layer in the being of the self or the highest power or faculty within the self which controls and motivates its behavior. Nor is spirit the mediated relation between two phenomena. Spirit is not the third element of the self as a *negative unity* which is established through the dialectical association of two phenomena neither of which can be clearly isolated from the other.[4] When Kierkegaard says that the self is spirit, he means that spirit is a *positive third* element which itself posits the relation of two dialectically opposing moments and in so doing posits[5] itself as the self.

[3] In designating the self as a synthesis, Kierkegaard uses five expressions: finitude and infinitude, body and soul, reality and ideality, necessity and possibility, and time and eternity. An analysis of these five expressions of the self as a synthesis constitutes the second part of this chapter.

[4] *SUD*, p. 146.

[5] Here the term "posits" means "to establish." At this point, it is difficult to be more precise about the meaning of the term. Both this and the following chapter are devoted to the development and clarification of this notion. For now, it is sufficient to realize that spirit both establishes and is established by the synthesis which it posits. The manner in which spirit posits the different synthetic expressions of the self is discussed in the remainder of this chapter, and the manner in which spirit is posited by the synthesis which it posits is the subject of Chapter III.

There are three key terms involved in this definition of the self: spirit, relation, and synthesis. And in order to understand the assertion that the self is a relation which relates itself to itself, we must be clear about how these three terms function in the definition. We have observed that the self is triadic in structure because it involves spirit and the two elements of the synthesis. Kierkegaard denies that the self can be understood exclusively in terms of the two elements of the synthesis. The self is not merely a relation of the two elements of the synthesis. If this were the case, according to Kierkegaard, the self would merely be the *negative* relation of the two elements of the synthesis. When Kierkegaard says that the self relates itself to itself, he means that the self relates itself as spirit to itself as a synthesis. Consequently, the self's relating itself to itself means that the self is not merely a relation of two elements but is a relating to a relation (synthesis). The self is not *in* the relation, as it would be if it were a relation of two elements, but is a relating *to* a relation (synthesis).

Ultimately, "the relation is the positive third term."[6] That is to say, the relation is the instant in which spirit relates to the synthesis first by reflecting it, second by bringing it to consciousness, and third by actualizing it in existence.

In the following section of this chapter, we shall observe that each expression of the self as a synthesis is determined by the manner in which spirit constitutes the synthesis. Spirit is the structuring principle of the self. Man experiences himself as constantly in the process of becoming. And when the existential thinker thinks on his existence as in the process of becoming, he thinks the principle of becoming as spirit, and the different ways in which the synthesis gets structured depends upon how spirit is becoming at any particular point in its growth. That is to say, the specific structure of each expression of the self as a synthesis is determined by the manner in which spirit constitutes and

6 *SUD*, p. 146.

unites the relation. The second section of this chapter is exclusively concerned with demonstrating this point.

The final aspect of the definition informs us that the self in relating itself to itself relates itself to another.

> Such a derived, constituted, relation is the human self, a relation which relates itself to its own self, and in relating itself to its own self relates itself to another.[7]

The implications and importance of this transcendent referent will be discussed under the category of freedom in this chapter.

The remainder of the chapter is devoted exclusively to an analysis of the What-Being of the self. It is not possible, however, to discuss the different syntheses without discussing at the same time the way in which the self relates them; consequently, there will be some discussion of spirit as well, although a more detailed discussion of spirit will be taken up in Chapter III, which deals with the problem of unity. The different synthetic expressions of the self will be discussed in the following order:

Finite-Infinite: Concrete
Body-Soul: Spirit
Reality-Ideality: Consciousness
Necessity-Possibility: Freedom
Time-Eternity: Temporality

In the analysis of these expressions of the self as a synthesis, three questions are crucial to the unfolding of our attempt to identify the ontological foundation of Kierkegaard's thought. These questions are: (1) What is the specific content of each expression of the synthesis? (2) Does the content of each synthesis significantly differ from the content of the other expressions of the self as a synthesis? (3) How are these different syntheses related if in fact their content differs?

7 *Ibid.*

EXPRESSIONS OF THE SELF AS A SYNTHESIS

Finite-Infinite: *Concrete*

Kierkegaard's most general and abstract expression of the self as a synthesis is his designation of the self as a synthesis of the finite and the infinite.

Who thinks of hitching Pegasus and an old nag to one carriage for a ride. And yet this is what it is to exist (*existere*) for one compounded of finitude and infinitude.[8]

Less metaphorically, Kierkegaard expresses the meaning of being so constituted: "For the self is a synthesis in which the finite is the limiting factor and the infinite the expanding factor."[9] To say that the self is finite is to affirm that it is limited by its *factical* being. The finite aspect of the self is not an empty abstraction. Rather, the self's facticity is a thoroughly concrete aspect of the self which includes its sex, race, personal appearance, emotional stability, talents, interests, abilities, and weaknesses[10] as well as its more general, yet concrete, natural environment and social, political, and cultural milieu.[11] Moreover, the self does not determine its own facticity but, on the contrary, experiences itself as already in it and determined by it.[12] The Heideggerian term, thrownness (*Geworfenheit*), is appropriate here.[13] The self can neither get behind its facticity in order to lead itself into a *factical* situation of its own choosing nor can it disregard its facticity in the projection of its own future possibilities.[14] Furthermore, the self, as immersed in existence and

---

[8] *Søren Kierkegaard's Journals and Papers*, ed. and trans. Howard V. Hong and Edna H. Hong, 2 vols. (Bloomington, Ind.: Indiana University Press, 1967-1970), I, 55.

[9] *SUD*, p. 163.

[10] Søren Kierkegaard, *Either/Or*, vol. II, trans. Walter Lowrie (Princeton University Press, 1959), II, 220.

[11] *E/O*, II, 267.   [12] *E/O*, II, 337.

[13] Martin Heidegger, *Being and Time*, trans. John Macquarrie and Edward Robinson (New York: Harper and Row, 1962), passim.

[14] *E/O*, II, 337.

becoming, experiences itself as carried along by its own time and by social, political, and cultural change. One may, without self-contradiction, speak of the limitlessness of finitude in the sense that the *limiting* pole of the self is constantly expanding. Kierkegaard frequently identifies the self's finitude with the world.[15] Here the term does not have a cosmological meaning but simply signifies the sheer, brute givenness of all that *is* in relation to the existing, becoming self.

The significance of the infinite is its capacity for *expansion*, and imagination (fantasy) is "the medium of the process of infinitizing."[16] Imagination is the maker of infinity in the sense that it opens up the self's own horizon of meanings.[17] Imagination ranges free of the self's facticity by positing a multiplicity of meaning possibilities without regard for its finite limitations. The more fertile the imagination, the richer and more multiple are the possibilities for existence which it discloses and explores. Kierkegaard expresses this point when he writes that "the intensity of this medium is the possibility of the intensity of the self."[18] The term passion rather than intensity more aptly expresses the sense of this thought, and here it means that the process of imaginative representation always outdistances the present existential condition of the self by saturating it with various existence possibilities which promise to extend the quality of the self's existence beyond its present moment.[19] Indeed, the quality of existence is most intensely experienced in

---

[15] *E/O*, II, 206-207, 212-213, 225.

[16] *SUD*, p. 163. Imagination and reflection are co-operative aspects of the process of "infinitizing." However, they perform separate and distinct functions. Here only imagination is discussed. Reflection and its relation to imagination will be discussed in the section on consciousness.

[17] Fahrenbach, *Kierkegaards Ethik*, pp. 16-17.

[18] *SUD*, p. 164.

[19] Søren Kierkegaard, *Concluding Unscientific Postscript*, trans. David Swenson and Walter Lowrie (Princeton University Press, 1941), p. 176.

those instants of passion when the self leaps toward its imaginatively represented future.

It is only momentarily that the particular individual is able to realize existentially a unity of the infinite and the finite which transcends existence. This unity is realized in a moment of passion. In passion, the existing subject is rendered infinite in the eternity of the imaginative representation, and yet he is at the same time most definitely himself.[20]

It seems contradictory to assert that the subject is existentially expanded through imagination while at the same time remaining itself. How is it possible for the subject simultaneously to remain itself and to become another through imagination? It would seem more logical to regard the imagination as that which opens the future to new possibilities by which the self substantively transcends itself. But Kierkegaard insists that while the imagination *infinitizes* the self, it does not make the self something other than it already is.

It is precisely the self's attempt to escape into the infinity of the imagination which Kierkegaard deplores. When the fantastical becomes a mode of existing, imagination itself becomes the authoritative medium of existence.[21] This is a contradiction because the medium of imagination can well open up possibilities for existence, but it cannot legitimately become the medium of existence. As soon as the self volatilizes itself in its imagination and abandons its strenuous task of remaining in existence while living in the possibilities of the infinite, it becomes fantastical. When, for example, the self indulges in abstract sentimentality, feeling such

20 *Ibid.*
21 This form of existence is best illustrated in Kierkegaard's "The Diary of a Seducer." See Kierkegaard, *Either/Or*, vol. 1, trans. David F. Swenson and Lillian M. Swenson (Princeton University Press, 1959), 1, 297-443.

pity for the human race in general that it can no longer feel pity for itself or another existing individual, then its feeling has become fantastical. Or, when a scholar aspires to acquire infinite knowledge about nature, world history, politics, or culture and fails to understand himself, his knowledge becomes fantastical. And, finally, when the self wills a possibility which bears no relation whatsoever to its facticity, it wills an abstraction, and thus, becomes fantastical in willing. Consequently, "when feeling, or knowledge, or will have thus become fantastic, the entire self may at last become so. . . ."[22]

The task, then, of the self is to become neither finite nor infinite but to become concrete in a synthesis of the two poles.[23]

> Most men have complacent categories for their daily use, and resort to the categories of the infinite only upon solemn occasions; that is to say, they do not really have them. But to make use of the dialectic of the infinite in one's daily life, and to exist in this dialectic, is naturally the highest degree of strenuousness; and strenuous exertion is again needed to prevent the exercise from deceitfully luring one away from existence, instead of providing a training in existence.[24]

Kierkegaard continues that "a genuine human being, as a synthesis of the finite and the infinite, finds his reality in holding these two factors together, infinitely interested in existing."[25] One can with justification say that Kierkegaard's life and authorship were devoted to the fulfillment of this task.

The most general and abstract co-ordinates of Kierkegaard's ontology have now been established. It is now appropriate to begin a discussion of the different and more

22 *SUD*, p. 165.   23 *SUD*, p. 162.
24 *CUP*, pp. 79-80n.
25 *CUP*, p. 268; cf. *SUD*, p. 162f.

concrete expressions of this synthesis of the finite and the infinite in the concrete.[26]

Body-Soul: Spirit

The major significance of Kierkegaard's discussion of the body-soul opposition in *The Concept of Dread* is its introduction of the notion of the dynamic nature of the self as a synthesis which is in the process of becoming. No new information about the content of the ontological co-ordinates of the self is added in his discussion of the body and the soul. This duality refers essentially to the same phenomena designated by the categories, the finite and the infinite.[27] Kierkegaard says in the second volume of *Either/Or* that we have "on the one side the whole world [body], and on the other side one's own soul."[28] Body means here not an extended, mathematically calculable substance like Descartes' *res extensa*, but the on-going, consistently changing facticity of each existing individual subject. Body means, in the words of George Price, "bodily events" and not a static and unchanging phenomenon.[29]

Kierkegaard's use of the term soul is more enigmatic. In the pseudonymous writings and the edifying discourses, he

---

[26] The self is a synthesis of the finite and the infinite, but for the self to exist finitely or infinitely, and not as infinitely finite (concrete), is for the self to exist "aesthetically." The first volume of *E/O* is a representation of the complex hierarchy of aesthetic existence possibilities which range from complete immersion in facticity-finitude-(Don Juan) to its dialectical opposite, total immersion in imagination-infinitude-(Johannes the Seducer). Kierkegaard's rich prose in this volume describes in clear detail these various existence possibilities with their respective moods and outlooks on life. I make this point in order once again to bring out the distinction in Kierkegaard's writings between the ontological principles of the self's being and the existence possibilities which they make possible.

[27] T. H. Croxall, *Kierkegaard Studies* (London: Lutterworth Press, 1948), p. 106; George Price, *The Narrow Pass* (New York: McGraw-Hill, 1963), pp. 36-37; Fahrenbach, *Kierkegaards Ethik*, pp. 12-14.

[28] *E/O*, II, 224.   [29] Price, *The Narrow Pass*, p. 37.

uses the same terms in three different ways.[30] There is, then, a semantic problem in determining which usage of the word, if any, has a technical significance for Kierkegaard. Its occurrence in biblical passages quoted by Kierkegaard provides no information as to how he uses the term himself.

The term is also used as a synonym for self,[31] and this usage also tells us nothing about its technical sense.[32] But the term also designates the animating power of the self.[33] It refers to that aspect of the self which distinguishes it in its ideality from its sensuous, bodily aspect. The soul is the source of possibility; it is that aspect of the self which may be totally absorbed into the infinite realm of its projected possibilities when the self abandons the *factical* side of its being.[34] Indeed, the power of the soul should be both feared and respected, for it is the origin of those imaginative *thought productions* in which the self may lose itself when it fails to act.[35] The concept, then, refers essentially

[30] Walter Lowrie in a letter to John Copp indicated that he translated only the Danish word, *sjael*, as soul. John D. Copp, "The Concept of Soul in Kierkegaard and Freud" (Diss. Boston University, 1953), p. 191.

[31] *E/O*, II, 224-226. Kierkegaard, "To Acquire One's Soul in Patience," *Edifying Discourses*, trans. David and Lillian Swenson (4 vols., Minneapolis: Augsburg Publishing House, 1943-1962), II, 67-87; "To Preserve One's Soul in Patience," *Edifying Discourses*, III, 7-37.

[32] Both Eduard Geismar, *The Religious Thought of Kierkegaard* (Minneapolis: Augsburg Publishing House, 1937), p. 37f., and Reider Thomte, *Kierkegaard's Philosophy of Religion* (Princeton University Press, 1948), p. 110, have gone awry in their discussion of the meaning of Kierkegaard's use of the term by treating it as a metaphysically distinct entity enduring within the body, yet rooted in God and destined for harmony with him, rather than recognizing that Kierkegaard "religiously" employs this term as a synonym for the self in his theological discussions of the self in the edifying discourses mentioned in the preceding footnote.

[33] Donald Tweedie, "The Concept of Anxiety in Kierkegaard and Heidegger" (Diss. Boston University, Boston, 1957), pp. 130-131.

[34] *SUD*, p. 160.

[35] *E/O*, II, 170; cf. *CUP*, p. 105.

to the imagination, and it is in this sense that it has a technical connotation.

Now as I have already indicated, the importance of this particular expression for the self as a synthesis is its introduction of the dynamic character of the synthesis as well as its introduction of the concept of spirit as the third and synthesizing element. For Kierkegaard, the self is not a bundle of metaphysically distinct and enduring entities. The self is, on the contrary, a dialectical relationship in which the physical and the psychical events of the synthesis are constituted as a synthesis by a *positive third* element, viz., spirit.

According to Kierkegaard, the Hegelian notion of mediation has destroyed the old philosophically respectable terminology: thesis, antithesis, synthesis,[36] by positing the synthesis as a negative unity constituted by the dialectical relation of thesis and antithesis. The very first triad of Hegel's *Logic* provides an illustration. Being and nothing are thesis and antithesis, and becoming is the logically necessary synthetic unity constituted by the dialectical relation of being and nothing.[37] Indeed, every synthesis in the *Logic* is a logically necessary mediation of the thesis and antithesis. And each mediation is a negative unity in the sense that it must of necessity now become itself a thesis opposed by an antithesis which logically necessitates a higher negative unity by virtue of their intrinsic opposition. But Kierkegaard maintains that the Hegelian synthesis is really only a mediation[38] and that there can be no synthesis without a positive third element.[39] Spirit is not the third moment in the dialectical development of self-consciousness, as with Hegel, but the positive third element in his triadic definition of the self

---

[36] Kierkegaard, *The Concept of Dread*, trans. Walter Lowrie (Princeton University Press, 1957), p. 11.

[37] G.F.W. Hegel, *The Logic*, trans. from *The Encyclopedia of the Philosophical Sciences* by William Wallace (Oxford: Oxford University Press, 1965), pp. 158-163.

[38] *CD*, pp. 10-11.   [39] *CD*, p. 76.

which posits the self as a synthetic unity. Spirit is the positive third element which binds the two elements of the synthesis into a unity.

Prior to the appearance of spirit, the self is "soulishly determined," and is, indeed, posited as a negative unity. To be soulishly determined means to exist in immediate unity with one's natural condition. Kierkegaard equates this soulish determination with a state of ignorance and innocence.[40] In Hegelian terminology, it is a state of immediacy in which the constitutive elements of the self have not been elevated to the level of self-consciousness. And, for Kierkegaard, without self-consciousness there can be no distinction between the self as reality and as ideality. Consequently the synthesis cannot be posited as such.[41] This means that in the condition of immediacy, idea and reality correspond. That is to say, there is no existential separation between ideality and reality, between possibility and necessity, between time and eternity. The self, in a word, has no history. So long as the spirit is dreaming, the self is an ignorant and an immediate self, a self for which there is no disproportionality between body and soul, a self totally absorbed in the infinite successiveness of time.

To exist as soulishly determined means to exist in accord with one's natural and cultural immediacy. It means living according to the categories of nature and culture totally devoid of an awareness of one's self as a self. But with the inflection of spirit, this soulish determination of the self in its natural and cultural immediacy becomes conscious of itself as real and ideal, is challenged by the possibility of its own freedom, and is stratified as a being which is in both time and eternity. Kierkegaard writes in *The Concept of Dread* that in the human self the relation of body and soul is principally thought not as the immediate endurance of a natural

---

[40] *CD*, p. 37f.

[41] Kierkegaard aesthetically describes this immediacy in which the ideal is only implicitly present, and hence, not consciously posited and ethically chosen, in "The Aesthetic View of Marriage" in *E/O*, II, 3-159.

unity but as a division to be synthesized in a self-relation, because in the self-relation it is not the soul but spirit which is the determinant of the relation.[42] With this thought, a genuinely new structural relation is established within the self whose synthetic character cannot be logically inferred from a simple relation between two elements.

Kierkegaard is probably in no respect more indebted to nineteenth century German Idealism than he is with respect to his concept of spirit. Boehme, Fichte, Schelling, and Hegel all stand in the background of the development of Kierkegaard's notion of spirit. However, it is not my intention here to enter into a study of the historical roots of his conception of spirit,[43] but rather to determine its place and significance in the development of Kierkegaard's view of the self.

It is my view that the remaining three expressions of the self as a synthesis are all necessarily entailed in the dynamic, developing, unfolding nature of spirit which Kierkegaard has introduced in relation to the body-soul duality. We may here briefly anticipate the relation between Kierkegaard's notion of spirit and the three remaining expressions of the self as a synthesis to be discussed below.

First, "consciousness is spirit."[44] The body-soul duality, when soulishly determined, is not self-conscious. It is, indeed, sentient in the sense of being aware of its presence in space and time, but it is not conscious of itself as body and soul, i.e., as finite and infinite. Its ignorance, its immediateness, has not been disturbed by the penetration of spirit.

[42] *CD*, p. 44.

[43] For detailed discussions of Kierkegaard's relation to German Idealism with respect to the notion of spirit see James Collins, *The Mind of Kierkegaard* (Chicago: Regnery, 1953), pp. 204-206; George Price, *The Narrow Pass*, pp. 73-77; Walter Schulz, *Die Vollendung des deutschen Idealismus in der Spatphilosophie Schellings* (Stuttgart: W. Kohlhammer Verlag, 1955), pp. 274-280; Niels Thulstrup, *Kierkegaards Forhold Til Hegel* (Copenhagen: Gyldendal, 1967).

[44] Kierkegaard, *De Omnibus Dubitandum Est*, trans. T. H. Croxall (Stanford, Cal.: Stanford University Press, 1958), p. 151.

41

But "the instant the spirit posits itself, it posits the synthesis, but to posit the synthesis, it must first permeate it differentially. . . ."[45] Kierkegaard is suggesting that for the spirit to posit itself it must necessarily involve the other elements of the synthesis. In order to do that, it must first permeate the synthesis differentially in order to bring these elements to the level of consciousness so as to comprehend the meaning and possibility of both.

Second, spirit is freedom.[46] When spirit is posited, the self becomes aware of itself as a self-conscious being which is related to itself as a possibility. A new element has now emerged, not self-consciousness, for it is already present, but a certain modification of it, viz., freedom. This relation between spirit and freedom is noted by Kierkegaard in a comment on dread.

> Thus dread is the dizziness of freedom which occurs when the spirit would posit the synthesis, and freedom then gazes down into its own possibility, grasping at finiteness to sustain itself.[47]

> The person who really becomes spirit, for which he is intended, at some point takes over his entire being (by choosing himself as it is called in *Either/Or*. . .).[48]

And third, it can be shown that the self is a temporal synthesis in consequence of being a body-soul synthesis. Temporality is posited by the unfolding development of the existing, individual spirit.

> The synthesis of the eternal and the temporal is not a second synthesis but is the expression for the first synthesis in consequence of which man is a synthesis of body and soul sustained by spirit. No sooner is the spirit posited than the instant is there.[49]

---

[45] *CD*, p. 44. [46] *CD*, p. 81. [47] *CD*, p. 55.
[48] *SKJP*, I, 78. [49] *CD*, p. 79.

The remainder of this chapter will explore the details and implications of each of these expressions of the self as a synthesis in order to determine how each particular synthetic expression of the self sheds more light on Kierkegaard's understanding of the self and its central and inestimably important position in his thought.

Reality-Ideality: Spirit (as Consciousness)

The discussion of Kierkegaard's understanding of consciousness as the synthesis of reality and ideality is here preceded by a brief discussion of the Hegelian view of consciousness in *The Phenomenology of Mind*,[50] because, as is frequently the case, Kierkegaard's concepts are polemically developed in opposition to their Hegelian definitions.

Hegel maintained that Kant was fundamentally mistaken in separating the concepts of truth and reality.[51] In Kant's view, the real is theoretically unknowable, and truth is a property of judgments which expresses what of the real can be taken in by human intuition and organized by the categories of the understanding. But Hegel was to argue that the most one could mean by the real is the true, and he set out to describe human experience in such a way that the Kantian distinction between reality and truth could be abolished.

For Hegel, experience, or what he calls sense-consciousness,[52] consists in immediate sensations. These sensations are present in consciousness and lack any relationships or temporal connections. In opposition to the immediacy of sense-consciousness, there arises the intellectual awareness of the mediate nature of experience, in which gradually the universal laws, by which the brute data of experience are related to each other, are discovered. The awareness of these

50 G.F.W. Hegel, *The Phenomenology of Mind*, trans. J. B. Bailey (New York: Harper and Row, 1967).
51 Hegel, *The Logic*, pp. 119-120.
52 Hegel, *The Phenomenology of Mind*, pp. 149-179.

relationships on this initial and lowest level of experience leads to an understanding of a fixed and necessary order of things which simply are self-identical and stand in external relations to each other. For Hegel, the emergence of these necessary, self-identical, and abstract concepts occurs through the process of what he calls reflection (understanding—*Verstand*).[53] Furthermore, knowledge does not stop here, for each concept, when taken as an abstract, self-identical concept, breaks down in its inadequacy. Each concept leads out of itself and into its own opposite by a dialectical movement, which is facilitated by Hegel's redefinition of the classical principle of identity.[54] The analysis of any concept leads dialectically to the contradiction of the concept, thereby revealing the interrelated nature of all experience, and ultimately leading to an understanding of the nature of reality. The concept of the real does not lie in the immediacy of sense-consciousness. On the contrary, reality lies at the end of the process of understanding (*Verstand*)—reflection—and reasoning (*Vernunft*). Reasoning is the dialectical development of the interrelatedness of all concepts abstracted by reflection, which development yields reality.[55] Reality, then, lies at the end of the process of reflection and reasoning and not at its beginning.

Here there is a clear threefold movement in Hegel's dialectical epistemology. First, there is immediacy with its sense-consciousness. Second, there is the abolition of this manifold character of immediacy through the process of reflection, wherein all thoughts appear as fixed, definite, and self-identical. Third, the stage of genuine reality appears in reason, where the content of immediacy is located in the dialectical interweaving of the concepts which were abstractly separated by reflection. Hegel argues that consciousness is the lowest level of human awareness; it is the level at which the knower is aware of what constitutes his

---

[53] Hegel, *The Logic*, pp. 92-94.   [54] *Ibid.*, pp. 212-215.

[55] This process of Reasoning is the enterprise undertaken by Hegel in *The Logic*.

knowledge as external to himself. Reflection designates the power of the abstract understanding to terminate the indiscriminate flux of immediacy and to give birth to definite thoughts which demand further interrelation as concepts. And, finally, reason dialectically schematizes these concepts into a rational, coherent, and necessary unity.

It is at this point that Kierkegaard raises crucial objections to Hegel's whole method of thinking. His primary differences with Hegel lie in his understanding of the relation of reflection and consciousness (*Bevisthed*). As we have noted, reflection in Hegel's view refers to the capacity of the understanding to penetrate immediacy and to give birth to abstract thoughts. But Kierkegaard defines reflection as the possibility of the relationship of reality and ideality, and consciousness as the relationship itself.[56] Reflection is the possibility of the relationship in the sense that, as disinterested, the classifications which it posits are dichotomous in nature, e.g., reality (immediacy) and ideality (mediacy).[57]

The term *immediacy* expresses the raw character of what is experienced and the fact that it has not been brought into relationship with ideality by reflection. Immediacy is indefiniteness[58] in the sense that nothing has been marked off from anything else, given its limit, or defined.

> In immediacy the falsest and truest things are equally true. In immediacy the most possible and the most impossible things are equally actual.[59]

Hence, the questions of what is true and what is actual never arise in immediacy, for something above immediacy is required. For Kierkegaard, what is given, that which must be presupposed and underlies the very possibility of knowledge, is what is found in immediacy. An immediate awareness or a pre-reflective awareness is present when the self is an undifferentiated body-soul unity. Immediacy is not

---

[56] Kierkegaard, *DODE*, p. 150.   [57] *DODE*, pp. 152, 151.
[58] *DODE*, p. 147.   [59] *DODE*, p. 149.

yet mediated by reflection and brought into a complex of identities, differences, and relationships.[60]

Kierkegaard then asks the question of how truth could arise. It appears that truth arises through the judging of certain statements as untrue. The inquirer after truth has been led by something to consider that certain contents of his awareness should be rejected as false. "In inquiring about truth the mind has been brought into a relationship with something else";[61] immediacy has been broken. It has been broken open or penetrated by what Kierkegaard calls word or speech.

> But how is immediacy annulled? By mediacy, which annuls immediacy by presupposing it. What then is immediacy? It is reality. What is mediacy? It is Word. How does Word annul Reality? By talking about it. For that which is talked about is always presupposed. Immediacy is reality. Speech is ideality.[62]

Reality is the actual world, the world of the senses, the world of cognition, loving, perception, playing, in so far as it is not infinitely reflected upon. The ideal, non-sensuous order, however, is only come upon reflectively, i.e., mediately. Speech penetrates the silence and dumbness of immediacy. But with the emergence of speech, one also comes to recognize that the word is not the thing. On the contrary, the word expresses thought, idea; while immediacy, now left behind, as it were, by the word, expresses reality. Immediacy is identified with reality and mediacy with ideality. Thought does not possess reality.[63]

[60] *DODE*, p. 147.   [61] *Ibid.*   [62] *DODE*, p. 148.

[63] The difference between Kierkegaard and Hegel on this point can be demonstrated by showing how Kierkegaard agrees with Hume and Kant. For Hume, immediacy is found in the lively impressions which lose their vividness when transposed into ideas. Knowledge for Hume is a frustrated effort to reconstruct in idea the vivid world of impressions. For Kant, that which underlies experience is the *ding-an-sich* which cannot be cognitively expressed as it is in itself but is merely shaped by the intuitions of space and time and defined by the categories

We are not yet at the point of consciousness. Kierkegaard maintains against Hegel that consciousness is not reflection. Consciousness is a relationship which presupposes reflection, and "reflection is the possibility of relationship."[64] Now, for Kierkegaard, there are two types of reflection, finite and infinite reflection. When reflection is finitely determined, it posits the synthesis from the standpoint of the factical and not from the standpoint of the infinite. The self in finite reflection determines itself through the conditions of immediacy rather than positing ideality in order to establish the difference. The self becomes in this case dialectical with respect to the world. Kierkegaard calls this reflective action the quantitative reflection of immediacy.[65]

Reflection is also infinite. It cannot stop itself when it reaches the point of its most abstract determination.[66] Reflection is halted only by individual resolve,[67] and it assumes its proper task when it is brought into a functional coherence with imagination. The function of imagination representation is crucial to the establishment of the two poles of the self's being which are necessarily prerequisite for the emergence of consciousness. The functional coherence of imagination and reflection must be regarded as an essential and constitutive condition for the possibility of the self's relating itself to itself. It is reflection's penetration into the facticity of the existing individual subject and into its imagi-

---

of the understanding. The "real" lies behind knowledge and is forever inaccessible to human intuition and understanding. With Hume and Kant reality lies behind conceptualization and language and is inaccessible to both language and thought. Kierkegaard in *DODE* seems to be aligning himself with this position in opposition to the Hegelian epistemology which in reason completely mediates all differences between the thing and knowledge of it.

[64] *DODE*, p. 150.

[65] *SUD*, pp. 166-168. This type of reflection is described in *E/O*, 1, "The Shadowgraphs," and "The Rotation Method," and the level of consciousness which it makes possible is discussed in *SUD*, pp. 175-194.

[66] *CUP*, p. 102.   [67] *CUP*, p. 103.

native projections which makes consciousness possible as the synthesis of reality and ideality.

This functional coherence of imagination and reflection operates as follows. Imagination projects possibilities of meaning without regard for the existing individual's facticity. Reflection, which is also present in the infinite horizon of ideality but retains a relation to reality, determines the decisive ideal with respect to the self's facticity.[68] Imagination ranges completely free of the limitations of facticity, positing multiple meaning possibilities, but reflection is related to the factical givenness of the existing subject.[69] That is to say, reflection pays attention to the factical self, and it makes the relation possible in terms of that which is specifically and existentially possible for the self. In this manner, reflection establishes reality and ideality, in contrast to the imagination, which explores all possibilities in the limitless realm of infinity. Reflection is possible in the medium of the infinite, in conjunction with imagination, only in so far as it posits ideality. This reflected difference of reality and ideality is posited only when reflection withdraws from the romanticism of the imagination and pays attention to the existing individual's finite facticity. "The poetical ideal is always a false ideal, for the true ideal is always real."[70] That is to say, the ideality of imagination must itself be reflected if ideality is to bear a direct and ethical relation to the self.

In the false forms of imagination and reflection—fantastical and endless reflection—their accomplishment in its negativity is seen as the fantastical flight into the romantic and poetic illusions of infinitude. The real task of the self, at this point in its development, is to enable reflection to posit the finitely determined self (reality) as infinitely determinable (ideality). These reflected dichotomies now may impinge on each other so that a relationship between the

[68] Fahrenbach, *Kierkegaards Ethik*, p. 18.
[69] *CUP*, pp. 175-177; cf. *E/O*, II, 270.
[70] *E/O*, II, 214.

48

two becomes possible.[71] This original synthesis or relationship is consciousness.

Now, as we have seen, Kierkegaard believes that the dialectical relationship which Hegel sets forth in *The Phenomenology of Mind* between sense-consciousness and reflection leaves reality behind in immediacy, and is not recovered as pure rationality by the dialectical advance of reason beyond reflection. Moreover, we have seen that for Kierkegaard reflection is nothing more than the possibility of a relationship between the real and the ideal and that a positive third, viz., consciousness, is what first constitutes the relationship. Perhaps it is clearer to say that the third is the relationship. So now we have immediacy, reality, and reflection, ideality, as the condition of the possibility of consciousness, spirit.

To understand consciousness as the original synthesis in which the opposing moments of reality and ideality are established and related to each other, it is first necessary to deny that consciousness is a determinate power or faculty in man. Consciousness is rather awareness of the self's being. It is the activity of being conscious of oneself as real and ideal. That is to say, consciousness means self-consciousness. It is not, as with Hegel, a moment in the development of Mind. Nor is it, as with Fichte, consciousness of the pure abstract self, the *I-am-I*.[72] Consciousness is spirit, and the remarkable thing about the world of spirit, says Kierkegaard, is that when One (primordial unity) is divided, it always becomes Three and never Two as is the case with Hegel. Consciousness, therefore, as the third factor must presuppose reflection.[73] Consciousness is the decisive third element of the self which is the collision of the reflected contradictions of reality and ideality. Without opposition and friction between reality and ideality, both would enter into an innocent partnership, and there would be no collision; hence there would be no consciousness.

[71] *DODE*, p. 150.
[72] *CUP*, pp. 107-108, 169, 176-177, 179; cf. *CD*, p. 128.
[73] *DODE*, p. 151.

49

Reflection is the mere disinterested process of setting thing against thing in collision. Consciousness is the place where this process takes place, indeed it is the energizing force behind the process. . . . Consciousness is essentially the manifestation of this collision and the opposition denoted thereby.[74]

Spirit, then, as consciousness, is not simply the locus of the collision. Kierkegaard hints at an active role for spirit by referring to it as that energizing force which is responsible for the collision. (This positive activity which Kierkegaard cautiously attributes to spirit will be more fully discussed in the following chapter. For now, it is sufficient for our analysis of consciousness to say that spirit is the Reality of the collision of the contradictions of reality and ideality as self-consciousness.)

A brief comparison of the German word *Bewusstsein*, which Hegel uses for consciousness, and the Danish term *Bevisthed*, which Kierkegaard uses in *De Omnibus Dubitandum Est*, should make Kierkegaard's meaning of the term more definite and clear. The meaning of *Bewusstsein* conveys the sense of the being-for-consciousness of things which are referred to. What is being designated is not a reference of consciousness to itself, which for Hegel is *Selbstbewusstsein*, but the simple presence in consciousness of phenomena of which the subject is aware. The Danish *Bevisthed* refers more explicitly to the state of being aware as such. There is a self-reflexive character in the Danish term which refers to an awareness of awareness.

Danish, to my knowledge and this is based on the *Dansk Ordbog* of Christian Molbech, Kbh. Gyldendal, 1833, used by SK possesses no word which corresponds strictly to the German *Bewusstsein*. And Molbech gives the following sense for *Bevisthed*: "the characteristic of being aware of one's own existence, to have knowledge of it and of one's self. 2. the capacity in thinking to be itself something, to be a certain known thing. (See *Selvbevisthed*)."[75]

It is clear how Kierkegaard makes the contrast between reflection and consciousness. Reflection is really what the Hegelians call *Bewusstsein*, involving an awareness of a manifold of thoughts but no self-awareness. Kierkegaard no doubt congratulated the Danish language in not having a term, corresponding to *Bewusstsein*, just as he congratulated it for having a term for repetition (*gentagelse*) but no term corresponding to the German *aufgehoben*.[76]

The fundamental character of the type of consciousness which we are here discussing may be brought into sharper focus by contrasting very briefly the two ways in which, according to Kierkegaard, reality and ideality can be brought together. In the first instance, one "can bring reality into relationship with ideality."[77] This action is the movement of theoretical consciousness in the establishment of knowledge which is disinterestedly expressed in the ideality of abstract concepts and language. "What is said is meant to express [non-personal] reality and in this I have brought reality into relationship with ideality." In the second instance, ideality is brought into relationship with reality. If what is expressed is my personal reality, "then I have brought ideality, [i.e., something I think] into relationship with reality." Theoretical consciousness yields scientific knowledge, and practical consciousness yields self-knowledge.

I have identified consciousness as the positive third which unites or synthesizes reality and ideality as the products of reflection, but we have not, as yet, really defined it. Kierkegaard explicitly identifies consciousness with interest. Consciousness cannot become the relationship of these dialec-

75 Robert Horn, "Kierkegaard and His Contemporaries," unpublished lectures (New York: Union Theological Seminary, Spring 1966).
76 Kierkegaard, *Repetition*, trans. Walter Lowrie (London: Oxford University Press, 1941), p. 52.
77 *DODE*, p. 149.

51

tically opposing moments unless it is interested in them. Without interest, there can be no relation between the two. Kierkegaard says that

> ideality and reality strive against each other to all eternity, so long as there is no Consciousness, i.e., no interest—no consciousness to have any interest in the strife.[78]

Consciousness is not the relation of ideality and reality as a negative unity; it is that which stands between them as an intermediate activity. Self-consciousness is not the dialectical mediation of the products of reflection, but, as we have said, it is a positive third which unites these opposite moments, if they are to be united at all.

> Reflection is the possibility of relationship. This can be stated thus: Reflection is "disinterested." Consciousness on the contrary is relationship, and it brings with it interest or concern; a duality which is perfectly expressed with pregnant double meaning by the word "interest" (Latin "interesse," meaning (1) "to be between," (2) "to be a matter of concern").[79]

Self-consciousness is also, according to Kierkegaard, infinite consciousness vis-à-vis finite consciousness. That is to say, it is a form of consciousness which is made possible by the preceding activity of infinite vis-à-vis finite reflection.[80]

Immediacy is, as we have seen, the absence of reflection, or, more precisely, it is the absence of infinite reflection. Immediacy, as *Either/Or* I shows, is itself characterized by stages, and the movement through it is a dialectical movement from total unconsciousness (Don Juan) through finite

---

[78] *DODE*, p. 153.   [79] *DODE*, pp. 151-152.

[80] Again I refer to *E/O*, I, and *SUD* for Kierkegaard's aesthetic and phenomenological descriptions of the movement of consciousness from total unconsciousness to the verge of infinite consciousness (self-consciousness), which we are here discussing.

consciousness ("The Shadowgraphs" and "The Rotation Method") to abstract consciousness ("The Diary of a Seducer"). In the first instance, the absence of consciousness is to be attributed to the absence of reflection. In the second instance, finite consciousness is to be attributed to finite reflection. Here the opposition is the opposition of the real and a finitely reflected finite ideal. And in the third instance, consciousness is abstract, because it is lost in the infinity of the imagination. True consciousness, however, is both finite and infinite in the sense that it is the contradiction of the real repeated as ideal so that an opposition between the two is established.

In the closing paragraph of *De Omnibus Dubitandum Est*, Kierkegaard refers to this process we have been describing as repetition.[81] He writes that "when we speak of Repetition we get collision, for Repetition is only conceivable of what existed before." Again, "there is opposition here, because that which was existing exists again in another manner." The immediate body-soul unity has been repeated as a conscious opposition and conflict. Reflection breaks open this immediate unity and establishes this opposition of reality and ideality which, when united by spirit's interest in the opposition, gives rise to self-consciousness.

Spirit's realization as self-consciousness is, then, the initial effort of the self to relate itself to itself. Now the stage is set for the completion of the self-relating task.

Necessity-Possibility: Spirit (as Freedom)

The next stage of the self's development may now be stated. Kierkegaard writes that

the problem is to transform repetition into something inward, into the proper task of freedom, into freedom's highest interest, as to whether, while everything changes, it can actually realize repetition.[82]

[81] *DODE*, pp. 153-155.   [82] *CD*, p. 17n.

Self-consciousness logically precedes the actual repetition of the self in existence. The problem now becomes whether the repetition of consciousness can be actualized.[83] Spirit's interest now passes beyond the activity of consciousness and emerges as the activity of freedom whose highest interest is likewise repetition. Spirit now emerges as the action between necessity and possibility.[84] Spirit is freedom[85] and is now ultimately expressing itself in the dialectical relation of necessity and possibility. Spirit ultimately realizes itself as the freedom to relate necessity and possibility.

The character of this self-relating act which gives birth to the existential concreteness of the existing individual subject can be more readily comprehended through an examination of the categories of possibility and necessity.

For Kierkegaard, necessity has both logical and existential connotations. In the first instance, necessity applies to the realm of objective knowledge.

> The spheres with which philosophy properly deals, which properly are the spheres for thought, are logic, nature, and history. Here necessity rules and mediation is valid.[86]

But Kierkegaard is especially concerned with the problem of logic. For him logic provides both the *a priori* principles by which thought operates and definitions. He was primarily concerned with the principles of identity, contradic-

---

[83] Action is defined by Kierkegaard in the following way: "The real action is not an external act but an internal decision in which the individual puts an end to the mere possibility and identifies himself with the content of his thought in order to exist in it. This is the action." *CUP*, pp. 302-303.

[84] It must be remembered that the dialectically opposing moments of each synthesis are posited by spirit in accord with the nature of its development. Spirit now manifests itself as the interest of freedom in the actual realization of the repetition which occurs in consciousness; consequently, the categories of reality and ideality are now transformed by spirit into the categories of necessity and possibility. Spirit is now conscious of itself as possible.

[85] *CD*, p. 81.   [86] *E/O*, II, 178.

tion, and excluded middle, which he thought Hegelian Logic had seriously distorted by having redefined them in a way that they introduced movement into logic and, thereby became the ontological principles by which all existence was to be explained.[87] In Kierkegaard's mind movement (κίνησις)[88] is present only in existence and not in the realm of abstract thought.

> Everything which comes into existence proves precisely by coming into existence that it is not necessary, for the only thing which cannot come into existence is the necessary, because the necessary *is*. . . . Nothing whatever exists because it is necessary, but the necessary exists because it is necessary or because the necessary is.[89]

Necessity in the first instance, then, refers to the objective knowledge of theoretical thought and especially to the logically necessary determinations of thought.

Logical necessity is less important for Kierkegaard's discussion of the self than is existential necessity. He argues against Hegel that necessity is not a synthesis of possibility and actuality[90] but that actuality is a synthesis of necessity and possibility.[91] He refers to necessity as "one's limit" and as a "sequence of consonants" which cannot be uttered without the addition of possibility.[92] To suggest that the self is limited is to say that there are real and distinct boundaries which necessarily contain all the factical ingredients which ever will be available to the existing subject for the fulfilling of its task to become itself. Moreover, these ingredients constitute the "sequence of consonants" which cannot be spoken or appropriated without the vowels of reflection and

---

[87] Hegel, *The Logic*, pp. 214, 220-223. And for Kierkegaard's criticisms of Hegel, see *Philosophical Fragments*, David Swenson translation revised and Niels Thulstrup introduction and commentary trans. Howard V. Hong (2nd ed. rev.; Princeton, New Jersey: Princeton University Press, 1962), pp. 89-111.

[88] *PF*, pp. 90-93.   [89] *PF*, pp. 91-92.   [90] *PF*, p. 92.
[91] *SUD*, pp. 168-169, 173.   [92] *SUD*, p. 169, 171.

possibility. In its second sense, necessity refers to the self's concrete and factical limits. And it is the category's very concreteness which, when separated from possibility, is the principle of certain forms of inauthentic existence. Kierkegaard describes two of these, fatalism and philistinism, in *The Sickness Unto Death* as types of human existence which are inauthentic, because they are submerged in necessity and, therefore, divorced from possibility.[93]

The category of possibility is one of the most dynamic in Kierkegaard's ontology. The references to it in the pseudonymous works are very frequent, but the following appear to me to express the substance of its meaning. First, "possibility is the only saving remedy."[94] Possibility saves the self from the suffocating grip of necessity. Without possibility the self would be reduced to an unintelligible, unutterable, and meaningless "sequence of consonants." Second, "the possible corresponds precisely to the future."[95] Real possibility is not something which is lost to the past and to which the self is related only in memory. On the contrary, possibility is in the future and that towards which the self projects itself in hope.[96] Third, the existing subject is "educated by possibility . . . and in accordance with his infinity."[97] Further, authentic possibility is never the possibility of this or that finite possibility. If possibility is infinite, and only the self is infinite, then the self must be the content of its possibility. The self is "infinitely concrete."[98] What Kierkegaard means by this term is that possibility is the possibility of what the self already is in its immediacy, though now imaginatively reflected in the dimension of infinity.

When the discoveries of possibility are honestly administered [by imaginative reflection], possibility will then

[93] *SUD*, pp. 173-174.   [94] *SUD*, p. 172.   [95] *CD*, p. 82.

[96] *E/O*, I, 220f. We must not forget that possibility and necessity are dialectically related; consequently, memory and hope as existential outlooks are also dialectically related.

[97] *CD*, p. 140.   [98] *E/O*, II, 219.

disclose all finitudes but idealize them in the form of infinity. . . .[99]

Fourth, and in relation to the third point considered above, possibility is absolute. Possibility is related to the self as a morally binding authority. It is the content of the ethical *ought* which characterizes the nature of the individual's existence. In *Either/Or* Kierkegaard writes that to refer to the self as possible is too aesthetic and that it is better to refer to the self's possibility as the self's task.[100] Here Kierkegaard points out the ethical nature of possibility in terms of its moral authority for the individual. This explains the statement made in Chapter I about the self's being related to itself as an ethical task. The following passage from *The Concept of Dread* is illuminating.

> . . . if one is to learn absolutely, the individual must in turn have the possibility in himself and himself fashion that from which he is to learn [i.e., imaginatively reflect it as the substance for consciousness and as the task for freedom], even though the next instant it does not recognize that it was fashioned by him, but absolutely takes the power from him.[101]

Here we have an imaginative blending of Socrates and Kant. From Socrates, Kierkegaard learned that the possible is in oneself as the eternal. And from Kant, Kierkegaard learned the moral power of possibility over man. The imaginatively reflected ideal, after one has become self-conscious evokes a moral sense of duty and responsibility quite independently of its projection.

And, finally, "possibility is . . . the heaviest of all categories."[102] Why is this so? Because, through its integral association with freedom, it is the most consequential for the existential content of human existence. The failure to actualize one's possibility is the source of despair, melancholy,

---

[99] *CD*, p. 141.   [100] *E/O*, II, 256.   [101] *CD*, p. 140.
[102] *Ibid.*

suffering, guilt, and sin. Kierkegaard's brilliant descriptions of the concrete existential patterns of individual subjectivity are anchored to this "heaviest of all categories." Moreover, the descriptions of the existential phenomenon of risk and "the leap," with its "fear and trembling," are likewise hinged to this principle of the self's being.

Sløk stresses as particularly important this relation between necessity and possibility because the self's task of realizing itself as a relation of opposite moments is not a matter of "partial qualitative determinations," but of "the decisive determinations of the whole."[103] Sløk implies that the categories of necessity and possibility are the most potent expressions for the being of the self, because they entail the being of the finite and the infinite which is, by reflection, raised to the level of being-conscious of oneself as ideal and real, which is then posed as a possibility for freedom. They are the final moments in the self's development prior to its being brought into existence through freedom.

But is it not contradictory to speak of the self's relating itself to itself as a relating of necessity and possibility? The thought of possibility invites the notion of freedom, while necessity suggests its opposite. How can a man be free when necessity prevents him from exercising his freedom? How can freedom overcome the necessity of the unfree, the given situation in which the self finds itself? How can a self become its possibility when an equally strong force hampers self-realization? What more can the self expect than the agony of being caught in an irreconcilable tension between what it is and what it can become? And, in such a tension, how can one speak of freedom at all? Kierkegaard's answer, paradoxically, is that the self's necessity is its possibility. We have noted that one form of despair is the floundering of the self in abstract possibilities which are unchecked by necessity.

[103] Johannes Sløk, *Die Anthropologie Kierkegaards* (Copenhagen: Gyldendal, 1954), pp. 26, 54, 57, 62.

The self becomes an abstract possibility which tires itself out with floundering in the possible, but does not budge from the spot, nor get to any spot.[104]

The self which ventures into "poeticized" possibilities neither departs from the spot of its beginning nor advances to a spot beyond itself. The key is to realize that the task of becoming is to realize oneself, as it were, "on the spot."

For precisely the necessity is the spot; to become oneself is precisely a movement at the spot.[105]

To make it more difficult, Kierkegaard adds, and not incidentally, that in becoming oneself one "cannot relinquish anything in this whole, not the most painful, not the hardest to bear. . . ."[106] The self then is not independent. It is, in fact, dependent upon that which it is, and when it seeks to avoid what it is by becoming something it is not, despair is the result. "On the spot" movement, then, implies the appropriation of what one already is.

However freely he develops, an individual can never reach that point where he is absolutely independent, because true freedom consists in appropriating what is already given. Consequently, the individual is, through freedom, absolutely dependent upon that which is already given.[107]

With this appropriation of the given in the movement of spirit, the self's being as a relation which relates itself to itself is completed.

Now what is this freedom which ultimately and only is free to choose that which is necessary? What does Kierke-

104 *SUD*, p. 169.   105 *Ibid.*; cf. *E/O*, II, 181.
106 *E/O*, II, 220.

107 *Søren Kierkegaards Papirer*, ed. P. A. Heiberg, V. Kuhr, and E. Torsting, 20 vols. I-XI 3 (Copenhagen: Gyldendal, 1909-1948), III A 11. All translations from this edition of the *Papirer* are mine unless otherwise indicated.

gaard mean by freedom? As we have seen in our analysis of the different syntheses of the self, the self is defined as the dialectical element in the opposing moments which constitute the elements of the synthesis. We have also noted that spirit is that in the relation which relates the self to itself. Spirit is first identified as consciousness. Here spirit is the being of being aware, and is constituted in the collision of reality and ideality. Self-consciousness posits the self as possibility. Now the self as a relation is taken a step further. Kierkegaard says:

> But the synthesis is a relationship, and it is a relationship which, though it is derived, relates itself to itself, which means freedom.[108]

In a journal entry Kierkegaard makes the assertion that "motion [freedom] also belongs in the sphere of spirit."[109] In *The Concept of Dread*, he also refers to spirit's possibility in the individual as freedom's possibility.[110] Spirit is now expressing itself in the dialectical relation of necessity and possibility. Spirit ultimately realizes itself as the freedom which relates necessity and possibility.

But the identification of freedom with the self as existing spirit still leaves undefined the actual nature of freedom. What is freedom which is the self? Kierkegaard answers that freedom is fundamentally and essentially the power of "being able."[111] Freedom is essentially not choice, resignation, repentance, or faith; it is fundamentally not any of these specific types of action which designate a concrete movement of the self in relating to itself as possibility and necessity. No, freedom is that essential "being able," that

---

108 *SUD*, p. 162.

109 *SKP*, IV B 117. This is quoted from Lowrie's introduction to *R*, p. 19; cf. *R*, p. 119.

110 *CD*, p. 81.

111 *CD*, p. 40. In *SUD* Kierkegaard refers to the self as κατὰ δύναμιν. Liddell and Scott's *Greek-English Dictionary* translates this idiom as "to the best of one's power."

fundamental power by which all these concrete movements of the self in its various stages of existence are made possible. (This distinction between freedom and its forms as existential action will be a continuing issue in Chapters III, IV, V, and VI.)

Kierkegaard would agree with Heidegger that freedom adds nothing new to man, but only in the sense that for Kierkegaard the self *is* freedom. What is new is the way in which this power of "being able" is appropriated and used. Existential newness is related to the form which freedom takes. It should also be noted that freedom and possibility are not identical. Freedom *is* that which swings between necessity and possibility. Further, the exercise of freedom is not necessary. It is possible for the self not to choose. If one identifies freedom with choice as Sartre does, then freedom is necessary. For Kierkegaard, choice is only one expression of freedom; hence it is not necessary. Sartre argues that by not choosing one makes a choice. While this is true —and Kierkegaard would have to admit it—it is not true for him in an existential sense. For Kierkegaard it is possible not to choose, because choice presupposes consciousness, and it is possible to remain unconscious, i.e., unaware of oneself as possible. *Either/Or* represents this distinction between not choosing and choosing, between aesthetics and ethics.

Kierkegaard defends this interpretation of freedom through a logical analysis of the categories of possibility, necessity, and actuality, which are central to this notion of freedom. Part of his reason for doing this may have been his desire logically to undergird the most important category in his ontology. But it is more probable that he undertakes the logical analysis of freedom in order to rescue it from an identification with the Hegelian logical category of mediation.

Two entries in his journal reflect the problem, and his way of resolving it.

Freedom and motion is perhaps one of the most difficult problems in all philosophy.[112]

Perhaps what we most need now to throw light on the relation between logic and ontology is a study of the concepts of possibility, actuality, necessity. [113]

Kierkegaard's efforts logically to separate the notions of mediation (*aufgehoben*) and freedom demonstrate his intention of placing freedom in the realm of ontology and not in the realm of logic.

Another more lengthy passage succinctly states the problem and his way of resolving it.

Transition is becoming. In the sphere of logic transition is mute, and in the sphere of freedom it becomes. So when possibility in logic qualifies itself as actuality, it merely disturbs the hushed reticence of the logical process by talking about motion and transition. In the sphere of freedom, on the other hand, there is possibility, and actuality emerges as transcendency. Therefore, when even Aristotle said that transition from possibility to actuality is a κίνησις he was not talking about logical possibility and actuality of freedom, and therefore he quite rightly posits motion. [114]

Three major points appear in this entry.

First, Kierkegaard argues that to talk about the transformation of possibility into actuality in logic is idle talk which "only disturbs the hushed reticence of the logical possibility." He writes in *The Concept of Dread* that

[112] *SKP*, V C 27. This is quoted from Gregor Malantschuk, *Kierkegaard's Way to Truth*, trans. Mary Michelsen (Minneapolis: Augsburg, 1963), p. 79.

[113] *SKJP*, I, 199.

[114] A journal entry (IV B 117) quoted by Walter Lowrie in his introduction to his translation of *R*, p. 21.

in logic every movement is an immanent movement, which in a deeper sense is no movement, as one will easily convince oneself if one reflects that the very concept of movement is a transcendence which can find no place in logic.[115]

Kierkegaard says that Hegelian Logic relies on the negative, and that if everything comes to pass in that way then "nothing comes to pass."[116] On the contrary, change comes about by a transcendence which refers to a cause in the sense of a subjective, passionate decision. For Kierkegaard, "nothing can come into existence by virtue of a logical ground but only by a cause."[117]

The second point follows upon the first. Transition in logic is mute, because "the change involved in coming into existence is actuality, i.e., a change in actual life, not in thought only: transition takes place with freedom."[118] Becoming or existential change in existence is brought about by freedom. The requirements of freedom cannot be accommodated within the confines of systematic thought, since human existence and action require real freedom as well as thought. Kierkegaard argues that in the realization of possibility something over and above thought must enter in as a motive principle. In mediation the actual is present immanently in the possible,[119] whereas in the movement of freedom the actual emerges from the possible in a transcendent way.

The third point is that transition from possibility to actuality emerges as a transcendency. If freedom is a transcendent cause which cannot be thought, then its product, as it were, is a transcendency in the sense that it too cannot be grasped and described by thought. The existential con-

---

115 *CD*, p. 12.
116 See Hegel's *Logic*, pp. 171 and 219 for his discussion of negation.
117 *PF*, p. 93. 118 *Ibid.*
119 Hegel, *The Logic*, pp. 265-268.

tent of the moment of passion in which the possible is actualized defies conceptualization.

Finally, spirit may stand in relation to a divine "other."

> If this relation which relates itself to its own self is constituted by another, the relation doubtless is the third term, but this relation (the third term) is in turn a relation relating itself to that which constituted the whole.[120]

> But the decisive affirmation comes only when a man is brought to the utmost extremity, so that humanly speaking no possibility exists. Then the question is whether he will believe that for God all things are possible—that is to say whether he will believe.[121]

What Kierkegaard intends by the phrase "no possibility exists" is not important for the discussion here. Its meaning will receive attention in the last two chapters. It is important now to be aware that the relation is established and that the establishing power, as the power of all possibilities, is experienced when no other possibility is left for the self.

To say that the self is established is not to say that it has been given a specific, concrete possibility, a specific destiny, but only that it can ultimately become itself—whatever that may be—according to the "power of all possibilities." The self includes no specific possibilities as necessarily its own; it is simply initially identical with the power of being able.

The self as we find it in a reflexive analysis of existence is simply a synthesis of finitude and infinitude which spirit as freedom is responsible for actualizing in existence. As we shall see in the second part of this book, the different ways in which spirit may relate to the synthesis give rise to the variety of modes of existence which Kierkegaard so vividly describes in his pseudonyms. Put another way, it is the attempt of spirit to reconstruct this synthesis in existence as an actuality rather than allowing it to continue as a mere

---

[120] *SUD*, p. 146.   [121] *Ibid.*, p. 171.

human possibility that constitutes the different modes of human existence, including Christian existence. Existence in all its modes grows out of the life of spirit understood as consciousness and freedom.

All existential actions of spirit are contingent and not necessary. That is to say, spirit is under no ontological, moral, or religious necessity to make any choice, including the choice of a divine "other." The appearance of God, then, in the development of spirit is made possible because spirit is free. But this does not entail in any sense the necessity of making God part of the ontological structure of the self. Rather, it is precisely because the self is what it is, that religious existence can become a genuine human possibility. It is in this sense that spirit may relate to a divine "other," thereby making it the existential ground of the self. Kierkegaard's conception of the self does not depend upon any Christian *Weltanschauung*. He avoids this move by making freedom the very essence of the self. The assertion of dependence is itself an act of freedom and only in this freely established relation-with-an-"other" can the divine "other" come into existence in the life of an individual. Hopefully, this relation of the self (being) to Christian existence will be made more clear and explicit in the fifth and sixth chapters of this book.

Time and the Eternal: The Instant

Kierkegaard begins his discussion of this expression of the self as a synthesis by accepting the definition of time as infinite succession.[122] He then immediately proceeds to protest that under this definition of time, it is impossible to distinguish the dimensions of temporality, because they are not inherently present in time. Temporality is not implicit in time. The problem, argues Kierkegaard, is that the present cannot find a foothold in infinite successiveness, whereby time can be divided so that the past and future can emerge.

[122] *CD*, pp. 76-77.

But precisely because every moment, like the sum of moments, is a process (a going-by) no moment is a present, and in the same sense there is neither past, present, nor future.[123]

No moment is itself present, because it itself is infinitely divisible; therefore, there can be no duration, no staticity in time such that a before and an after can be established. Kierkegaard continues that the problem with this view of time is that the present is incorrectly considered as a moment of time. Such a mistake makes of the present something "infinitely void" and "infinitely vanishing."

Kierkegaard counters this view of the present with the claim that "the present is the eternal, or rather the eternal is the present, and the present is full." And only by introducing the eternal present into time is it possible to establish the temporal dimensions of past, present, and future. Kierkegaard refers to the introduction of the eternal present into time as the "instant," which he describes as "the first reflection of eternity into time."[124] More specifically,

the instant is that ambiguous moment in which time and eternity touch one another, thereby positing the *temporal*, where time is constantly intersecting eternity and eternity constantly permeating time. Only now does that division we talked about acquire significance: the present, the past, and the future.[125]

Spirit's establishment of the synthesis introduces the eternal into the dialectic of the self's becoming, because spirit itself is the eternal.[126] Prior to the establishment of the self as a synthesis, the eternal spirit is absorbed in the infinite on-goingness of time. But when spirit breaks open the innocent unity of the self and establishes the self as a synthesis, the instant appears.[127] Now this conjunction of time

---

[123] *CD*, p. 77. [124] *Ibid.*, pp. 77-79.

[125] *CD*, p. 80. [126] *CD*, p. 81.

[127] "No sooner is the spirit posited [in the synthesis] than the instant is there." *CD*, p. 79.

and the eternal which is accompanied by spirit occurs in two tightly knitted stages.

The initial collision of time and the eternal occurs in consciousness. In the instant of consciousness, spirit synthesizes its bodily reality, which is subject to the on-goingness of time, and its eternal ideal, which appears in the future.[128] This collision of reality and ideality in consciousness is simultaneously the intersection of time and the eternal in consciousness. Kierkegaard expresses this when he writes that "the synthesis of the soulish and the bodily . . . is accomplished only when the spirit posits at the same time along with this the second synthesis of the eternal and the temporal."[129] Therefore, the initial stage of the instant occurs in consciousness.

But no sooner is the future, eternal ideal grasped in consciousness than it slips into the past. "The instant and the future posit in turn the past."[130] The on-goingness of bodily reality as subject to time passes the ideal object (self) of consciousness by, thereby making it past. Consequently, the ideal self is now in the past as necessity and must be again posited in the future—now as spirit's possibility. And if spirit, as freedom, actualizes its possibility the second stage of the instant is established in the existential unification of time and the eternal. In this synthesis of time and the eternal, the self gains eternity.

Kierkegaard writes in his journal that "in eternity a person is not in the succession of time, and being *eterno modo* is the most intensive punctuality."[131] By punctuality Kierkegaard means presence. The punctual present is the instant in which past and future are synthesized as presence. This instant is the negation of time in the sense that its succes-

[128] Kierkegaard asserts that "the eternal means first of all the future. . . ." *CD*, p. 80.

[129] *CD*, p. 81.

[130] *CD*, p. 80. Cf. "If the instant is posited so is the eternal—but also the future which comes again like the past." *Ibid.*, p. 81.

[131] *SKJP*, I, 842.

siveness is momentarily negated. This instant is "brief and temporal indeed, like every moment; it is transient as all moments are; it is past, like every moment in the next moment. And yet it is decisive, and filled with the Eternal. Such a moment ought to have a distinctive name; let us call it the 'Fullness of time.' "[132] Spirit gains eternity, i.e., presence, as a creature of time and, therefore, it is no sooner gained than it is lost to the past in the on-goingness of time. Eternity, then, once again becomes spirit's possibility.

It is now possible to see that spirit as the eternal in the process of becoming in time expresses basically and fundamentally the task and the problem facing the self. The entire development of the self from its beginning as reflected, through the emergence of self-consciousness, to its achievement as freedom must be comprehended within the categories of time, eternity, and temporality. The self as reflected exists in time and eternity. The foundation of the moments of reality and necessity as reflected is time, while the moments of ideality and possibility as reflected are eternal. But the awareness of the collision of these opposing moments in consciousness posits temporality as the field upon which the ultimate challenge of self-realization must be met. Self-consciousness is the awareness of oneself as both real (past) and ideal (future), and freedom realizes itself by uniting in existence itself as necessary (past) and itself as possible (future).

The importance of Kierkegaard's understanding of time and eternity for an understanding of his thought as a whole cannot be overestimated. The expression of the self as a synthesis of time and the eternal is important in the sense that the other expressions of the self as a synthesis are all affected by this basic and fundamental fact that spirit's task of gaining eternity is enormously complicated by its inextricable confinement to time. The self is constantly being swept along in time. Its facticity is constantly being added

[132] *PF*, p. 22.

to, so that the self is constantly a task for itself. But the category of the eternal is equally fundamental, because it expresses the notion that the self is not necessarily lost in the infinite successiveness of time, but is capable of transforming time into future and past which may be united in the present.

SUMMARY

The purpose of this chapter has been to delineate the self-structure which, according to Kierkegaard, is universally inherent in all human beings. Kierkegaard's five expressions of the self as a synthesis are, as we have seen, constitutive of an ontology. This analysis has determined what constitutes this ontology, through a detailed description of the unique aspect of the self contained in each expression of the self as a synthesis.

Each synthesis is not merely a restatement of the other four syntheses but expresses a particular aspect of the being of the self not expressed in the others. It is not possible to comprehend the being of the self in its entirety until each synthesis has been examined and until the interrelations of the five syntheses have been illuminated. Furthermore, we have seen that the being of the self is constituted not only by its synthetic structure but also by a dialectical process, a movement of spirit from immediacy to actuality, which both constitutes and is constituted by the interrelationships of the five expressions of the self as a synthesis. Now this fivefold structure of the self and the movement of spirit by which the five elements are related constitute an abstract description of a process which occurs throughout the dialectical development of the self. It is the abstract form by which the self develops. The movements from aesthetics to ethics, from ethics to Religiousness A, and from Religiousness A to Religiousness B all occur within the framework of this form. Before attempting to interpret these movements in terms of the underlying self-structure in Chapters IV, V, and VI, it is necessary now to undertake a discussion of the relation of spirit to the problem of unity.[133]

[133] It might be objected that any ontology which is confined to a discussion of human being, excluding nature and God, is at best a regional ontology and possibly only a philosophical anthropology. I do not think that Kierkegaard's doctrine of the self can be called a philosophical anthropology, for such an anthropology attempts simply to provide a theory of man without investigating the question of being. Martin Buber's thought strikes me as an example of this kind of anthropology. But philosophers like Hegel, Heidegger, and Sartre are concerned to discuss not simply man but, more basically, the question of being and the nature of the relation of that question to an analysis of man. Heidegger's and Sartre's earlier works hinge on the notion of the inseparability of these two questions. Although Kierkegaard's ontology is very different from those found in *Being and Time* and *Being and Nothing*, I shall be arguing that Kierkegaard's distinction between self and individual existence operates on the assumption that the resolution of the question of Being cannot be divorced from an analysis of human existence. More specifically, for Kierkegaard, being is disclosed in an analysis of existence as the necessary condition of its possibility.

It is true that the concept of human being developed by Kierkegaard in his doctrine of the self omits the reality of God. For Kierkegaard, the God question is an existential question, not an ontological one. Discussions of God appear in his descriptions of the ethico-religious stage of existence, not in his ontology. At least this is the case in the pseudonyms. But in the journals, there are two passages which suggest that Kierkegaard may have been willing to extend the dimensions of his ontology to include God: "God is really the *terminus medius* in everything a man undertakes; the difference between the religious and the purely human attitude is that the latter does not know it—Christianity is therefore the highest union between God and man because it has made the union conscious" (*SKJ* #487). "Christianity really presupposes that eternity engages a man absolutely. Christianity knows the remedy of this concern" (*SKJP*, 1, 844). These two passages seem to suggest that there is an ontological unity between God and man. This is a surprising suggestion since Kierkegaard in the pseudonyms is so anxious to deny this very Hegelian notion. It is precisely this position with which he takes issue in the theology of his teacher, Martensen. At any rate, I do not think it possible to argue that Kierkegaard includes God as a dimension of the ontology developed in terms of the doctrine of the self in the pseudonyms. Further work must be done on these and related passages in the journals to discover their implications for the ontology in the pseudonyms.

As for nature, it does not receive the attention it should in Kierkegaard's pseudonyms. Whether a view of nature can be ontologically developed in Kierkegaard is a question that I have not investigated. Since, then, Kierkegaard's descriptive ontology does omit nature and God in fact, though not necessarily in principle, it may be that we must call it a regional ontology in its present form in the pseudonyms.

CHAPTER III

The Dialectical Development
of Spirit

IN the preceding chapter, we explored the sense of Fahren-bach's term *Was-Sein*, and observed how the specific struc-ture of each expression of the self as a synthesis is deter-mined by the manner in which spirit constitutes and unites the relation. It is equally true, although it has not been em-phasized until now, that the dialectical development of spir-it is limited by what I have analyzed as *Was-Sein*. More explicitly, spirit is limited by that which it constitutes. To say that spirit is limited by that which it constitutes means that spirit cannot in any manner fulfill its own being apart from its involvement with these dialectically opposing mo-ments of the self which we have conceptualized as syn-theses. Furthermore, to argue that spirit constitutes these syntheses does not imply that they dialectically emerge from spirit. Rather, such an assertion means that spirit ful-fills its own being by bringing to consciousness and realiz-ing in existence the contradictions already implicitly present in the existence of the potential self.[1]

The examination of aesthetic immediacy revealed the presence of the finite and the infinite aspects of the self prior to the emergence of spirit by which they are positively related to each other. To this extent, spirit is always made possible through the given elements of the synthesis. Spirit, if it is to fulfill its being, must discover and realize itself within an already established set of limitations. The exist-ence of spirit is the action by which a relation, whose con-

[1] Kierkegaard, *The Concept of Dread*, trans. Walter Lowrie (Prince-ton University Press, 1957), p. 121.

stitutive moments are given to it prior to the emergence of spirit, is existentially actualized. Therefore, spirit's fulfillment of its own being is made possible through the preliminary and reflected establishment of a relation of two moments which we understand as a synthesis. The dialectical development of spirit occurs, of necessity, within this synthetic framework.[2]

Now we have seen that spirit ultimately emerges as freedom and that spirit as freedom is dialectically dependent upon the prior emergence of spirit as self-consciousness. The task before us now is to examine more thoroughly the dialectical relation between consciousness and freedom in the developing life of spirit. In turning from an analysis of *Was-Sein* to an analysis of *Wie-Sein*, I am not now taking up for discussion a new phenomenon. The uniting of the self as a synthesis constitutes the dialectical development of spirit, and I shall now turn to this development of spirit by which the synthesis is achieved. In Chapter II, I concentrated on the structure of the self as a synthesis of two opposing and contradictory moments. Now, in this chapter, I shall concentrate on the very internal activity of spirit by which the structure of the self as a synthesis is constituted. This internal activity of spirit which is driven forward by the dialectical relation of consciousness and freedom gives rise to the progressive development, movement, of spirit. In conjunction with the examination of the nature and the course of this movement, we shall re-examine the concepts

[2] Kierkegaard writes that the "soulish-bodily synthesis in every man is planned with a view to being spirit." Kierkegaard, *The Sickness Unto Death*, trans. Walter Lowrie (Princeton University Press, 1954), p. 176. The self as a synthesis of the finite and the infinite becomes spirit in the degree that spirit understands itself as the synthesizing power of the self as finite and infinite. The dialectical development of spirit is a process in which spirit understands itself in relation to the self as the power by which the self is related to itself. The expanding consciousness of spirit entails the increasing incorporation of the self by spirit. Therefore, we can speak of this process as one in which the self becomes spirit.

73

of immediacy and unity as the *terminus a quo* and the *terminus ad quem* of movement.

SELF-KNOWLEDGE: THE DIALECTICAL INTERPENETRATION OF CONSCIOUSNESS AND FREEDOM

The process described in Chapter II is an ever-recurring cycle through which the potential self must continually pass in its drive toward its final realization in existence. Each completion of the cycle, each mediation,[3] projects the self into a new immediacy. That is to say, each new immediacy constitutes, on the one hand, an actual and higher degree of consciousness and freedom, and on the other hand, a potentially still higher degree of consciousness and freedom.[4] As we have observed, the dialectical interaction of consciousness and freedom constitutes the movement of spirit. Before proceeding to a discussion of the meaning of the concepts of immediacy, movement, and unity, it is necessary to examine more closely this relation of consciousness and freedom.

As we have seen, Kierkegaard first relates spirit to self-consciousness and then to freedom as that point at which "self-consciousness is most concentrated and most normally itself."[5] In *The Concept of Dread*, Kierkegaard writes that "freedom is infinite and does not arise out of anything,"[6] and, consequently, cannot be explained by any antecedent. This assertion that freedom "does not arise out of anything"

[3] The term "mediation" will be used, hereafter, to refer to one full revolution of the cycle described in Chapter II.

[4] The section in *SUD*, "Despair Viewed Under the Aspect of Consciousness," explicitly illustrates the major and the more subtle gradations in the development of consciousness. And, in discussing the intention of this section, Kierkegaard refers to "gradation[s] in the consciousness of the self" (p. 210), and to the "potentiation in the consciousness of the self." *SUD*, p. 244.

[5] George Price, *The Narrow Pass* (New York: McGraw-Hill, 1963), p. 37.

[6] *CD*, p. 100.

reflects another distinctly Kantian theme in Kierkegaard's thought, viz., the *a priori* nature of freedom. Kierkegaard argues that if freedom can be explained it does not arise out of itself and, hence, is not infinite—we would say *a priori.* Rather, it would arise out of reason; consequently, reason, as the rationale of freedom, would be logically prior to freedom. Moreover, a rational explanation of the origin of freedom would, in Kierkegaard's view, reduce it to necessity. In Kierkegaard's mind, this is the case with and the crucial error in Hegel's concept of freedom. For instance, Kierkegaard argues that "to want to say that man sins necessarily is to want to construe the curve of the leap as a straight line."[7] To exchange the curve of the leap for a straight line is to want to explain sin as a logically necessary ontological state rather than a result of human freedom.[8] Rationally to explain freedom would require a degree of self-transcendence which would take the existing subject completely out of existence and time, and such transcendence is available, according to Kierkegaard, to God alone.[9]

Indeed, the task confronting each individual is not to explain one's freedom by venturing into heady metaphysical speculation but, on the contrary, to become conscious of oneself through freedom.[10] Such an achievement reflects nothing less than the total acceptance of responsibility for one's existence, and such an ethical accomplishment is all that a finitely existing spirit can legitimately expect of itself. Moreover, the complete acceptance of responsibility for one's existence—this means to become completely free—

7 *Ibid.*

8 Sin, on the contrary, like freedom "presupposes itself" and "cannot be explained." *CD*, p. 100. I have already noted in Chapter II that freedom is a transcendent cause beyond the confines of human thought, and that its product is a transcendency because it cannot be grasped and explained by reason.

9 Kierkegaard, *Concluding Unscientific Postscript*, trans. David Swenson and Walter Lowrie (Princeton University Press, 1941), pp. 107-108.

10 *The Journals of Søren Kierkegaard*, ed. and trans. Alexander Dru (Oxford: Oxford University Press, 1938), #825.

rather than the vain striving for metaphysical explanations, is what peculiarly distinguishes and dignifies man as man.

The self is a self-constituting process, and the self's awareness of its freedom and its production of that freedom are not separable. Now it may appear self-contradictory to assert that the self produces freedom when we have just maintained that freedom is infinite and cannot arise out of anything. Perhaps the distinction which Blass makes between freedom's being-in-itself and freedom's being-for-itself will be helpful here.

> As being-in-itself (*Von-sich-her-sein*) freedom is not dependent and is, consequently, absolute and unconditional. As being which relates to itself (*Auf-sich-Bezogensein*) freedom is always realized through the relating of the self as a relation to itself.[11]

That is to say, freedom in its original and undeveloped potential[12] is simply given and is, therefore, absolute and unconditional. Freedom is produced to the extent that as a given potentiality it is actualized by the act of relating the self as a relation to itself. As we have seen, this self-relating act occurs first as self-consciousness and, then, as the repetition of the content of consciousness in existence.

In Chapter II, the distinction was made between to-be-self-conscious and to-be-in-existence, and I argued that the former necessarily preceded the latter in the development of spirit. While this distinction is schematically valuable for tracing the development of spirit, it obscures the fact that the movement from self-consciousness to its repetition in existence is a single movement by which self-understanding is achieved.[13] The schema in Chapter II presents the dis-

---

[11] Josef L. Blass, *Die Krise der Freiheit im Denken Søren Kierkegaards* (Duesseldorf: A. Hen, 1968), p. 56.

[12] Kierkegaard describes this state in *CD*, pp. 37-38, as the "dreaming . . . sleeping" condition of spirit.

[13] To avoid semantic confusion, the following distinctions will hereafter apply to the terms self-consciousness, self-awareness, on the one

torted impression that self-consciousness is tantamount to self-understanding and is itself not a moment of understanding. But in a journal entry Kierkegaard writes that "to understand one's life is to be spirit."[14] Spirit has already been characterized as interest. Spirit is essentially interested in itself. Interest implies the action of finding out about something, of discovering; and in the case of spirit, self-understanding is the goal or outcome of spirit's interest in itself. In other words, spirit as interested in itself seeks to find out about itself, to know itself. This goal is fulfilled in the repetition of self-consciousness in existence. An extensive, but important, passage from *The Concept of Dread* will help to clarify this notion of spirituality.

The most concrete content consciousness can have is consciousness of itself, not the pure self-consciousness, but

---

hand, and self-understanding, on the other. Self-consciousness and self-awareness are synonymous and refer to the reflexive state of consciousness in which the self becomes conscious of itself as a synthesis of reality and ideality. Self-understanding, however, refers to the actualization or completion of self-consciousness, i.e., to the repetition of self-consciousness in existence. The term "understanding" now makes it possible to see as unified a phenomenon which up to this point could only be presented schematically and, hence, as fragmented into separate and distinct elements.

Kierkegaard never provides a dictionary definition for the terms *Forstand*, translated by Swenson in *PF* as "reason" and by Swenson and Lowrie in *CUP* as "understanding." We can be certain that *Forstand* represents neither the objective activity by which the categories are neatly arranged nor cogitation devoid of subjective content. *Forstand*, understanding, entails a source of energy derived from the subject's infinite interest in himself. The material upon which it reflects is both the subject's experience and the content of his imagination. Together this material is reflected as an ethical possibility intended for actualization. For a discussion of the confusion created by the English translation of *Forstand* as both "reason" and "understanding," see Robert Widenman, "Kierkegaard's Terminology—and English," *Kierkegaardiana* (Copenhagen: Munksgaard, 1968), VII, 113-130.

[14] *Søren Kierkegaards Papirer*, ed. P. A. Heiberg, V. Kuhr, and E. Torsting, 20 vols. I-XI 3 (Copenhagen: Gyldendal, 1909-1948), X³ A 76.

the self-consciousness which is so concrete that no author . . . has ever been able to describe such a thing, although such a thing is what every man is. This self-consciousness is not contemplation; he who thinks that it is has not understood himself, for he sees that he himself is meanwhile in the process of becoming and so cannot be a finished object of self-contemplation. This self-consciousness is, therefore, a deed, and this deed in turn is inwardness, and every time inwardness does not correspond to this consciousness, there is a form of the demoniacal as soon as the absence of inwardness expresses itself as dread of its acquisition.[15]

This means that the existing subject does not understand himself as freedom until he is, in fact, free. Self-understanding is the result of an act and not of contemplation. That self-understanding is a deed means that the completion of self-consciousness is not what is described in Chapter II, but is, on the contrary, the repetition of consciousness in existence. One does not truly understand himself until the content of self-consciousness has been inwardly appropriated, i.e., acted upon in existence.[16] That is to say, the exercise of one's freedom actualizes and completes self-consciousness, because only in an act of freedom does the self know itself as freedom. Therefore, when, as self-conscious, the self appears to itself as possible and the interest of spirit emerges as the freedom to realize this self, the self's knowledge of itself as free remains hypothetical until the act of freedom is consummated in existence.

Self-understanding, then, is fulfilled in action and remains incomplete at the level of self-consciousness. This point hinges on what Kierkegaard means by to know. First, to know means primarily to know oneself.

---

[15] *CD*, p. 128.

[16] "The real action is not an external act but an internal decision in which the individual puts an end to the mere possibility and identifies himself with the content of his thought in order to exist in it. This is the action." *CUP*, pp. 302-303.

The law for the development of the self with respect to knowledge, in so far as it is true that the self becomes the self, is that the increasing degree of knowledge corresponds with the degree of self-knowledge; that the more the self knows the more it knows itself. If this does not occur, then the more knowledge increases, the more it becomes a kind of inhuman knowing for the production of which man's self is squandered....[17]

Knowledge, then, which is relevant to the development of the self, must always be self-knowledge.

Second, and equally important, one knows a thing only when its concept has been actualized as an existential reality through an act of the existing subject. That is to say, knowledge is not knowledge for me unless it possesses an existential reality which I alone am capable of imposing upon it.[18] Consequently, the collision of reality and ideality in self-consciousness is incomplete, in so far as self-understanding is concerned, until it is repeated in existence. Therefore, knowledge of oneself as freedom remains an hypothesis, an assumption—albeit one upon which the self must act—as long as the repetition in existence of self-consciousness remains a possibility. The self cannot know that it is free until it acts upon the hypothesis that it, in fact, is free.[19]

Therefore, actual and complete knowledge of oneself as a relation of finitude and infinitude fully realized in existence through and as freedom is subsequent to the act by

[17] *SUD*, p. 164.

[18] *CUP*, p. 284. Cf. "The aesthetic and intellectual principle is that no reality is thought or understood until its *esse* has been resolved into a *posse*. The ethical principle is that no possibility is understood until each *posse* has become an *esse*." *CUP*, p. 288.

[19] In a journal entry, Kierkegaard refutes Descartes' placing thought over freedom in his *cogito ergo sum* and declares that Fichte is more correct when he asserts: "I act (*handler*); therefore I am." Kierkegaard argues that consciousness of freedom never precedes the act but is either simultaneous with or subsequent to the act which proceeds upon the assumption that one is free. *SKP*, IV C 11.

which it is achieved. Self-knowledge is the consequence of the two-fold act by which the self relates itself to itself, first in consciousness and then in existence as freedom.[20] One of the most lucid passages in Kierkegaard's thought which illustrated the dialectical relatedness of consciousness and freedom and implicitly implies the dialectically developing character of the self will help, at this point, to carry the analysis a step further.

> Generally speaking, consciousness, i.e., consciousness of self, is the decisive criterion of the self. The more consciousness, the more self; the more consciousness, the more will, and the more will the more self. A man who has no will at all is no self; the more will he has, the more consciousness of self he has also [and, consequently, the more self].[21]

The passage states that will depends upon consciousness, that, in turn, consciousness depends upon will, and that without will there is no self. Furthermore, the use of the term *more* implies the existence of gradations in the development of the self. We have already observed how freedom depends upon self-consciousness and how self-knowledge

[20] "['Know yourself'] cannot be the real goal of life if it is not also the beginning. The ethical individual knows himself; but this knowledge is no mere contemplation. It is a reflection upon himself which itself is an action, and therefore I have deliberately used the expression 'choose oneself' instead of 'know oneself.'" *E/O*, II, 261. Cf. "And this is the wonderful thing about life, that every man who gives heed to himself knows what no science knows, since he knows what he himself is; and this is the profundity of the Greek saying (know thyself), which so long has been understood in the German way as pure self-consciousness, the airiness of idealism, surely it is high time to understand it in the Greek way, and then again in such a way as the Greeks would have understood it if they had had Christian presuppositions. But the real 'self' is first posited by the qualitative leap." *CD*, pp. 70-71.

[21] *SUD*, p. 162. Will is for Kierkegaard a synonym for human freedom. "Freedom is the will." *E/O*, II, 180. For a discussion of Kierkegaard's dependence upon German Idealism for this identification, see Price, *The Narrow Pass*, p. 75f.

depends upon both consciousness and freedom, but what is new here is Kierkegaard's assertion that consciousness depends upon will (freedom).[22] In what sense can this be the case?

Self-consciousness is reflexive because it results from reflection which bends back upon what is already the case. That which is reflected and grasped in consciousness is already there. That is to say, the content of self-consciousness is already a reality but as unreflected and, hence, as unconscious, in the history of the individual self.[23] Without reflection, there is no self-consciousness; without self-consciousness, no freedom; and without freedom, no self-understanding. By passing through this cycle, a new and still higher self-knowledge emerges. But now this self becomes a new, immediate subject for the repetition of this cycle, which in turn eventuates in a still higher form of self-knowledge.[24] For example, consciously to persist in resignation produces a new immediacy, i.e., a new but unconscious self, viz., the self as suffering.[25] The task now becomes one of reflecting on suffering so that it may become the content of self-consciousness and, ultimately, may be acted upon through freedom.[26] Only in this way can the self come to know itself as suffering even though it already is suffering, but unconsciously so. The task is always one of achieving "transparency,"[27] i.e., of understanding the immediacy in which one finds oneself. Persistence in suffering, in turn, produces a

[22] For Kierkegaard, all expressions of freedom are acts of the will.

[23] The state of unconsciousness as the result of the absence of reflection will be further explored below in the section on immediacy.

[24] Kierkegaard says the more consciousness, the more will, and the more will the more self. The implications of the term more will have to wait for the sections below on movement and unity. Here I am simply trying to show that the repetition of the cycle described in Chapter II constitutes the development of spirit.

[25] *CUP*, pp. 468-469.

[26] *Ibid.*, pp. 396-397.

[27] Kierkegaard never explicitly defines this term. He uses it to mean self-understanding in *SLW* (p. 435) and *SUD* (p. 147).

new immediacy, viz., guilt.[28] Now the self must again penetrate guilt with reflection, incorporate it into one's consciousness and then act upon it in order to know that one
is guilty.[29]

Self-understanding, then, at any given point within the
development of spirit is incomplete because it becomes the
terminus a quo of a higher reflection which begins anew the
cycle of reflection, self-consciousness, and action which terminates in self-understanding. Remembering that spirit is
freedom, it can be said that the process by which spirit attains an understanding of itself is a process of actualization,
comprehension, of oneself as freedom. The ultimate goal of
the self's development, as I have attempted to show, is to
become completely free. At that point, spirit's development
is complete, and the final *terminus ad quem* of being completely conscious of and responsible for oneself is actualized.

This self-constituting process begins in a unity of original
immediacy and terminates in a unity of attained immediacy.
We shall now pay closer attention to the meaning of these
two phenomena and to the meaning of the phenomenon of
movement by which the two are connected.

IMMEDIACY: THE DORMANCY OF SPIRIT AS CONSCIOUSNESS AND FREEDOM

As we have seen, the immediate individual is "soulishly"
determined. The immediate individual is dialectically related to his natural, cultural, and social surroundings.[30] The

---

[28] *CUP*, pp. 468-469.

[29] This stretch of the development of spirit occurs in the ethical
stage as it is described in *CUP*. In Chapter V a detailed examination of
these movements of spirit will be made in terms of the schema developed in Chapter II.

[30] *CD*, p. 37. Cf. "The immediate man . . . is merely soulishly determined, his self or he himself is a something included along with 'the
other' in the compass of the temporal and the worldly, and it has only
an illusory appearance of possessing in it something eternal. Thus the

immediate self, which finitely reflects, is finitely conscious and, hence, finitely free.

> Inasmuch as this view [that life is the pursuit of pleasure, the view of immediate consciousness] is split into a multiplicity one easily perceives that it lies in the sphere of [finite] reflection; this reflection, however, is only a finite reflection, and the personality remains in its immediacy.[31]

The self, which is not infinitely reflected, is not aware of itself as a synthesis of the finite and the infinite. In immediacy, then, ideality and reality are synonymous.

> "Immediacy is fortune," for in the immediate consciousness there is no contradiction [between the self as finite (real) and infinite (ideal)]; the immediate individual is essentially seen as a fortunate individual and "the view of life natural to immediacy" is one based on fortune.[32]

Kierkegaard expresses this state of affairs in another way by saying that the immediate self is an ignorant self and, as such, is "soulishly" determined.

> Innocence [immediacy] is ignorance. In his innocence man is not determined as spirit but is soulishly determined in immediate unity with his natural condition. Spirit is dreaming in man.[33]

---

self coheres immediately with 'the other' wishing, desiring, enjoying, etc. . . ." *SUD*, p. 184.

[31] Kierkegaard, *E/O*, II, 188. Cf. "This is pure immediacy or else an immediacy which contains a quantitative reflection. Here there is no infinite consciousness of the self. . . ." *SUD*, p. 184; cf. *CD*, p. 140.

[32] *CUP*, p. 388.

[33] *CD*, p. 37. Kierkegaard occasionally replaced the term "immediacy" with the term "innocence" in order to substitute his ethical emphasis for Hegel's logical emphasis. *CD*, p. 32. Moreover, Kierkegaard argues that as an enduring reality and not a logical concept, it cannot be mediated (*aufgehoben*) in the Hegelian sense of the word. "Innocence is not an imperfection with which one cannot be content to stop but must go further; for innocence is always sufficient unto itself. . . ." *Ibid.*, p. 34.

In immediacy, spirit is dreaming and, hence, asleep. As such, it is inactive and does not disturb the enduring body-soul unity. Consequently, when the self is an undifferentiated body-soul unity, the self's awareness, consciousness, is immediate or pre-reflective. Properly speaking, therefore, "immediacy has no self."[34]

But immediacy is also characterized by spirit's desire to fulfill itself.

> There comes a moment in a man's life when his immediacy is, as it were, ripened and the spirit demands a higher form in which it will apprehend itself as spirit. Man, so long as he is immediate spirit, coheres with the whole earthly life, and now the spirit would collect itself, as it were, out of this dispersion, and become in itself transformed, the personality would be conscious of itself in its eternal validity.[35]

The entirety of immediacy is penetrated with the darkness of dread and melancholy (despair) resulting from the failure of spirit to advance beyond immediacy to the level of infinite consciousness. Kierkegaard persuasively illustrates this point in a description of Nero's insatiable desire for pleasure:

> The immediacy of spirit is unable to break through, and yet it demands a metamorphosis, it demands a higher form of existence. . . . The spirit constantly desires to break through, but it cannot attain the metamorphosis, it is constantly disappointed, and he would offer it the satiety of pleasure. . . . The spirit wills to break through, wills that he shall possess himself in his consciousness, but

[34] Kierkegaard's description of the aesthetic sphere is a description of the different life styles (stages) of immediacy. He denies the presence of the self in this sphere when he writes that "great as the differences within the aesthetic domain may be, all the stages have this similarity, that spirit is not determined as spirit but is immediately determined." Kierkegaard, *E/O*, II, 185.

[35] *E/O*, II, 193.

that he is unable to do, and the spirit is repressed and gathers new wrath. He does not possess himself. . . .[36]

As we have seen, immediacy is a state which is not necessarily mediated. It is a state sufficient to itself, and it is possible for spirit defiantly to repress itself by refusing to comprehend and to actualize itself as freedom. It is possible for spirit to remain in sleep by stifling its internal tendency toward self-understanding and in so doing to submit itself to the agony of despair. Continuing with the characterization of Nero's desperation, Kierkegaard writes:

> Then the spirit within him gathers like a dark cloud, its wrath broods over his soul, and it becomes an anguishing dread which ceases not even in the moment of pleasure.[37]

The inner restlessness of the anguished spirit then recoils upon itself in despair.

> However, the spirit will not let itself to be mocked, it revenges itself upon you, it binds you with the chain of melancholy . . . and the gloom of melancholy grows denser around you. . . .[38]

Now this restless, dreaming, ignorant spirit encroaches upon the body-soul unity. Spirit, in order to grasp itself, must "relate to its situation."[39] That is to say, spirit's own

---

[36] *Ibid.*, pp. 190-191.   [37] *Ibid.*, p. 190.

[38] *Ibid.*, pp. 208-209. There is neither time nor space for extensive analyses of dread and despair. Both are mentioned here in order to bring out the internal desire of spirit for its actualization and its recoiling upon itself in despair when the fulfillment of the desire is frustrated. For detailed studies of dread, see: T. H. Croxall, *Kierkegaard Studies* (London: Lutterworth Press, 1948); Donald F. Tweedie, "The Significance of Dread in the Thought of Kierkegaard and Heidegger" (Diss. Boston University, 1954); Arland Ussher, *Journey Through Dread* (New York: Devin-Adair, 1955). For detailed studies of despair, see: Croxall, *Kierkegaard Studies*; G. Clive, "Sickness Unto Death in the Underworld: A Study in Nihilism," *Harvard Theological Review*, 1958; H. V. Martin, *Kierkegaard* (London: Epworth, 1950).

[39] *CD*, p. 40.

actualization depends upon its entering into relation with the self as a synthesis and upon its relating this synthesis to itself.

> Man is a synthesis of the soulish and the bodily. But a synthesis is unthinkable if the two are not united in a third factor. This third factor is the spirit. In the state of innocence man is not merely an animal, for if at any time in his life he were merely an animal, he never would become a man. So then the spirit is present, but in a state of immediacy, a dreaming state. For as much as it is present, it is in one way a hostile power, for it constantly disturbs the relation between body and soul, a relation which endures, and yet does not endure, inasmuch as it has endurance only by means of the spirit. On the other hand, it is a friendly power which has precisely the function of constituting the relationship.[40]

Spirit is, on the one hand, a hostile power which destroys the comfort and illusion of ignorance and, on the other hand, a friendly power which constitutes the struggle for self-knowledge by relating the self to itself.

Having now observed the incipient and unfulfilled spiritual desire of immediacy, I shall now turn to an examination of the body-soul unity in the condition of immediacy.

Ideality and possibility are reality and necessity, infinitized as eternity. Ideality and possibility are reality and necessity, viewed from the point of view of self-consciousness and freedom.

> When the discoveries of possibility are honestly administered, possibility will then disclose all finitudes but idealize them in the form of infinity.[41]

Now we can amplify this point with the proposition that immediacy *is* the self as a synthesis, but as unreflected. There are a number of passages in *Either/Or*, II, which in

[40] *Ibid.*, p. 39.   [41] *Ibid.*, p. 141.

a general way reflect this point. The following, rather lengthy, passage is one of the most lucid.

> The self which the individual knows is at once the actual and the ideal self which the individual has outside of himself as the picture in likeness to which he has to form himself and which, on the other hand, he nevertheless has in him since it is the self. Only within him has the individual the goal after which he has to strive, and yet he has the goal outside him, inasmuch as he strives after it. For if the individual believes that the universal man is situated outside him, that from without it will come to him, then he is disoriented, then he has an abstract conception and his method is always an abstract conception and his method is always an abstract annihilation of the original self. Only within him can the individual acquire information about himself.[42]

Having noted that immediacy is characterized by the restlessness of spirit, which is interested in its realization through self-understanding, we can now see that immediacy is also characterized by the presence of both poles of the synthetic structure of the self, but as unreflected.

Remaining faithful to his style, Kierkegaard discusses aesthetically this complex philosophical point. He conceals this point in *Either/Or*, II's long, and often repetitive discussion concerning the relation between first love and marriage. In these discussions, first love stands for immediacy,[43] and immediacy is characterized by a unity of contradictions which constitute the self.

> It is sensuous and yet spiritual; it is freedom [possibility] and yet necessity; it is in the moment, is definitely in the present tense, and yet it has in it an eternity.[44]

[42] *E/O*, II, 263; cf. *ibid.*, pp. 42, 266-267, 279, and *CD*, p. 140.
[43] *E/O*, II, 20, 46, 95.
[44] *Ibid.*, II, 61. Cf. *Ibid.*, II, 42; *CD*, p. 47; *CUP*, pp. 262-263.

But first love is this unity of contradictions "not by virtue of reflection but immediately."[45] That is to say, these contradictions are present immediately and are only potentially related to the self since at this point spirit has not conceived and realized itself in terms of these contradictions. Kierkegaard lapses into Hegelian terminology to express this point.

> First love remains an unreal *an-sich* which never acquires inward content, [i.e., never *fur-sich*] because it moves only in an external medium.[46]

That is to say, this unity of contradictions is not internalized and, therefore, remains external to spirit. Marriage, however, has brought these contradictions to consciousness and appropriated them;[47] consequently, marriage has an inward infinity, vis-à-vis the external infinity of first love.[48] Marriage vis-à-vis first love is a style of life in which the universal, implicitly present in first love, is raised to the level of self-consciousness and brought into existence in the act of the marriage vow.[49]

Now reflection inflicts the first pain of becoming. It is the initial invasion of immediacy by which it is raised to the level of self-consciousness. Reflection breaks down the primitive state of immediacy. However, reflection does not occur necessarily any more than does the collision of its results in self-consciousness. It is entirely possible for immediacy to endure, i.e., for the universal self to remain hidden in and commensurate with immediacy. The universal is not necessarily mediated even though it is implicitly in immediacy, because the mediation of universality depends upon the voluntary action of spirit.

> For this universal can very well coexist with and in the particular without consuming it; it is like the fire which burned the bush without consuming it.[50]

---

[45] *E/O*, II, 46.   [46] *Ibid.*, II, 95-96.
[47] *Ibid.*, II, 148. Kierkegaard refers to conjugal love as consciousness.
[48] *Ibid.*, II, 62.   [49] *Ibid.*, II, 90ff.   [50] *Ibid.*, II, 266.

But immediacy tends towards its actualization. Innocence, immediacy, is, however, "a determinant oriented towards freedom."[51] Moreover, we have seen that reflection initiates the process of mediation and that the process itself dialectically unfolds in a manner which cannot be violated.[52]

Immediacy is essentially characterized, then, as a unity which is ignorant of itself. Spirit dreams; the unified self is not reflected. Ignorance prevails. We also noted in Chapter II that there is movement within immediacy. In pure immediacy, there is a total absence of consciousness. There is absolutely no reflection. Pure Immediacy is pure sensuousness (body).[53] In later stages of immediacy the self is finitely reflected and, therefore, finitely conscious. That is to say, the self's reality collides with a finitely reflected ideality.[54] The final moment of immediacy is one of infinite reflection

---

[51] *CD*, p. 109; cf. *CUP*, pp. 33-34, 226, 262-263.

[52] Kierkegaard argues that reflection is infinite and he maintains against Hegel that for a beginning to be made reflection does not end itself once it has reached the most abstract determinant of being. Kierkegaard asserts, on the contrary, that for a beginning to be made the process of reflection must be arbitrarily breached, "then the beginning so made cannot be absolute; for it has come into being through a μετάβασις εἰς ἄλλο γένος." *CUP*, p. 103. The Greek phrase is taken from Aristotle's *Analytica Posteriora* (*Works*, I, 75ᵃ) and means "transition to another sphere." Here the phrase suggests that reflection has been broken off by a phenomenon alien to it. There has been a transition from reflection to another sphere. Reflection does not stop itself but is stopped by the will. This implies that the reflected self is itself arbitrary. If reflection is arbitrarily breached by the will, then reflection's product has no claim to finality. The reflected self, as arbitrary, is a guess—at best, a risk—and yet one's entire existence depends upon it.

[53] This state of being is aesthetically illustrated in the character of Don Juan, *E/O*, I, 43ff.

[54] This state of being is aesthetically illustrated in "The Shadowgraphs" in *E/O*, I, 163-215. The major portion of Kierkegaard's description of immediacy in the first volume of *E/O* illustrates, aesthetically, the movement through the stages of finite reflection into infinite reflection. The movement is characterized by both an increasing distrust of the finite and an ever-deepening penetration into the infinity of the imagination.

in which the self achieves the dialectically opposite pole of pure sensuousness, viz., pure infinity or infinite reflection.[55] But within this stretch of the development of consciousness, the self never acquires infinite self-consciousness. In spite of all this movement the self remains essentially ignorant because the body-soul unity remains fundamentally undisturbed.[56]

In the opening pages of this chapter, I used the phrase *new immediacy*. An objection may arise concerning the continued usage of the term once the stage of immediacy (aesthetic stage)[57] is mediated. How is it possible to continue to speak of immediacy? Kierkegaard himself does not hesitate to refer to marriage, a form which the ethical stage may

[55] This state of being is illustrated in "The Rotation Method" and "The Diary of a Seducer" in *E/O*. This total penetration into the infinity of the imagination, Kierkegaard describes as "inwardness with a jammed lock." *SUD*, p. 206.

[56] The following lengthy passage illustrates, in a general way, the movement here under discussion: "When immediacy is assumed to have self-reflection . . . there is somewhat more consciousness of the self. . . . Here there is in fact a certain degree of observation of oneself. With this certain degree of self-reflection begins the act of discrimination whereby the self becomes aware of itself as something essentially different from the environment, from externalities and their effect upon it. . . . He understands by the aid of reflection that there is much he may lose without losing the self; he makes admissions, is capable of doing so, and why? Because to a certain degree he has dissociated his self from external circumstances, because he has an obscure conception that there may even be something eternal in the self. But in vain he struggles thus: the difficulty he stumbled against demands a breach with immediacy as a whole, and for that he has not sufficient self-reflection or ethical reflection; he has no consciousness of a self, which is gained by the infinite abstraction from everything outward, this naked, abstract self (in contrast to the clothed self of immediacy) which is the first form of the infinite self and the forward impulse in the whole process whereby a self infinitely accepts its actual self with all its difficulties and advantages." *SUD*, pp. 187-188; cf. *E/O*, II, 195, 229.

[57] Kierkegaard, *Stages on Life's Way*, trans. Walter Lowrie (Princeton, New Jersey: Princeton University Press, 1940), p. 430.

take, as immediacy.[58] He also refers to the more general category inwardness as immediacy.[59] And he does so with good reason, for the definition of immediacy as ignorance continues to apply to the self which is conscious of itself as a synthesis of the finite and the infinite. Full understanding of the self as a synthesis of finitude and infinitude does not occur with spirit's initial mediation of the self through which it emerges as conscious of itself as a synthesis of finitude and infinitude. Spirit develops in stages and cannot move from complete ignorance of itself to total understanding in one movement. This has been illustrated by the preceding brief discussions of the movement within the aesthetic and ethical stages. Consequently, each stage of spirit's development is an immediacy to the extent that it continues to be ignorant of itself as spirit.

Even though structurally things are different once the self attains the ethical stage, partial ignorance still characterizes spirit. That is to say, in the initial mediation, the self becomes a synthesis of the finite and the infinite in existence for the first time. The three constituents of the process first emerge with the completion of the initial mediation. Future mediations involve, then, not the inflection of finitude, infinitude, and spirit as a synthesis into the dialectical process, but an ever-deepening understanding of the reality of the relation of finitude, infinitude, and spirit. Each new mediation carries the process a step further toward completion by further constricting the bounds of ignorance. This self-constituting process, then, is one of self-discovery and is finalized only when the self totally understands itself.

We should now recapitulate this section before proceeding further. It has become evident that the term immediacy refers to two interrelated phenomena. On the one hand, there is the unreflected self which endures immediately as the body-soul unity. By dividing this unified synthesis

---

[58] E/O, II, 96, 98; cf. SKJP, I, 972.
[59] Kierkegaard, CD, p. 126.

against itself, that is, by reflecting this unity, immediacy is shattered. On the other hand, immediacy is spiritual ignorance. Spirit overcomes ignorance of itself by establishing a relationship with the self as a synthesis, and in mediating this synthesis, spirit drives toward full understanding of itself. However, even though immediacy is shattered when the self is infinitely reflected, it continues to cling to spirit as long as it is in any degree characterized by ignorance.

The initial reflection of the body-soul unity reflected simply this unity and nothing more. As unreflected, the self had neither substance nor a relation with spirit. However, once this unity is mediated, there is something more. First, body becomes this definite, specific body, and soul this definite, specific soul. That is to say, body becomes *my* body, and soul *my* soul. Second, the initial mediation of this body-soul unity eventuates in an act which holds the two poles together in existence. The *more,* then is the personal concreteness of the two elements of the self and the act which unites them in existence. That is to say, the *more* is self-particularity and spirit.[60] Future mediations, however, involve still more. This *more* may apply to the self's particularity since, as subject to time, its facticity is constantly being expanded. But the *more* applies primarily to spirit. Spirit's mediation of the self's particularity involves it in a dialectical penetration of itself by which it progressively actualizes and understands itself as freedom.

[60] Freedom (spirit) initially manifests itself as the possibility of possibility (*CD*, p. 38). Freedom is the possibility of any and all possibilities. Why? Freedom is initially aware simply of itself. This initial awareness comes as dread, which Kierkegaard defines as the reflex of freedom at the thought of itself. When freedom enters into relation with the body-soul unity, it becomes concrete. It is no longer the possibility of possibilities but the possibility of this definite, specific possibility. By relating itself to the self as a synthesis, freedom abandons itself as the possibility of possibilities for a concrete, specific, definite possibility through which it may actualize itself. Apart from this abandonment, there is no opportunity for freedom to become itself. Therefore, freedom forfeits its infinity for its concretion. Cf. *CD*, p. 55.

MOVEMENT: THE EXPANSION OF SPIRIT AS CONSCIOUSNESS AND FREEDOM

The movement which characterizes the development of spirit is not a quantifiable phenomenon. It is not subject to the quantitative determinations of time. It is not a movement which is measured by the ages or phases of life, nor is it a movement which is determined by the fortuitousness of time. While it is always subject to the on-goingness of time, experienced as seriality, spirit creates its own medium of time, experienced as temporality, i.e., as a conflation of past and future in the instantaneous present. This movement is also not an external, linear movement in which achievement or advancement can be visibly measured. That would make it an aesthetic movement, i.e., a movement in which the finite self remains dialectical with respect to the world and subject to the quantitative determinations of time. Kierkegaard frequently refers to knights, heroes, scholars, and prominent citizens who achieve admirable accomplishments but who never know themselves as spirit. One is reminded of Kierkegaard's comment that the most comical thing in the world is the professor who knows everything there is to know but himself.

Movement is also not being considered here in terms of Kierkegaard's stages of existence. We are here avoiding any discussion of the relation of the stages in terms of the development of spirit for two reasons. First, Kierkegaard refers to the relations of the stages in a wide variety of places and not always consistently in the same way.[61] In spite of all the work which has been done in this area, the subject continues to deserve considerable attention, and there is neither time nor space for such an analysis here. Second, it

---

[61] The following is a partial listing of the places in which Kierkegaard either fully or partially discusses the relation of the stages of existence: *E/O*, II, 182-195; *R*, pp. 21-22; *CD*, pp. 96-98, 100-101; *CUP*, pp. 144-145, 256, 347-348, 387, 400, 450, 473n., 494, 498-499, 507; *SLW*, p. 430; and *SUD*, p. 210.

has already been established that Kierkegaard's theory of the self, with which this book is concerned, and his descriptions of the stages of existence, which they make possible, are two separate phenomena.[62] While the second part of this essay attempts to illustrate how the structure of the ethical and theological selves must be understood in terms of this theory of the self, a full scale analysis of the existential topography of the ethical and religious stages and their relationship is also far beyond the scope of this essay.

The discussion of movement, which follows, is concerned exclusively with the sense of the terms more and concreteness in relation to the development of consciousness. "On the spot" movement is a deeper penetration, a deepening consciousness, of the spot. In *The Concept of Dread,* Kierkegaard writes: "The more concrete the content of consciousness, the more concrete is the understanding. . . ."[63] The task is now to determine what Kierkegaard means when he speaks of more consciousness and an increasing concreteness of consciousness.

Kierkegaard states that spirit

dedicates itself more and more profoundly to the task of existing, and with the consciousness of what existence is,

[62] Gregor Malantschuk so clearly describes Kierkegaard's dependence upon his theory of the self in the full development of his stages of existence that his ideas seem worth quoting at length. "An examination of the structure of the stages shows that Kierkegaard builds his whole theory on a very simple presupposition: that man is a synthesis of two completely different qualities. . . . The theory of the stages, which is the basis of Søren Kierkegaard's whole authorship, is constructed on the premise of the synthesis in an amplified form—as in the theory of the stages—which gives Kierkegaard the consistency and the accuracy characteristic of his thinking." Malantschuk, *Kierkegaard's Way to Truth,* trans. Mary Michelsen (Minneapolis: Augsburg, 1963), pp. 20-22. Cf. "The three stages are dialectical moments in the consciousness of freedom." Louis Dupre, "The Constitution of the Self in Kierkegaard's Philosophy," *International Philosophical Quarterly,* III, 506.

[63] *CD,* p. 127.

penetrates all illusions, becoming more and more concrete through reconstructing existence in action.[64]

Within each mediation there is increasing concreteness. First, the self is a relation of reality and ideality, and, then, that relation is made more concrete as a relation of necessity and possibility. Now, it can be added that successive mediations entail increasing concreteness. The reference in the above passage to the penetration of all illusions suggests that spiritual understanding, which depends upon spirit's relating the self to itself, itself comes in stages or a process. The reference to illusions, and not to a single illusion, and to more and more concreteness implies development. This development of spiritual understanding, in turn, implies that the action whereby spirit relates the self to itself is a repeated and developing action, which becomes more concrete as the illusions (ignorance) of spirit's relation to the self are penetrated and cast aside. Concreteness, then, refers to the quality of the action of spirit which is made possible by the degree of consciousness achieved by spirit. Therefore, the formula applies: the more consciousness, the more concreteness. But what is meant by more consciousness?

Reflection always reflects what is already the case. Reflection turns back on the reality of spirit, i.e., on what is already the case, and reflects this reality as the subject matter for consciousness. Reflection is the condition for bringing to consciousness what is already the case. Self-consciousness is the condition for expressing in existence what is already the case, and the existential expression of what is already the case is the condition for understanding it. This much is already clear to us.

It can now be added that spirit concretely understands itself reflexively.[65] Only in looking back does spirit go for-

64 *CUP*, p. 387.

65 The following discussion cannot easily be documented. Remaining faithful to his style, Kierkegaard always employs the principle of

ward in existence. More precisely, existence unfolds with the pushing back of the bounds of ignorance or, conversely, with the increase in the depth of consciousness. Spirit understands itself as that which it already is. By mediating what it already is, i.e., its reality, spirit penetrates more deeply into itself. To bring into existence what spirit already is means that spirit concretely understands itself as that which it already is. The reality of spirit is not necessarily identical with its expression in existence. The distance between the reality of spirit and its expression in existence is a distance which must be covered by mediation. For mediation brings spirit to itself in existence.

Each action of spirit which relates the self to itself as a synthesis of the finite and the infinite in existence, i.e., each existential expression of spirit, terminates in a new and higher spiritual reality which itself must be mediated if it is to be truthfully expressed in existence. Reflection constantly reflects more. Initially, infinite reflection reflects the body-soul unity. Subsequently, there follows a dialectically related series of reflections of the body-soul-unified-by-spirit. Each of these reflections penetrates deeper into the true nature of this synthesis and, consequently, more concretely reflects the true nature of the synthesis. Each action of spirit terminates in a higher spiritual reality, i.e., a potentially more concrete expression of spirit. Reflection, then, turns back to this reality and initiates the mediation of that particular level of spiritual reality, whereby it is ultimately expressed and understood in existence. Spirit, which becomes more concrete with each mediation, is simultaneously extended beyond the bounds of its own understanding of itself and, hence, becomes subject to a further mediation and a still more concrete expression of itself. One could say

---

movement here being discussed and never discusses it theoretically in any significant detail. Two places where this principle is most clearly evident in its application is in his discussions of existential pathos (*CUP*, pp. 347-493) and the gradations of consciousness (*SUD*, pp. 175-207).

that this restless and demanding spirit is always outrunning itself and must constantly catch up to itself by mediating itself over and over again. Put another way, the existential expression of spirit is always a step behind spirit's reality. Spirit always expresses and understands what is already the case, i.e., its reality, and in this act of existential expression and understanding it is extended beyond itself as understood.

On the one hand, each time spirit relates the self to itself, it does so with more consciousness of itself. That is to say, each time spirit relates the self to itself, it does so with a degree of consciousness exceeding the degree of consciousness involved in the preceding actions of spirit. On the other hand, each relating of the self to itself by spirit terminates in a new and higher level of spiritual reality which is subject to a higher reflection and, hence, to a higher degree of consciousness. The *more* pertaining to consciousness, then, is simply the increasing awareness of the true nature of spirit's relation to the self, which spirit relates to itself. The more conscious of itself spirit is, the more concrete it can become in its existential expression. The more concretely spirit is existentially expressed, the more it understands itself. Therefore, the ultimate goal of this movement is total consciousness, which is the necessary condition of total understanding. In such a condition, the self is totally reflected, the spot is totally penetrated by consciousness; consequently, the movement of spirit reaches its final point.[66]

[66] It is interesting to note that the higher levels of consciousness are qualified by higher intensities of dread, passion, and despair. As it turns out, this phenomenon is attributable to the increasing awareness of the difficulty of spirit's uniting these opposing moments of the self. Each advance in consciousness is an advance in the awareness of the difficulty of achieving the synthesis. In a sense, then, the moments are pushed farther apart with each advance in consciousness. "More" consciousness means greater awareness of how distant the self is from itself. Therefore, each increase in consciousness is accompanied by a

97

As we have seen, Kierkegaard refers to this movement as one which goes forward in existence by going backward in consciousness.[67] It is a forward movement because spirit presses ahead to its most concrete existential expression. It is a backward movement because spirit regresses into itself toward full consciousness of itself. The process, in Kierkegaard's words, is one of the "reconstruction of existence in action"[68] through spirit's return to itself in self-consciousness. In his analysis of despair, Kierkegaard maintains that spirit remains in despair until this process of reconstruction is completed.[69] Metaphorically, he describes the process in this way:

> For here applies what the fairy-tale recounts about a certain enchantment: the piece of music must be played through backwards; otherwise the enchantment is not broken.[70]

In other words, to break the *spell*—it can hardly be called an enchantment—spirit must go forward in existence by going backward in consciousness to an awareness of what it already is. The analysis of movement is at this point complete, and we are now in a position concretely to analyze the phenomenon of unity as the outcome of this movement.

---

similar increase in dread, passion, and despair. Kierkegaard's existential descriptions of the varying intensities of dread (*CD*), passion (*CUP*), despair (*SUD*), and melancholy (*E/O*) are all grounded in the advances of spirit's consciousness of itself as responsible for the unification of these moments. Each of these phenomena are subjects for separate analyses in terms of the theory of the self which is being advanced in this essay.

[67] *CUP*, pp. 468-469, 475.   [68] *Ibid.*, p. 387.

[69] "However a self, every instant it exists, is in process of becoming, for the self κατὰ δύναμιν [potentially] does not actually exist, it is only that which it is to become. In so far as the self does not become itself, it is not its own self; but not to be one's self is despair." *SUD*, p. 163. Cf. *SKJP*, I, 750.

[70] *SUD*, p. 177.

UNITY: THE CULMINATION OF SPIRIT AS CONSCIOUSNESS AND FREEDOM

The preceding analyses of immediacy and movement have disclosed that immediacy is a unity which is increasingly conscious of itself as a unity to be actualized in existence. Immediacy is constituted by both unity and a level of consciousness which is dialectically related to each concrete existential expression of unity. The unity of reality and ideality in self-consciousness (spirit) makes possible the unity of possibility and necessity by freedom (spirit) which, in turn, becomes the subject of a higher unity in consciousness and existence, etc. Immediacy is, then, an existential condition constituted by the dialectical relatedness of unity and consciousness.

In the *Concluding Unscientific Postscript*, Kierkegaard refers explicitly to unity as the highest interest and achievement of spirit.[71] "Immortality [unity] is the most passionate interest of subjectivity [spirit]. . . ."[72] Moreover, the question of existential unity is not an academic but an ethical one and can only be raised when spirit has become conscious of itself as spirit.[73] Once spirit becomes conscious of itself "immortality [unity] precisely is the potentiation and highest development of the developed subjectivity [spirit]."[74] That

[71] *E/O, CD, SUD*, and *CUP* all describe the same phenomena, viz., the dialectical development of spirit. But they do not always employ the same terminology. Immortality and subjectivity are two important terms in *CUP* and refer to the same phenomena which *E/O, CD*, and *SUD* refer to as unity and spirit. Kierkegaard refers to immortality as the "unity of infinitude and finiteness" (*CUP*, p. 156) and to subjectivity as an unfolding process of development. "For the development of subjectivity consists precisely in his active interpenetration of himself by reflection concerning his own existence, so that he really thinks what he thinks through making a reality of it." *Ibid.*, p. 151. Cf. *Ibid.*, pp. 63, 141-143, 146, and *SKJ*, #1376. Gregor Malantschuk points out these identifications in *Kierkegaard's Way to Truth*, pp. 81-83. Cf. *Ibid.*, pp. 62, 141-142.

[72] *CUP*, p. 155.   [73] *Ibid.*, p. 154.   [74] *Ibid.*

is to say, the highest potentiality of spirit is its unification of the finite and infinite aspects of the self. Through the unification of finitude and infinitude, spirit actualizes its highest potentiality. Kierkegaard writes that "precisely at the moment when I am conscious of my immortality I am absolutely subjective."[75] That is to say, at the moment spirit fully understands itself as the unifying power of body and soul, spirit becomes itself absolutely. Conversely, when finitude is eternally identical[76] with infinitude through the unifying power of spirit, spirit fully understands itself. Unity, then, means ultimately "being the same."[77] Unity is the falling away of the contradiction between what the self is in its finitude and what it infinitely ought to be. For the self to be the same means that spirit has completely united what the self is with what it ought to be. When the radical break between ideality and reality in self-consciousness and, hence, between possibility and necessity in existence is eradicated by the unifying power of spirit, the self becomes eternally identical with itself.

To be eternally identical with oneself, i.e., to be transparent, can be understood in two ways. First, it means, as we have seen, the unification of finitude and infinitude. Second, it means that spirit has absolutely become and understood itself in existence. We are here looking at the same phenomenon from two different perspectives. In the first instance, finitude and infinitude are coalesced by the power of spirit. In the second instance, spirit has, by unifying finitude and infinitude, fully actualized and understood itself in existence. There is an inseparable dialectical interdependence here. On the one hand, the unification of finitude and infinitude depends upon spirit, and, on the other hand, spirit's understanding of itself in existence depends upon its uniting finitude and infinitude. Even in the final moment of the dialectical development of spirit, then, we cannot free ourselves of this duality which was noted at the begin-

[75] *Ibid.*, p. 155. [76] *Ibid.*, p. 157. [77] *Ibid.*

ning of this chapter. In existence, this phenomenon is indeed understood as a unified and single experience. But to explain this phenomenon adequately it must always be viewed from the two perspectives. We are now in a position to advance our understanding of this notion of unity by examining four related points.

First, it should be apparent by now that the concept of unity under discussion here refers to the unification of the constitutive elements of the self by spirit and not to the unity of the stages of existence. Kierkegaard frequently discusses the unity of the stages,[78] but, again, we must avoid the temptation to lapse into a discussion of an existential phenomenon which is constituted by the integration of the ontological coordinates of the underlying self-structure. A discussion of how the existential content of each stage is taken up into the succeeding stages far exceeds the limitations of this essay.[79] The parallel problem of how the unity

[78] *CUP*, p. 311; *E/O*, II, 150.

[79] Emmanuel Hirsch has rightfully reprimanded much of the Barthian-influenced Kierkegaard scholarship for viewing the development of spirit as one which excludes rather than includes the preceding stages of its development. "The manner in which we in Germany usually understand the *Postscript* is roughly as follows: It describes the ethical and the religious solely for the purpose of distinguishing these from the Christian religiosity as being non-Christian and without faith in the paradox. This interpretation deserves the gold medal in stupidity to see who could say the most stupid thing about Kierkegaard. The *Postscript* intends to make clear that everything Christian which does not possess the unconditionality of the ethical and the depth of religious suffering and religious guilt is illegitimate and religious aestheticism, a paganism in Christian disguise." Emmanuel Hirsch, *Kierkegaard-Studien* (Gutersloh: C. Bertelsmann, 1933), II, 802-805, as translated by Reider Thomte, *Kierkegaard's Philosophy of Religion* (Princeton University Press, 1948), pp. 102-103. Hirsch is one of the first scholars to challenge the notion that the stages of existence do not constitute a process. As this passage indicates, Hirsch is anxious to demonstrate that the stages are integrally related. But it is our contention that the self's movement is not explained by referring to the stages, but, on the contrary, that the development of the stages is

of the self-structure is itself constitutive of the unity of the stages must also be bypassed. The extensive analyses which both problems deserve far exceed the bounds of this essay since the subject here under discussion must be confined to an analysis of the unity of the constituents of the dialectical development of spirit.

Second, the ethical emphasis with which Kierkegaard imbues the development of spirit is made much more specific and concrete once we turn to the issue of unity. Where, initially, we spoke of man's ethical responsibility for himself, we may now speak of the task of achieving a unity of body and soul by spirit in existence. Unity is a goal which is won or attained. Existential unity is neither simply given nor inevitably or automatically achieved. It is, on the contrary, a task which springs from the "problematic situation of polarity"[80] and which is recovered through the sustained ethical striving of the existing individual. The reintegration of body and soul by spirit in existence is the goal and the ethical duty of every individual.

> No doubt immediacy can be attained again—but the nonsense of *The System* is that it is attained again without a break.
>
> Immediacy is attained again only ethically, immediacy itself becomes the task—you "shall" attain it. . . .
>
> People who have no conception of spirit talk in this way: When immediacy is lost, one can never recover it. And in order to illustrate it properly . . . they add: A girl can lose her innocence but she never recovers it. But spiritually the following is true: if I cannot recover innocence, then all is lost from the beginning, because the

---

explained by reference to the self as a process. To account for Kierkegaard's view of movement, we must ultimately appeal to his notion of the self and not to the stages of existence.

[80] Harvey Smit, *Kierkegaard's Pilgrimage of Man* (Grand Rapids: Eerdmanns, 1965), p. 43.

primary fact is simply that I and everyone have lost innocence.

If for a moment I omit the specifically dogmatic aspects of the cooperation of spirit, etc., I can define rebirth this way: it is immediacy won ethically.[81]

Attention has already been brought to the fact that Kierkegaard discovers within the existing subject an implicit duty to exist. This Apollonian tone in existence is reenforced by the absence of any logico-ontological necessity in the dialectical development of spirit. This unfolding of spirit proceeds, if at all, from each individual's response to his duty, accepting full responsibility for the unique development of his own freedom. The additional point here being made is that Kierkegaard explicitly associates this duty with the ultimate outcome of the development of spirit, viz., the attainment of immediacy.

The third point is that unity is not achievable conceptually. As we have already seen, the medium of thought is not existence or actuality but possibility. "Abstract thought can get hold of reality only by nullifying it, and this nullification of reality consists in transforming it into possibility."[82] All that is said about existence in the language of abstraction is stated as possibility, and this applies to the problem of the unification of existence as well.

Abstract thought closes up the trilogy. Just so. But how does it close the trilogy? Is abstract thought a mystic something, or is it not the act of the abstracting individual? But the abstracting individual is the existing individual, who is as such in the dialectical moment, which he

---

[81] *SKJP*, I, 972. Cf. "Immediacy or spontaneity is poetically the very thing we desire to return to . . . but from a Christian point of view, immediacy is lost and it ought not be yearned for again but should be attained again." *SKJP*, II, 1942. Cf. *CUP*, pp. 151, 309, 310n; *CD*, p. 44; *SLW*, pp. 435-436; *SKJP*, II, 1123.

[82] *CUP*, p. 279.

cannot close or mediate, least of all absolutely, so long as he remains in existence. So that when he closes the trilogy, this closure must be related as a possibility to the reality or existence in which he remains.[83]

The unification of existence in thought is merely an hypothesis which is related to the abstract thinker as an ethical possibility. To conclude that existence is unified in thought, on the one hand, abrogates existence which is the only medium in which unity can be achieved, and, on the other hand, suppresses spirit which is the only power by which unity can be achieved. To exist means to abandon reflection in order to actualize existence through spirit's unification of the self as both finite and infinite. The concrete act of existing requires the abrogation of reflection; therefore, reflection alone is powerless to unify the self in existence.

The fourth and final point stresses that unity is not final or absolute. To be in existence means to be subject to the on-goingness of time. Unity cannot have existential finality as long as the individual remains subject to time. The infinity of time constitutes an ever-expanding facticity which means that constant adjustments must be made by reflection. Time is an inescapable snare because it denies the existing individual a lasting resting place this side of his own death. Time introduced an unstable and constantly changing factor into the self as a dialectical moment; and as long as the self remains in existence, it cannot be absolutely, finally, mediated. To rationalize one's existence into a unity would require, then, that the individual transcend his own death in order to view objectively his earthly life from its beginning to its conclusion.

While unity, then, is achieved neither by thought nor once and for all, it is, nevertheless, the culminating moment of existence in which the finite and infinite aspects of the self are united by freedom. But this union of the synthesis

[83] *CUP*, p. 279.

is only momentary as long as the subject remains in existence.

> It is only momentarily that the particular individual is able to realize existentially a unity of the infinite and the finite which transcends existence. This unity is realized in the moment of passion. Modern philosophy has tried everything and anything in the effort to help the individual to transcend himself objectively, which is a wholly impossible feat; existence exercises its restraining influence. . . .[84]

Kierkegaard rejects modern philosophy because, by holding passion (action)[85] in contempt, it also holds existence in contempt. And, for Kierkegaard, passion (action) alone is constitutive of existence.

> . . . And yet passion is the culmination of existence for an existing individual—and we are all of us existing individuals. In passion the existing subject is rendered infinite in the eternity of the imaginative representation, and yet he is at the same time most definitely himself. The fantastic I-am-I is not an identity of the infinite and the finite, since neither the one nor the other is real; it is a fantastic rendezvous in the clouds, an unfruitful embrace, and the relationship of the individual self to this mirage is never indicated.[86]

Kierkegaard's dilemma is clear. By insisting on the existential quality of unity, he inevitably submits it to the ongoingness of time, and, therefore, to a momentary and contingent character. Further, though confined to time, the individual by thinking projects himself as possibility into the medium of eternity. The abstract thinker is an existing

[84] *CUP*, p. 176.

[85] Action and passion refer to the same event, viz., the act of freedom by which spirit attempts to unify finitude and infinitude in existence.

[86] *CUP*, p. 176.

subject; consequently, the individual is caught in an unresolvable tension between time and eternity. From the standpoint of time, the tension is resolved into a unity only momentarily, and from the standpoint of thought the tension will inevitably arise again. The constant mediation of this tension is the task of spirit. Existential unity is achievable by spirit alone and has being only in the realm of spirit which exists enigmatically between time and eternity.

The attainment of unity, then, is an existential and momentary fulfillment of an ethical task. This final unity is a return to immediacy, but it is a return to an immediacy in which the self is fully conscious of itself. This return to immediacy depends upon the full development of consciousness. For consciousness to become fully concrete it must pass through a process of development. Finitude and infinitude become concrete when they are initially and infinitely reflected; and although time continues to alter the concrete content of both, no process of development is required before their concreteness is fully grasped. Spirit, on the contrary, does not so easily become transparent to itself. Spirit's clear and correct comprehension of its situation does not entail its most clear and concrete comprehension of itself. The most clear and concrete comprehension of itself requires a process of consciousness-expansion which is made possible by the continual efforts of spirit to integrate its situation, i.e., to unify the synthesis. Consequently, the synthesis must wait for spirit to comprehend itself fully as freedom before it can be united with itself. There is no stronger evidence for Kierkegaard's argument that the synthesis must be united by a positive third factor. The two elements of the synthesis are powerless to unite themselves, except as a negative unity[87] and must wait for spirit to comprehend itself fully before they can finally be united.

The most concrete expression of unity depends upon the complete annulment of ignorance or, conversely, upon the full expansion of consciousness. All the major differences

[87] *SUD*, p. 146.

between original and attained immediacy hinge on this distinction between ignorance and full consciousness. On the one hand, original immediacy is an *abstract unity* which is accidental in nature. Abstract immediacy is not at all concrete, because spirit dreams and body and soul are not differentiated by spirit. In the initial act of differentiation, body, soul, and spirit take on concreteness. Furthermore, abstract immediacy is a *negative unity*, because the self is constituted by the dialectical relation between body and soul. This relation is undisturbed by spirit. And this negative unity is *accidental* in character because it is subject to the fortuitousness of time and to worldly fate, i.e., fortune and misfortune.

On the other hand, attained immediacy is a concrete positive unity which is intentional in nature. This attained immediacy is fully *concrete* because, on the one hand, body and soul are differentiated, i.e., infinitely reflected, and, on the other hand, spirit fully understands itself as spirit as the result of successfully uniting body and soul in an existential unity. Furthermore, this unity is a *positive unity* because, as we have seen, the body-soul unity is an existential phenomenon fully constituted by spirit. And this positive unity is *intentional* in nature, because it is permeated by the intentionality of spirit and, hence, overcomes the fortuitousness of time and the arbitrariness of the world.

In summarizing, we can see that, initially, body and soul negatively cohere because they have not been differentiated by infinite reflection. Spirit coheres restlessly with this body-soul unity as total ignorance. This unity which has not been differentiated by spirit is not comprehended; therefore, it remains in ignorance. Ultimately, the unity of immediacy after reflection is a positive, existential unity of finitude and infinitude in and by which spirit totally understands itself as spirit.

This completes the analysis of *Wie-Sein*. Having concluded the discussion of both aspects of the being involved in the dialectical structure and development of spirit, we are now in a position to determine how this ontology influences and manifests itself in Kierkegaard's presentation of ethics and religion. As I have already mentioned, there is insufficient time to examine the stages of ethics and religion, taking fully into account the existential topography of each stage of existence, the relation between the two stages, and the different fictional and non-fictional characters whom Kierkegaard uses to illustrate the dread, existential pathos, and despair of both stages. The goal of the second part of this essay is considerably more modest since it attempts only to disclose the structure of both stages in terms of their enhancement of both consciousness and freedom.

THE TASK OF EXISTING

PART TWO

Introduction

THE structure of the ethical and ethico-religious stages of existence is to be comprehended in terms of the dialectical development of spirit. Freedom's drive toward the existential unification of the two elements of the self's *Was-Sein* gives rise to the reality of the existing individual. In the following chapters we shall see that the task of the reconstitution of this existential unity is an ethical one. And the existing individual is an individual who accepts the task of ethics and attempts in his own unique and particular existence, through striving to unite himself in existence, to understand himself.

The self and existence are not synonymous. The self is the being of the individual, and existence, as we shall see, is constituted by the individual's ethical responsibility for actualizing the self or his being. Every human being is characterized by the possession of this self-structure. The existing individual, however, is particular. The particularity of existence is constituted by the manner of the individual's relation to his being.[1]

There is a dialectical relation between the self and existence. Each individual's ethical task of actualizing and un-

[1] It is very difficult to express this relation to the self and the existing individual. The phrase "his self" most adequately expresses this relation, but it is grammatically incorrect and, thus, should not be used. The third person pronouns "himself" and "itself," therefore will be used, and the reader is warned to keep in mind that the use of these pronouns, hereafter, expresses almost without exception, a relationship between the individual and the self. Where possible, the more correct "one's self" will be used.

111

derstanding himself gives rise to existence.[2] This task occurs as a process. We shall see how the momentum of this process is generated by using the following formula: The more the existing individual understands himself, the more concretely he exists; and the more concretely he exists, the more he understands himself. The ethical task of actualizing and understanding the self-structure gives rise to existence. In Chapters Two and Three, we explored the structure and dynamic character of the self. Now it is important to disclose how ethics takes over the task of achieving self-understanding and how the process of realizing the task gives rise to existence.

In attempting to disclose how ethico-religious existence

[2] Here our study diverges from Fahrenbach's because he does not argue for the presence of a dialectical relation between the self and existence in the pseudonymous corpus. Fahrenbach's analysis of the self is a more explicit rendering of existence. The self and existence are essentially synonymous, the only difference being that the former is a more formal designation of Kierkegaard's conception of the latter. I shall be arguing in Part Two that the self and existence are not synonymous but that the self constitutes the being of the existing individual (existence), on the one hand, and that this relation between the existing individual and his being is not of a theoretical and objective nature, but is, on the contrary, ethical in the sense that the individual is responsible for actualizing his being in existence.

Sløk argues that the ontological categories are adequate only for describing the self which does not exist "before God," i.e., before the Absolute Paradox. Once the self understands himself as existing "before God," the ontological categories are replaced by theological ones. I will strongly oppose Sløk's position on the ground that the ontological categories cannot be replaced without doing away with the self also. Kierkegaard's ontological categories describe the being (selfhood) of the existing individual, and the individual does not lose or abandon his being when he exists "before God." On the contrary, his being is existentially actualized in the Christian encounter with God. When the individual exists "before God," the human situation does not so radically change that an entirely new set of categories is required to illuminate it. On the contrary, theological categories such as God, Christ, and sin are validly used only when situated within the wider ontology which Kierkegaard has already laid down.

112

is constituted by the existing individual's assumption of the ethical task of self-understanding, our discussion will be guided by three major questions. (1) What is the relation between Kierkegaard's ontology and his ethics? (2) How is his notion of ethical and ethico-religious existence constituted by this dynamic ontology? (3) How is knowledge (understanding) related to his notion of existence?

Part Two of this essay is comprised of three chapters. The fourth chapter attempts to define ethics, to demonstrate the manner in which the individual assumes through ethics the task of existing which is implicitly present in the self-structure, and to analyze the concept of choice as the act which brings the task of existence to consciousness. The fifth and sixth chapters are concerned with an analysis of the two levels of Kierkegaard's ethico-religious stage of existence in terms of the underlying self-structure.[3]

[3] In this analysis of religious existence, Kierkegaard distinguishes between Religiousness A and Religiousness B. I shall attempt to understand these two phenomena in terms of the ethical task which is implicitly present in the ontology. Hereafter, I shall refer to them, in accord with Kierkegaard's terminology, as the religion of Hidden Inwardness and the religion of Christianity.

CHAPTER IV

The Ethical Character of Existence

Two Definitions of Ethics

Ethics has two meanings in Kierkegaard's pseudonymous writings. It refers both to the process of self-understanding and to the ethical stage of existence. The former meaning refers to the self as a task whose fundamental possibility in life is self-understanding, and the latter meaning refers to that stage in the dialectical development of spirit in which the ethical requirement of ideality comes to consciousness. Since the more fundamental meaning of the term emerges, within the development of the ethical stage, I will first discuss ethics as a stage and then ethics as a process of self-understanding.

The function of the ethical stage of existence is to bring ideality into reality.

> Ethics would bring ideality into reality; on the other hand, its movement is not designed to raise reality up into ideality. Ethics points to ideality as a task and assumes that man is in possession of the conditions requisite for performing it.[1]

In the ethical stage of existence, the individual becomes conscious of himself as ideal and relates to this ideality as

---

[1] Kierkegaard, *The Concept of Dread*, trans. Walter Lowrie (Princeton University Press, 1957), p. 15. Cf. "The more ideal ethics is, the better. It must not let itself be disturbed by the twaddle that it is no use requiring the impossible; for even to listen to such talk is unethical, is something for which ethics has neither 'time' nor 'opportunity.'" *Ibid.*, p. 15.

114

a possibility,[2] which it is his duty to actualize. Moreover, the individual by accepting and fulfilling his task becomes the "true man, the whole man."[3] It is an ennobling and humanizing activity, and the ethical individual is confident of his own power to actualize this task which is before him.[4]

Now ethical ideality is the ideality of the self's existential reality. The ideality of ethics does not soar beyond man as a formal absolute abstractly conceived and formulated. On the contrary, ethical ideality proceeds from the ideality inherent in the self's given reality.

> This self which the individual knows is at once the actual [real] self and the ideal self which the individual has outside himself as the picture in likeness to which he has to form himself and which, on the other hand, he nevertheless has in him since it is the self. Only within him has the individual the goal after which he has to strive, and yet he has this goal outside him, inasmuch as he strives after it.[5]

[2] We have already noted that Kierkegaard prefers to speak of possibility as a task.

[3] *CD*, p. 17.

[4] J. S. Weiland has very accurately expressed this meaning of ethics in Kierkegaard: "Ethics is still an 'ideal' science: Ethics prescribes the moral law and puts the *Du Sollst* before man in all its ideality in the certainty of the '*Du kannst denn Du sollst*.' Ethics shows man his task without asking whether man has the power to fulfill it. Reflection upon the reality of man is superfluous on the ground of the certainty that 'to know the good is to do the good.'" J. Sperna Weiland, *Philosophy of Existence and Christianity* (Gorcum and Co., 1951), pp. 25-26. This view of ethics in *E/O* is modified in *SLW* and *FT*, and in *CUP* the task of self-understanding, "reflection upon the reality of man" in Weiland's words, replaces this notion of ethics.

[5] Kierkegaard, *Either/Or*, trans. Walter Lowrie (Princeton University Press, 1959), II, 263. Cf. "For he who lives aesthetically sees possibilities everywhere, they constitute for him the content of the future, whereas he who lives ethically sees tasks everywhere. The individual therefore sees this [his] actual [real] concretion of his as his task, his goal, his aim." *Ibid.*, II, 256.

The relation between reality and ideality is not one in which reality is confronted by a formal, abstract ideality to which it is morally subject.[6] Ethical ideality emerges not through abstract thinking, contemplation, or intuition but through the unconditional requirement upon the individual to be himself.[7] If ideality were derived in this former manner, reality would be directed toward an ideal alien to it, whereas, for Kierkegaard, the ideal is discovered in the real.

The distinction between reality and ideality rests in the consciousness of one's reality as a requirement. Ideality is the consciousness of one's reality as a requirement or a task. The self is related to its ideality as a possibility simply because of the "requirement of ideality."[8] Genuine possibility has no other origin. It is true that aesthetic and intellectual possibilities can confront the individual as tasks, but they are not genuine tasks because they are not genuinely possible. That is to say, such possibilities are not existential possibilities since they are not rooted in existence. Each individual is his only genuine, i.e., existential, possibility. Furthermore, each individual confronts his ideality as possible because his reality is for him a requirement.[9] For in the requirement existence is accentuated as possibility. Ethics

[6] *Ibid.*, II, 258-267.

[7] "The ethical then will not change the individual into another man but makes him himself; it will not annihilate the aesthetical but transfigure it." *Ibid.*, II, 257-268.

[8] *Søren Kierkegaard's Journals and Papers*, ed. and trans. Howard V. Hong and Edna H. Hong (Bloomington, Ind.: Indiana University Press, 1967-1970), II, 1785. The full nature of this requirement cannot be made clear until we discuss resignation and the God-relationship in the following chapter.

[9] It is important to note here that reality receives its determination as reality by ideality. Prior to the collision of ideality and reality, there was no self-consciousness, hence, no consciousness of one's reality. The self first becomes aware of its reality, i.e., its reality initially is defined or becomes determinate for him, as ideality. The self is not conscious of its own reality until it faces itself as a task, i.e., until it recognizes itself as ideal.

116

aims at action and existing in one's own ideality, and this alone constitutes one's ethical existence.

The claim of ethical ideality upon the individual is absolute. As absolute, ethical ideality is grounded in itself; consequently, ethics finds its sole purpose exclusively in itself. The task of ethics constitutes an immanent teleology in the sense that it has its *telos* exclusively in itself. As we have seen, the ethical is not something outside the personality standing in an external relation to it. "Personality manifests itself as the absolute which has its teleology in itself."[10] The absoluteness of ethics is derived from its inner teleology and from nothing else. The absolute character of the ideality of ethics would be negated if it were reduced to a passing moment in the wider, dialectical development of spirit. That is to say, if the dialectical development of spirit moves beyond the claim of ethical ideality, it loses the absolute quality of its claim on human nature.

Now Kierkegaard points to the nature of duty as evidence for the autonomy of the ethical individual. Duty is an "obligation arising from an inner necessity rather than one imposed by an outside compulsion. It is incumbent because it belongs to self-responsibility grounded in the nature of the self."[11] The term suggests that, for Kierkegaard, the ethical nature of the inward relation of the individual to himself is one of requirement. That is to say, duty prescribes the ethical nature of the relation of a finite human being to his infinite ideal. Duty itself is internally derived because the claim of ideality upon the individual is itself grounded in the individual's separation from himself rather than in his separation from a heteronomous ideal. The internal character of duty stems from the individual's first re-

[10] *E/O*, II, 267. Cf. "But the fact that the individual sees his possibility as his task expresses precisely his sovereignty over himself, which he never relinquishes. . . ." *Ibid.*, II, 256.

[11] George Price, *The Narrow Pass* (New York: McGraw-Hill, 1963), p. 177.

sponsibility to relate himself to himself and not to something external to himself.

> It is strange that the word duty can suggest an outward relation, inasmuch as the very derivation of the word (*Pligt*) indicates an inward relation; for what is incumbent upon me, not as this fortuitous individual but in accordance with my true nature, that surely stands in the most inward relation to myself. For duty is not an imposition (*Paalaeg*) but something which is incumbent (*Paalagger*). When duty is viewed thus it is a sign that the individual is in himself correctly oriented.[12]

The ethical individual who seeks to relate himself as real to himself as ideal, has, in Kierkegaard's words, "clad himself in duty, for him it is the expression of his inmost nature."[13] It is now the duty of the individual to actualize in existence his ideal self-consciousness.[14]

This first definition of ethics also entails the universality of ethics.[15] By universality, Kierkegaard means that ethics applies to everyone at every moment.

> The ethical is always requirement—and consequently it is the greatest possible backwardness and distance from the ethical to regard it as peculiar, as eccentricity, that is, as something especially for that particular individual.[16]

[12] *E/O*, II, 259.

[13] *Ibid.*

[14] Just as the requirement is accentuated in the God-relationship so also is duty accentuated as obedience in that same relation. But at this point in the development of spirit, no such accentuation is possible because there is no consciousness of God through which the accentuation is made possible.

[15] Kierkegaard, *Fear and Trembling*, trans. Walter Lowrie (Princeton University Press, 1954), p. 65.

[16] *SKJP*, I, 996. Cf. "The ethical begins straightway with this requirement to every person: You shall be perfect. . . ." *Ibid.* "But people are afraid of the true ethicist and would rather protect themselves against him by making him out to be unusually gifted so that his life loses the

On the one hand, every individual is subject to the obligation stamped upon existence by ethics, and, on the other hand, the ethical obligation is never superseded. Each individual is eternally subject to the requirement of the ethical. At no point is the requirement cancelled out of existence. Now the universality of the ethical requirement is grounded in the universality of the self-structure. The very possibility of the individual's being conscious of himself as a task and a duty is dialectically related to his conception of the self as a synthesis which relates itself to the self. Unless the self is conceived as a relation, the ethical consciousness of oneself as a task to which one has a duty is impossible. The very possibility of the requirement is situated in the relational nature of the self. Consciousness grasps the self as an unrealized relation, and it is in this separation of the individual from himself that the ethical requirement is grounded. An extended passage from the *Papirer* illustrates this point.

In the realm of genius, the realm of natural qualifications, the realm of the esthetic, what counts is: to be able. In the realm of the ethical: to be obliged. Therefore, the ethical is related to the universally human, whereas the esthetic is related to the differences between man and man. It would be a contradiction of the ethical to speak of "being obliged" if every human being did not have the conditions of being able if he himself only wills. In connection with the ethical, there are, therefore, no conditions; it is the unconditional ought which tolerates no conditions because it presupposes no conditions.[17]

---

power of being a requirement, for if it depends upon capacities, then it is nonsense to require of a person what has not been given to him." *Ibid.*, I, 989.

[17] *Ibid.*, I, 975. Cf. "For the universal man is not a phantom, but every man as such is the universal man, that is to say, to every man is assigned the way by which he becomes the universal man." *E/O*, II, 260.

The aesthetic emphasizes the particular, e.g., talents and abilities. Ethics emphasizes the universal *You Shall*. It would be ridiculous to require each man to become a musician; however, it is ethically incumbent upon each man to become himself. The aesthetic knows conditions. One is able to be a musician only if he is naturally musically inclined. Ethics knows no special conditions, because each man is potentially conscious of himself as a relation which he is free to relate or not to relate. Consciousness of the requirement is simultaneous with consciousness of freedom. No sooner is an individual conscious of himself as free than he is conscious of his duty to act.

To be obliged to do what one is able to do or to be universalizes human nature. Men are distinguished by their particularity, i.e., facticity, but man is one in being subject to the requirement to become what he is. Ethics, then, is a synthesis of the universal and the particular.[18] We never say that a particular man does duty or duties. On the contrary, we say, "He does his duty; I do my duty; you do your duty." An individual becomes universal by accepting his particularity as a duty.

> He who regards life ethically sees the universal, and he who lives ethically expresses the universal in his life, he makes himself the universal man, not by divesting himself of his concretion, for then he becomes nothing, but by clothing himself with it and permeating it with the universal.[19]

And the fulfillment of the universal in the particular is the realization of the ethical.

[18] *E/O*, II, 260.

[19] *Ibid.* In a similar vein, Kierkegaard says that "it is perfectly true, as people say, that the proper effect of ethics is to transform one's talents into one's vocation." *The Journals of Søren Kierkegaard*, ed. and trans. Alexander Dru (Oxford: Oxford University Press, 1938), #463.

To be the one man is not in itself anything so great, for that everybody has in common with every product of nature; but to be that in such a way that he is also the universal man is the true art of living.[20]

The ethicist, then, by obeying the absolute of duty escapes the incoherence and instability of the aesthetic individual who as a consequence of his ignorance of freedom is incapable of unifying himself as a synthesis of the finite and the infinite. He lives rather in the confident expectation of possessing the ability to become an autonomous and unified person.

Kierkegaard speaks of the aesthetic stage of existence as being dethroned from its dominating position in existence by the ethical. Ethics takes the aesthetic into itself and transforms it so that it loses its absolute claim upon existence, yet it retains its relative significance as the concrete givenness, facticity, of existence upon which the ethical absolute is imposed. But he never speaks of the ethical stage of existence as being dethroned by the religious stage. Kierkegaard writes that "the ethical is the absolute, and in all eternity the highest."[21] "The ethical is and remains the highest task for every human being."[22] "The ethical requirement is imposed upon each individual. . . ."[23] Also, ". . . the religious sphere . . . lies so close to the ethical that they are in constant communication with one another."[24] Kierkegaard, therefore, speaks of the "ethico-religious" stage.[25] In his view, the religious stage of existence possesses the ethical stage, and an individual must have been through the ethical in order to arrive at the religious.[26] There is therefore, no

[20] *E/O*, II, 261. Cf. "Only when the individual himself is the universal is it possible to realize the ethical." *Ibid.*, II, 260.

[21] Kierkegaard, *Concluding Unscientific Postscript*, trans. David Swenson and Walter Lowrie (Princeton University Press, 1941), p. 133.

[22] *CUP*, p. 135.   [23] *Ibid.*, p. 284.

[24] *Ibid.*, p. 144.   [25] *Ibid.*, pp. 387, 417, 430.

[26] *Ibid.*, pp. 124, 347. Kierkegaard, *Stages on Life's Way*, trans. Walter Lowrie (Princeton University Press, 1940), p. 430.

conflict between the ethical and the ethico-religious stages of existence[27]—only a dialectical interdependence.

Since we have not examined in detail the structures of the ethical and the ethico-religious stages of existence with respect to the problem of self-understanding (relating), these propositions cannot now have more than a general meaning for us. I am now simply trying to reenforce the already established claim that the ethical requirement to fulfill one's duty to oneself as ideal is not abandoned with the introduction to the ethico-religious stage of existence.

This notion can at this point in the essay perhaps be made more clear by turning to a discussion of the other definition of ethics which prevails in the pseudonymous corpus.[28]

The more basic meaning of the term refers to the possibility of self-understanding as the fundamental possibility of human existence.[29]

> The ethical individual knows himself, but this knowledge is not a mere contemplation (for with that the individual is determined by his necessity), it is a reflection upon himself which itself is an action. . . .[30]

[27] *CUP*, p. 103.

[28] The notion of ethics as a stage of existence in which the individual is dutifully related to his ideality is most thoroughly developed in *E/O*, II. The choice of oneself initiates the ethical stage, and its subsequent development is conceived in terms of duty to oneself, i.e., duty to actualize that which is chosen. *CUP* emphasizes the second notion of ethics, viz., self-understanding. Here the phenomena of choice and duty are practically unmentioned, while the process of inward reflection becomes the central theme. The issue is whether these two notions of ethics are complementary, contradictory, or unrelated in any sense. The argument which we will be following is that they are dialectically complementary. Ethics as self-understanding depends for its emergence as the fundamental possibility (task) of human existence upon the appearance of the ethical stage. And the content of the ethical stage contributes to the development of self-understanding.

[29] It is more fundamental because its meaning applies to a process which characterizes both the strictly ethical and the ethico-religious stages of existence.

[30] *E/O*, II, 263.

Two major points are made here. First, self-knowledge belongs to ethical consciousness, and second, such knowledge is achieved in action. It follows from the first point that any stage of existence which enhances self-knowledge is qualified by the broader sense of the ethical. And it follows from the second point that all self-knowledge is grounded in the decisive relationship of an individual to his possibilities.[31] Ethics here means that the individual's relation to any possibility is an ethical relation in the sense that the individual is always responsible for a decision in relationship to possibilities which preserves them in existence. Kierkegaard believes that ethics is "the power to demand actuality, the power to achieve presentness, the power to minimize the medium of imagination and to will to have only the medium of existence."[32] And it also means that the individual can understand himself only by being decisively related to possibilities. Thus, Kierkegaard can affirm that

> all Christian knowledge and generally all ethical knowledge is not what it is essentially when it is separated from its situation. A situation (actuality, that is, that a person expresses in actuality what he knows) is the *conditio sine qua non* for ethical knowledge.[33]

Ethical understanding, then, is decisive for all existence. This meaning characterizes both the ethical and the ethico-religious stages of existence since in both the individual is related to himself as possibility. Kierkegaard is perfectly consistent, then, in saying that ethical consciousness "is the authorization and the aim and the measure of human exist-

[31] We have already defined action as that event by which a possibility is existentially actualized.

[32] *SKJP*, I, 973. Cf. "Reality for the poet is merely an occasion, a point of departure, from which he goes in search of the ideality of the possible. The pathos of the poet is therefore essentially imaginative pathos. An attempt ethically to establish a poetic relationship to reality is therefore a misunderstanding, a backward step." *CUP*, p. 347.

[33] *SKJP*, I, 978.

ence."[34] The task of radically penetrating oneself so that one's self as it is becomes totally transparent is an ethical task. Again, in Kierkegaard's words, "it is essential to a man who is to live ethically that he become so radically conscious of himself that no adventitious trait escapes him."[35] Once this ethical task is accepted, the individual is of necessity, as we shall see, pushed beyond the bounds of the ethical into the ethico-religious stage of existence.

Now the relation between the two meanings of the term, ethics, is clear. Ethics as the task of self-understanding cannot challenge the individual as his primary task until he has become conscious of himself as a self and a task. Neither consciousness of oneself as a self nor consciousness of one's fundamental possibility as self-understanding are immediately given and disclosed in existence. Both must be discovered and appropriated in one's own existential development, i.e., in the dialectical development of spirit. The discovery and appropriation is the substance of the ethical stage of existence. Only by passing into the ethical stage of existence does the fundamentally ethical character of existence open up for consciousness. We might express the relationship between the ethical stage and the ethical task in this manner: the ethical choice is the initiation and the heart of the ethical stage of existence, and the individual's fundamental task of self-understanding involves the elaboration and clarification of that choice. This elucidating process constitutes the ethico-religious stage of existence in the dialectical development of spirit.[36] Before proceeding

[34] *Ibid.*, I, 922; cf. *SUD*, p. 201f. and *CUP*, pp. 291, 359.

[35] *E/O*, II, 258.

[36] Now neither the first level of the ethico-religious stage (Religiousness A), which terminates in repentance, nor ethics as a task of self-understanding, are abandoned once the second level of the ethico-religious stage of existence (Religiousness B) is reached. For, on the one hand, without Religiousness A, Religiousness B cannot come into existence. Christianity can only be dialectically understood. Without the requirement and the discovery of guilt in Religiousness A, Christianity cannot find a place in the development of the process of self-

to an analysis of the ethical choice, it is first important to consider briefly the relation of ethics and ontology in Kierkegaard's doctrine of the self.

The coincidence of ethics (in its second and broader meaning) and ontology is situated in the relation of existing (self-relating) and understanding (self-knowing). As we have seen, self-knowledge is gained through the existential actualization of one's possibilities. The only possibility open to the individual is himself. Consequently, the individual gains self-understanding only by realizing himself in existence.

Now the individual's fundamentally ethical task is made possible by the dialectical structure of the self itself. That is to say, unless the self is already a relation which potentially can relate itself to itself, there can be no task for ethics. Apart from the dynamic structure of the self, ethics, for Kierkegaard, is abstractly conceived and cannot be determined as an existential process. Ethics imposes on each individual the task of consciousness and clarifies the self-structure itself.

---

understanding. The existing individual remains Christian only so long as he remains guilty. To abandon guilt-understanding even for a moment has the immediate effect of destroying the existential reality of Christianity by converting it into either scholasticism or a cultural formality. And, on the other hand, it is completely false to assume that once that Religiousness A is taken up into Christian existence the task of self-understanding is abandoned. Religiousness B is the culminating stage in the development of self-knowing. It is erroneous to think that in the stage of Religiousness B, we gain understanding of the nature of God. The divine is a central aspect of this stage of existence but as a determinant by which the task of self-understanding is culminated. In terms of self-understanding, then, the stage of Religiousness B does not take us beyond man but to the very core of the nature of the self. Hence, the fundamental ethical task of self-understanding is not abandoned in Religiousness B but, on the contrary, finally reaches its culmination. The level of Religiousness B, like the preceding level of Religiousness A, in the ethico-religious stage, is a stage of self-understanding and, hence, remains within the second notion of ethics as a process of self-understanding.

THE CHOICE

Ethics as a stage of existence and as the task of self-understanding begins with the famous Kierkegaardian "choice of oneself." The choice of oneself establishes both the subject and the limits of the entire dialectical development of spirit. That is to say, in the choice, the individual understands himself as a task, and the elucidation of the nature and content of that task constitutes the further dialectical development of spirit. The entire movement of the spirit in terms of the development of self-understanding is a turning back upon and a penetration of this original choice so that the final outcome is one in which the choice itself has become a fully transparent phenomenon. The choice, then, both constitutes the task of understanding and becomes the subject matter of the task itself.

We must begin, then, with an examination of the choice itself. Our discussion can profitably hinge on two important passages from *Either/Or*.

> But what is it I choose? Is it this thing or that? No, for I choose absolutely, and the absoluteness of my choice is expressed precisely by the fact that I have not chosen to choose this or that. I choose the absolute. And what is the absolute? It is I myself in my eternal validity.[37]

> But what, then, is this self of mine? If I were required to define this, my first answer would be: It is the most abstract of all things, and yet at the same time it is the most concrete—it is freedom.[38]

The first passage affirms the absolute quality of the choice and its object, and the second states that the self, which is chosen, is freedom. These passages confront us with two fundamental problems. First, the choice is an expression of freedom. How, then, does spirit at this point in its development become conscious of itself so that the choice becomes

---

[37] *E/O*, II, 218.   [38] *Ibid.*

possible? And, second why is the choice and its object absolute? Or, better, in what sense are choice and its object absolute?

In answering the first question, we must examine briefly the way in which the aesthetic stage comes to its conclusion. As we have already noted, the aesthetic stage culminates in despair. The fully developed aesthetic consciousness thoroughly knows that the finite cannot grant happiness, and the aesthetic individual, consequently, loses himself in the infinity of the imagination. In the aesthetic stage of existence we find, on the one hand, the aesthete dabbling frenetically, anxiously, in the finite and, on the other hand, a slowly developing awareness of the futility of the finite along with a corresponding dialectical flight into the infinite. To the extent that the finite is mistrusted as a source of happiness, reflection is intensified and deepened without any awareness of the necessity for making the dialectical move of choosing oneself as a relation. Reflection and the degree of dabbling in the finite are, then, dialectically related. The more finite the self is the less reflective it is. And, conversely, the more reflective the self is the less finite it is. The hierarchy of moods which Kierkegaard describes in *Either/Or*, I, represents the different ways in which absorption in the finite and reflection are related. The aesthetic stage dialectically progresses from unreflective sensual immediacy (Don Juan), through the moods of grief (The Shadowgraphs), cynicism (The Unhappiest Man), imagination (The First Love), and boredom (The Rotation Method) into the final outpost of the aesthetic, "inwardness with a jammed look,"[39] or despair (The Diary of a Seducer).

The final refuge of the increasingly despairing aesthetic mind is the attitude of irony. The seducer knows what none

[39] This phrase means that the self is as completely absorbed in the infinity of the imagination as it is humanly possible to be. He has totally abandoned finitude by becoming imaginatively infinitized. He is, as it were, without a body. This is a conscious refusal to become oneself and, hence, is despair.

of the other aesthetes knows, viz., that the aesthetic is despair and that there is no refuge from despair in the aesthetic stage of existence. This the seducer knows, and his irony reduces everything to the status of possibility in the inwardness of self-reflection. He has overcome all attachment to the finite; he is too sophisticated, too talented, for that. And his irony, without a foothold in an eternal ideal principle, stresses the imaginative toying with possibilities at the expense of choosing himself as a relation of the finite and the infinite. In the aesthetic stage of existence, the regressive movement of reflection continues unabated unless a choice is made for a reflected possibility. A possibility remains a possibility when it is only reflected and not acted upon. Reflection, then, regresses infinitely, each possibility dissolving into others *ad infinitum* while at the same time the forward movement of the self continues.

> The lost wayfarer always has the consolation that the scene is constantly changing before him, and with every change there is born the hope of finding a way out. . . . It is in vain that he has many exits from his foxhole, at the moment his anxious soul believes that it already sees daylight breaking through, it turns out to be a new entrance . . . [and] he constantly seeks a way out, and finds only a way in, through which he goes back into himself.[40]

There is no refuge from despair in the on-goingness of time. The novelties of time are equally impotent to conquer the despair of the seducer. He does not know that the momentary happiness which he finds in his sexual conquest of Cordelia Wahl can be saved from its strictly momentary, i.e., timely, character by absorbing the relation in the eternal ideal of love. He does not know that he must choose Cordelia in order to bring the seduction itself under the category of the instant instead of the moment.[41]

[40] *E/O*, I, 304.

[41] The moment refers to the on-goingness of time in which the seducer lives. The instant refers to the impingement of the eternal upon time through an act of freedom.

He won her. As long as the fight lasted [i.e., as long as the seduction remained only a possibility] he noticed nothing; then she resigned herself, he was loved with all the emotion of a young girl—then he became unhappy, his melancholy awoke, he drew back, he could fight with the whole world but not with himself. His love made him indescribably happy for the moment; as soon as he thought of time he despaired.[42]

The despairing individual cannot get rid of himself, and the effort to do just that through reflection leads him still further into this labyrinth of self-deception. This reflective effort to escape this "gnawing canker" (despair) leads to even higher forms of reflective escape until one ultimately arrives at the awareness that there is no escape. At this point, the individual grounds himself in irony in order to live only for possibilities, fully aware that the momentary satisfaction of any one possibility will throw the individual back upon the immediate awareness that there is no escape, that his life, then, must be one of complete despair. In a real sense his life is one of momentary diversions and amusements which serve to assuage the pain of despairing existence. Throughout Cordelia's seduction we are constantly aware of the seducer's awareness of the contingency of the whole affair. The moment of the seduction brings to an end the experience of reflective enjoyment of the multifarious moods which he reflectively created and in which he imaginatively thrived. The seducer, then, abandons Cordelia as he must abandon all future lovers, because of his failure to grasp himself as eternal, whereby he might gain partial authority over time.

The next step beyond the despairing irony of the seducer is the irony of the true ironist. He is one who exists in the tension between the claims of the finite and the absolute claim posed by the ethical requirement. This more developed irony grounds itself in the claim of the ethical requirement and in so doing becomes the possibility of ethical un-

[42] *SKJ*, #468.

derstanding. The ironist is not yet, however, an ethicist; ethical existence is still only a possibility for him.

In irony, the *Was-Sein*, i.e., the underlying dialectical structure of the self as a relation of finitude and infinitude, comes to consciousness.

> Irony arises from the constant placing of the particularities of the finite together with the infinite ethical requirement, thus permitting the contradiction to come into being.[43]

The ironist penetrates all the delusions of finite consciousness by measuring them against the absolute requirement of infinity. Infinity appears at this point not as a specific requirement but merely as requirement. The ironist is only at this point conscious of himself as a requirement. As yet, he is not conscious of the specific content of the requirement. Ironical consciousness expresses the tension in the relation between the claims of finitude and infinitude, but the self, as yet, has not become an active relationship of the two.

> The ironist levels everything on the basis of humanity in the abstract, the humorist on the abstract God-relationship; for he does not enter concretely into this relationship, but it is just at this point that he parries by means of a jest.[44]

Both irony and humor express the tension of infinite consciousness. The finite is brought into relation with the infinite and yet, the infinite is not existentially actualized but is instead "parried with a jest." Now an ethicist may indeed employ irony as an incognito,[45] but "an observer may be de-

---

[43] *CUP*, p. 448.   [44] *CUP*, p. 401n.

[45] "But although such an individual's realization of infinite movement is given, it is not given that he is an ethicist. The latter is what he is solely and exclusively through maintaining an inner relationship to the absolute requirement. Such an ethicist uses irony as his incognito." *CUP*, p. 449. The ethicist uses irony as an incognito because

ceived if he accepts an ironist as an ethicist, for irony is only the possibility thereof."[46] The ironical individual is conscious of himself as a relation but has not yet acted upon that consciousness by actualizing the relationship itself. Ironical consciousness is the pre-condition of the choice of oneself as finite and infinite. So we see, then, that the development of ironical consciousness out of the aesthetic stage of existence makes possible choice of oneself as a relation.

Now for the choice to be absolute, the individual must choose himself as "infinitely concrete."[47]

> In thinking, I infinitize myself too, but not absolutely, for I disappear in the absolute. Only when I absolutely choose myself do I infinitize myself absolutely. . . .[48]

To infinitize oneself is to open oneself up to possibility. We have seen that one form of despair is constituted by the self's losing its footing in reality and escaping into the unreflected imagination. Kierkegaard is here saying that such a choice of oneself as infinite is not an absolute choice, because it has excluded the real self altogether. The self becomes absolutely infinite only when finitude is dialectically conceived as an infinite requirement. Kierkegaard means that the self is absolutely infinitized, i.e., becomes infinitely concrete, only when the individual chooses himself as a relation of the finite and the infinite.

The self which one strives to gain is one's own self; the existing individual does not divest himself of his facticity.

> But when one chooses oneself abstractly one does not choose oneself ethically. Only when in his choice a man

---

"he grasps the contradiction there is between the manner in which he exists inwardly and the fact that he does not outwardly express it." *CUP*, p. 450.

[46] *CUP*, p. 451. Cf. "There are thus three spheres of existence: the aesthetic, the ethical, the religious. Two boundary zones correspond to these three: irony constituting the boundary between the aesthetic and the ethical; humor, as the boundary that separates the ethical from the religious." *Ibid.*, p. 448.

[47] *E/O*, II, 219.   [48] *Ibid.*, II, 228.

has assumed himself, is clad in himself, has so totally penetrated himself that every movement is attended by the consciousness of a responsibility for himself, only then has he chosen himself ethically . . . only then is he concrete, only then is he in his total isolation in absolute continuity with the reality to which he belongs.[49]

It is important to note here that the aesthetic is not abandoned but transformed once the ethical choice is made. Indeed, and more to the point, to abandon one's facticity would make the choice impossible.

By the absolute choice the ethical [self] is posited, but from this it does not follow by any means that the aesthetical is excluded. In the ethical the personality is concentrated in itself, so the aesthetical is absolutely excluded or is excluded as the absolute, but relatively it is still left. In choosing itself the personality chooses itself ethically and excludes absolutely the aesthetical, but since he chooses himself and since he does not [cannot] become another being by choosing himself but becomes himself, the whole of the aesthetical comes back again in its relativity.[50]

In the choice, the individual chooses himself in its entirety, i.e., absolutely and in so doing "he does not become another man than he was before, but he becomes himself, consciousness is unified and he is himself."[51] Kierkegaard never espouses the complete abrogation of the aesthetic. If the individual is to choose himself ethically, he must choose himself concretely as a definite self. And he can only do this by including his aesthetical self. The unification of consciousness depends upon the unification of the self's factical

[49] *Ibid.*, II, 252.

[50] *Ibid.*, II, 181-182. We shall see in the discussion below on resignation how this formula of being absolutely related to the absolute and relatively related to the relative is picked up and clarified in *CUP*.

[51] *Ibid.*, II, 181.

being (finitude) and his ethical requirement (infinitude) through an act of freedom.

Now to choose myself as infinitely concrete is to choose myself as freedom. As long as the individual is unconscious of himself as a relation he is unconscious of his potential freedom. But in irony, the consciousness of myself as a relation emerges. But the individual maintains a strictly ironical stance in relation to this self at the expense of freedom. Only in the instant when the individual chooses himself as a relation which is a possibility for himself does his freedom come into existence. But even then freedom has an abstract character, because the individual chooses himself as a finite being who is faced with an infinite ethical requirement. Just what that requirement is in its concrete substance does not come to consciousness at this point.

> That which is prominent in my either/or is the ethical. It is therefore not yet a question of the choice of something in particular, it is not a question of the reality of the thing chosen but of the reality of the act of choice.[52]

The individual merely chooses himself as possible. One merely chooses to choose. That is to say, the individual does not choose himself as something in particular, e.g., a teacher, husband, politician, musician, revolutionary, or whatever, but he chooses himself in the much more abstract sense of being a finite being who is faced by an absolute and infinite ethical requirement. In this choice of his *Was-Sein*, then, he chooses himself as freedom. The choice to be ethical is the choice before the choice. It is the acceptance of oneself as radically free and responsible for oneself, and it is a choice made possible by the previous determination of consciousness.[53]

[52] *Ibid.*, II, 180.

[53] Kierkegaard writes that "the reality of spirit constantly shows itself in a form which entices its possibility. . . ." *CD*, p. 38. That is to say, spirit appears initially as self-consciousness and in so doing presents freedom with the possibility of itself.

But freedom itself remains abstract. The self as freedom has merely been chosen as freedom. The choice is the initial expression of freedom as freedom's choice of itself as possibility. The more concrete choice of myself as a specific and concrete possibility lies in the future; therefore, the full concreteness of myself as freedom itself remains a possibility and, hence, an abstraction. The establishment of the self as a concrete possibility is the pre-condition for freedom's becoming concrete. Moreover, freedom at this point has no understanding of its true nature. It is merely aware of itself.

Even though freedom appears as an abstraction in the choice, we can say that with the choice the self has come into existence. To relate oneself actively to oneself can only mean to choose oneself as freedom. Only when the existing individual realizes his freedom is his relation to himself actual; and at the instant in which this relation is actualized, the self becomes spirit. Now the further dialectical development of spirit comes to understand itself fully in existence.

It follows, then, that in the choice the concrete content of the self is produced in the sense that it is brought to consciousness and chosen as the individual's own responsibility. The choice produces the self by bringing the concrete content of the self's facticity to consciousness as a possibility realizable through freedom.

> The choice itself is decisive for the content of personality, through the choice the personality immerses itself in the thing chosen, and when it does not choose it withers away in consumption.[54]

The content of the choice immediately *is* and, therefore, is not created. However, if the self is to become what it *is*, the collision of the ideal *is not* with the real *is* must emerge in

[54] *E/O*, II, 167. Reider Thomte succinctly expresses it as follows: "The choice is an act of freedom, and it may well be said that in an act of choosing the individual produces himself." *Kierkegaard's Philosophy of Religion* (Princeton University Press, 1948), pp. 45-46.

consciousness, and freedom must accept as its task (possibility) the content of consciousness.

> The self did not exist previously, for it came into existence by means of the choice, and yet it did exist, for it was in fact "himself." In this case, choice performs at one and the same time the two dialectical movements: that which is chosen does not exist and comes into existence with choice; that which is chosen exists, otherwise there would not be a choice. For in case what I chose did not exist but absolutely came into existence with the choice, I would not be choosing, I would be creating; but I do not create myself, I choose myself.[55]

The whole background for Kierkegaard's discussion of the choice is the dialectically structured self. Until the individ-

---

[55] *E/O*, II, 219-220. Whenever Kierkegaard speaks of choice, he speaks also of despair, for together they constitute an inseparable phenomenon. "So then choose despair, for even despair is a choice . . . one cannot despair without choosing. And when a man despairs he chooses again—and what is it he chooses? He chooses himself, not in his immediacy, not as this fortuitous individual, but he chooses himself in his eternal validity." *E/O*, II, 215. The self makes the choice in the height of despair, i.e., when everything has lost its value and there is nothing left outside of himself to choose. He is, therefore, in his despair driven toward his absolute self. Price correctly sees the relation between despair and choice: "But when a man decides not to drift, he decides at the same time the point where he will anchor himself. This cannot be anything outside himself, because there is nothing outside him worth choosing. It must, therefore, be something inward . . . in this case, his own self, the only absolute left for him." Price, *The Narrow Pass*, p. 173. If the self is to choose himself, he must choose his despair, for he is despair. In the choice of despair, the aesthetical stage relinquishes its absolute claim upon the individual, and the way opens for the self to choose himself in his entirety, i.e., as a relation. Only through the deed of despair is it possible for the ethical to appear. "So then the choice of despair is ('myself')—for though when I despair it is true that, among all other things I despair of, I despair also of myself, yet this self of which I despair is a finite thing like every other finitude, whereas the self I choose is the absolute self, or myself according to its absolute validity." *E/O*, II, 223, 212-213.

ual becomes conscious of himself and chooses himself as a possibility, the self exists immediately as a possibility. Kierkegaard is saying that the dialectical structure of human existence comes into existence with the choice. The entire structure of the self is now in existence for the individual inasmuch as he has understood himself, albeit abstractly, in terms of this structure. Of course, the self has yet to become fully transparent for the existing individual, and the remainder of the dialectical development of spirit has precisely the purpose of completely clarifying this original choice.

The choice, then, is absolute because in the choice the absolute comes into existence.[56] Once the existing individual

---

[56] Kierkegaard frequently speaks of the emergence of the structure of the self in the choice as self-revelation as opposed to the self-concealment of the aesthetic stage of existence. "The ethicist has 'despaired' (the first part of *Either/Or*); in this despair he has 'chosen himself,' in and by this choice he 'reveals himself' (the expression which sharply differentiates between the ethical and the aesthetic is this: it is every man's duty to reveal himself). . . ." *CUP*, p. 227. In the aesthetic stage, the self endures as an immediate unity, i.e., a unity which is not conscious of itself. The self is, then, hidden, concealed, from itself, and the revelation of ethics is the manifestation of this unity as a task in existence. "The ethical as such is the universal, again, as the universal it is the manifest, the revealed. The individual regarded as he is immediately, that is, as a physical [body] and psychical [soul] being, is the hidden, the concealed. So his ethical task is to develop out of this concealment and to reveal himself in the universal." *FT*, p. 91. The self is, as it were, publicly identifiable through the existing individual's participation in the universal ideal. Judge William, for example, conquers the melancholy and despair of the aesthetic stage of existence by committing himself to the ideal of marriage. Judge William with an "infinite passion of resolve embraces the modest ethical task, and edified thereby stands self-revealed before God and man." *CUP*, p. 228. But, as we shall see, self-revelation turns back toward a deeper form of concealment with the introduction of religious consciousness. "Another author (in *E/O*) has properly carried the ethical back to the determination of self-revelation: that it is every man's duty to reveal himself. Religiosity on the other hand is the secret inwardness, but not,

has comprehended and chosen himself as his life-long task for which he and he alone is ultimately and completely responsible, the individual has penetrated to the very limits of his being. With the choice of the self, the existing individual, on the one hand, comprehends his *Was-Sein* as the absolute limit of what he is and can become, and, on the other hand, he comprehends his *Wie-Sein* by recognizing that he is free and has an absolute responsibility for becoming what he is.

But we must not conclude from all this that the choice, because it is absolute, is once and for all. It is not as though one chooses himself and then abandons the choice for higher levels of consciousness. Indeed, all further levels of consciousness are possible only if the existing individual continually chooses himself. There are two reasons for this. First, the factor of time is not escaped or neutralized in the choice. And, second, the further stages of consciousness are deeper incursions into this original choice. Both points are emphasized in the following passage.

> The beginning of an absolute decision in the medium of existence is the last thing in the world that can be characterized once for all, as something left behind . . . [for] the existing individual becomes concrete in his experience, and in going on he still has his experience with him, and may in each moment be threatened with the loss of it; he has it with him not as something one has in a pocket, but his having it constitutes a definite something by which he is himself specifically determined, so that by losing it he loses his own specific determination. As a consequence of having made a decision in existence, the existing individual has attained a more specific determination of what he is; if he lays it aside, then it is not he

---

please note an immediacy which needs to be brought out into the open, not an unclarified inwardness, but an inwardness whose clarifying determination it is to be hidden." *CUP*, p. 446n. Cf. *E/O*, II, 327 and *PF*, p. 96.

who has lost something; he does not have himself while happening to have lost something, but he has lost himself and must now begin from the beginning.[57]

Kierkegaard's first point is that the choice must constantly be remade, for only in the choice is the self determined as absolute. The decision does not eternally secure the absolute self. The self continues to grow. We cannot forget that the self is in time and its facticity is constantly expanding; therefore, the self can be continually determined as absolute only so long as the individual is constantly choosing himself. The on-goingness of time as a threat to the choice is illustrated in this long passage from *Either/Or*.

When the individual has grasped himself in his eternal validity this overwhelms him by its fullness. The temporal vanishes from before his eyes. At the first instant this fills him with indescribable bliss and gives him a sense of absolute security. If then he begins to gaze upon this bliss, the temporal advances its claim. This is scorned. What the temporal can give, the more or the less which now presents itself, is so very unimportant in comparison with what he eternally possesses. Everything comes with him to a standstill, he has, as it were, reached eternity before the time. He relapses into contemplation, he gazes at himself, but this gaze cannot fill up the time. Then it appears to him that time, that the temporal, is his ruin; he demands a more perfect form of existence, and at this point there comes to evidence a fatigue, an apathy, which resembles the languor which is the attendant of pleasure. This apathy may rest so broodingly upon a man that suicide appears to him the only way of escape. No power can wrest from him his self, the only power is time, but neither can that wrest from him his self; it checks him and delays, it arrests the embrace of the spirit with which he grasps his self. He has not chosen himself; like Narcis-

[57] *CUP*, pp. 436-437.

sus he has fallen in love with himself. Such a situation has
certainly ended not infrequently in suicide.[58]

Time constantly intrudes upon the choice reminding the
self of the unrelenting on-goingness of its factical being. In
the choice, the self is concentrated in the instant. The self's
facticity is united with its ideality in an act of freedom. The
past and the future intersect in the present instant, and the
individual thereby knows himself in his eternal validity.
However, if the individual fixes his gaze upon this one
choice, forgetting the timely progression of his being, time
sweeps the self beyond the choice, and its eternal validity
becomes a tormenting memory. The individual will then be
inclined to say: "What is the use? I exerted myself absolutely to come to an understanding of what I am only in the
next moment to have that knowledge swept away by time.
Existence is too tiring; it demands too much energy. I cannot possibly find in myself the strength to repeat the choice
over and over again. That is too much to ask of any man."
But such an individual cannot remain comfortably apa-
thetic. He now knows what it means to understand himself
in his eternal validity. And, though he may not find the
strength to choose himself again, he cannot settle back into
the naive apathy of immediacy, i.e., into an ignorance of
himself as eternal. He is caught, then, in a terrible tension.
On the one hand, he lacks the courage and the energy to
choose himself again, and, on the other hand, he knows that
a higher despair awaits his refusal to choose himself again
in the future. Suicide, Kierkegaard says, is a very likely consequence. And time in all of this is the culprit. Time necessitates a continual repetition of the choice in order that the
self may retain its eternal validity as a unity (present) of
the past (necessity) and future (possibility) through freedom's expression of itself as choice.

And, secondly the further development of the self beyond
the initial choice depends upon the choice itself for its development. If the individual for an instant stops choosing

[58] *E/O*, II, 235-236.

himself, the ground upon which the further development of spirit occurs disappears and along with it the possibility of further spiritual development. The individual has himself as absolute only as long as he chooses himself, and the loss of this crucial determination throttles altogether the further development of spirit. Consequently, if the individual refrains from choosing even for a moment, he loses himself absolutely and, hence, must begin all over again and from the beginning.

Only as long as the existing individual maintains himself in the choice is it possible for spirit, which comes into existence in the choice, to develop. To hold oneself constantly in the choice is to remain conscious of oneself as free and fully responsible for oneself as a task. The choice determines the content in which one will live and examine his life. The existing individual's factical being, which is brought to consciousness in the choice, constitutes the experiential network in which the individual must live and understand himself. This consciousness is absolutely indispensable for the further development of spirit. Kierkegaard refers to the further stages of spirit's development as resignation, suffering, guilt, repentance, and faith; and we may, by turning to *Concluding Unscientific Postscript*, see how they are related to choice and the ethical stage of existence which it brings into existence.

Before analyzing each of these levels of existence separately, we should examine Kierkegaard's own reasoning concerning the necessity for further movement subsequent to the choice.

> The ethicist in *Either/Or* had saved himself through despair, abolishing concealment in self-revelation; but here was in my opinion a difficulty. In order to determine himself in the inwardness of the truth as distinct from speculative philosophy, he had used the term despair instead of doubt; but still he had made it appear that by despairing in the very act of despair itself, as if *uno tenore*, he had been able to win himself. Had *Either/Or* proposed

to make it clear where the difficulty lies, the entire work would have had to have a religious orientation; *but in that case it would have been necessary to say in the beginning what, according to my ideas, should [can] be said only successively.* . . . The difficulty is, that the ethical self is supposed to be found immanently in despair, so that the individual by persisting in his despair at last wins himself. *He has indeed used a determination of freedom: to choose himself.* . . . But this avails nothing. *When I despair, I use myself to despair, and therefore I can indeed by myself despair of everything; but when I do this; I cannot by myself come back.* In this moment of decision it is that the individual needs divine assistance, while it is quite right to say that one must first have understood the existential relationship between the aesthetic and the ethical in order to be at this point; that is to say, by being there in passion and inwardness one will doubtless become aware of the religious—and of the leap.[59]

There appear to be three major points in this key passage. First, *Either/Or* culminates in ethical understanding, and it is, therefore, impossible to include anything in that work which is not of that level of consciousness. The existing individual is aware of who he is to the extent that what he is has been mediated by consciousness and existentially understood. Consciousness is the ultimate arbiter of existence, and the individual can only become existentially what has been mediated by consciousness. To have said more in that work than is possible for the stage of ethical understanding would have violated the principle governing its writing. Second, Kierkegaard says that choice is a determination of freedom. To speak of choice as a determination of freedom implies that freedom has other determinations, but what they are and how these further determinations are related to choice, we cannot know at this point.

[59] *CUP*, pp. 230-231. Italics mine.

And, third, Kierkegaard suggests that the religious stage of existence begins where the ethical leaves off but does not go beyond it. That is to say, religious understanding is dialectically dependent upon ethical consciousness and cannot abandon it without, at the same time, losing itself. Religious understanding only penetrates deeper into the beginning made by choice, thereby more fully clarifying the true nature of the beginning itself. More concretely, Kierkegaard seems to be saying that when the existing individual despairs of everything finite and chooses himself as infinite, it is impossible for the individual to come back to himself under his own power. By this phrase I take him to mean that it is impossible for the individual to become infinitely concrete without the aid of divine assistance. In this struggle to become infinite, freedom's consciousness of itself is expanded to the point where the possibility of the leap emerges. But, as we shall see, such a possibility necessarily depends upon the attainment of a certain level of consciousness. Indeed, one is unconscious even of the thought of the leap as a real possibility for oneself until a certain level of consciousness is reached.[60] It is the task of the following chapters to chart the development of the ethico-religious stage of existence.

[60] I do not mean to suggest here either that the consciousness emerging at the beginning of E/O, II, culminates in an empty consciousness or that this level of consciousness does not entail still higher levels of consciousness. In the first instance, there can be no consciousness which is not consciousness of something. Consciousness is always consciousness of something. And in Kierkegaard's case, the consciousness appearing at the beginning of E/O, II, with the choice is consciousness of the self. The choice is a choice of oneself as a synthesis of finitude and infinitude. With the choice, the triadic character of the self becomes the object of consciousness. Secondly, although the possibility of religious consciousness lies embedded in ethical consciousness as its fulfillment or completion, it is impossible at this point to investigate religious consciousness since the unfolding of ethical consciousness is a necessary condition for the appearance of religious consciousness.

CHAPTER V

The Religion of Hidden Inwardness

WE are now ready to move beyond the initial choice and the strictly ethical stage of existence which it makes possible to an analysis of the first level of the ethico-religious stage of existence. It is here in the religion of hidden inwardness that the existing individual comes to a more concrete understanding of the meaning of being a relation in which he freely exists and for which he is fully responsible. In the first and second sections of the chapter, we shall see how the notions of resignation and the God-relationship sharpen the meaning of choosing oneself as absolute. And the analyses of suffering, guilt, and repentance in the next three sections will disclose the way in which freedom more concretely is understood as incapable of uniting the self as an existential unity or relation.

RESIGNATION

Resignation is a higher understanding of the act of choice by which the existing individual relates himself to his self. That is to say, in resignation the individual gains a still higher understanding of what it means to confront himself as a task. The choice of oneself as infinitely concrete involves the higher consciousness of being absolutely related to the absolute and relatively related to the relative.[1] This

---

[1] Both absolute and relative relations have a psychological and a moral aspect. The psychological aspect of the relation expresses the attitude of the individual toward the object of the relation. In an absolute relation, the individual is totally and without reservation committed to an absolute. Put another way, the individual is ultimately concerned about the object of the relation. In a relative

formula for resigned consciousness is even present in *Either/Or,* although it is only implicitly present and not at all developed. Here Kierkegaard writes that "the ethical personality is concentrated in itself, so the aesthetical is absolutely exluded or is excluded as the absolute, but relatively it is still left."[2] Now in *Concluding Unscientific Postscript* the task consists in "the simultaneous maintenance of an absolute relationship to this absolute *telos,* and a relative relationship to relative ends."[3]

To choose absolutely means to be absolutely related to what one has chosen and relatively related to everything else which is not absolute. In the choice the self is grasped

---

relation, he is not ultimately concerned about the object of the relation. The moral aspect of the two relations concerns the character of the relation itself. If the object of the relation is absolute, the relation is necessary and should not be revoked at any time or under any circumstances. If the object of the relation is relative, the relation is contingent and can be revoked.

[2] *E/O,* II, 182.

[3] Kierkegaard identifies the absolute *telos* and an eternal happiness in the sense that the latter is a reward for the realization of the former. The individual becomes happy through becoming himself. "In the life of time the 'expectation' of an eternal happiness is the highest reward, because an eternal happiness is the highest *telos.* . . ." *CUP,* p. 360. The goal of ethical action is happiness. And the existential actualization of the self is the fulfillment of the individual's task and produces his happiness.

Happiness is not conceived by Kierkegaard as psychological contentment or the triumph of pleasure over pain. On the contrary, happiness is grounded in action. Happiness is, says Kierkegaard, "the absolute ethical good [which] can be proved only by the individual himself existentially expressing it in existence." *CUP,* 379. Happiness is rooted in the existential unification of the self as a relation of the finite and the infinite. It does not result from inaction or passivity but from the perfect exertion of freedom by which the individual's task is fully realized in existence. In this action and in this action alone is happiness to be achieved. Michael Novak's translation of *eudaimonia* as "well acting" perfectly expresses the meaning of happiness in Kierkegaard's writings. The action by which one's absolute *telos* is actualized is happiness. See Michael Novak, *The Experience of Nothingness* (New York: Harper and Row, Inc., 1970), pp. 69ff.

as absolute. The self as a synthesis of the finite and the infinite, i.e., as infinitely concrete, is the absolute. Now in resignation, Kierkegaard speaks of an absolute relationship to an absolute *telos*. The individual establishes an absolute relationship to himself as his own *telos*, i.e., as the task which the individual strives to actualize. Therefore, the individual in establishing an absolute relationship to his absolute *telos*, establishes an absolute relationship to himself.[4]

The choice of oneself as absolute involves the renunciation of all finite relations and ends as absolute. The renunciation of finitude as having an absolute claim upon the individual is the existential expression for becoming absolutely related to oneself as absolute. The individual now confronts himself not simply as an absolute but as an absolute to which he is absolutely related. In the renunciation of finitude as absolute, freedom is more rigorously, indeed irrevocably, bound to the task of actualizing the self as a synthesis of the finite and the infinite. The self as a relation which relates himself to himself is now permeated by an absolute responsibility for himself so that no other alternatives or possibilities are now open to him. The individual is in resignation absolutely bound to himself.

The only way to be related to an absolute is absolutely.

---

[4] The diversity of Kierkegaard's terminology is perplexing. Thus far we have used the terms *telos*, ideal task, absolute, infinitely concrete, and unity to describe the sense of Kierkegaard's definition of the self as a relation. Each term conveys a nuance of meaning so that it is impossible to grasp fully the nature of the self as a relation apart from an acquaintance with all the different ways in which Kierkegaard chooses to describe it. In Chapter III I spoke of the culmination of the development of spirit as the existential unification of the three constitutive elements of the individual's being. This ideal task can be described as the concrete rendering of the self as infinite through an act of freedom. Kierkegaard resorts almost exclusively to the use of the term, absolute *telos*, goal, in *CUP*. He uses this term here, because he is emphasizing not the structure of the self's goal but its movement toward the goal itself. Unity is the individual's absolute *telos*, and the movement toward this goal involves the spirit in the existential determinations of resignation, suffering, guilt, repentance, and faith.

And to be absolutely related to something means that it must be willed only for itself. One must not look for results or consequences external to the absolute relation, for then the relation itself is made secondary to an end external to it. An absolute relation is its own end, and only that which is an end in itself can be willed absolutely.

> All relative volition is marked by willing something for the sake of something else, but the highest end must be willed for its own sake. And this highest end is not a particular something [finite end], for then it would be relative to some other particular and be finite. It is a contradiction to will something finite absolutely, since the finite must have an end, so that there comes a time when it can no longer be willed.[5]

Here Kierkegaard reasons that what is absolute cannot be subject to finite willing or to finite ends. The absolute is an end in itself, and, therefore, is not subject to relative relations and ends. Furthermore, no choice is absolute because it is willed absolutely. Kierkegaard warns that willing a finite end absolutely results in a contradiction; therefore, to will a finite end absolutely does not make it absolute. The absolute, then, is not made absolute simply by being willed, but the will can only will absolutely when it wills the absolute.

The passage also states that finite ends have an end. Kierkegaard presumably means that finite ends can be fully and satisfactorily realized; whereas, there is never a time when the absolute is not willed. It must be willed eternally. The absolute does not have an end in the sense of being fully realized. It cannot be willed except as an end in itself, and the absolute is eternally willed.

Now in his discussion of resignation, Kierkegaard speaks negatively of the finite. In resignation, the individual is a "stranger in the world of the finite," and is completely sep-

[5] *CUP*, p. 353.

arated from "worldliness."[6] "In order that the individual
may sustain an absolute relationship to an absolute *telos* he
must first have exercised himself in the renunciation of relative ends, and only then can there be a question of an ideal
task . . ."[7] And the individual who renounces worldliness
"senses the pain of renouncing everything, the dearest
things he possesses in the world."[8] As we have seen, to renounce the world completely is the negative criterion by
which an individual determines whether he has in fact an
absolute relation to an absolute *telos*.

> He need only submit his entire immediacy with all its
> yearnings and desires to the inspection of resignation. If
> he finds a single hard spot, a point of resistance, it means
> that he does not have a relationship to an eternal
> happiness.[9]

And, "if the individual shrinks from this inspection, it is a
sign that he lacks a relation to an eternal happiness. But if
as a result of inspection, resignation finds nothing out of the
way, it is a sign that in the moment of inspection the individual does have a relationship to an eternal happiness."[10]

Kierkegaard writes that

> In proportion as the individual expresses the existential
> pathos (resignation—suffering—the totality of guilt-con-
> sciousness), in that same degree does his pathetic rela-
> tionship to an eternal happiness increase.[11]

These three forms of pathos are expressions of spirit's (freedom's) existential actualization of itself. But why must spirit express itself negatively? Spirit's initial expression of itself
upon coming to self-consciousness in the choice is resigna-

---

[6] *Ibid.*, p. 367.   [7] *Ibid.*, p. 386.   [8] *FT*, p. 51.

[9] *CUP*, p. 353. Cf. "On the other hand, the individual who sustains
an absolute relation to an absolute *telos* may very well exist in relative
ends precisely in order to exercise the absolute relationship in renunciation." *CUP*, p. 363.

[10] *Ibid.*, p. 354.   [11] *Ibid.*, p. 497.

tion. Here freedom understands itself as being absolutely related to the absolute in the act of negating all relative relations and ends. "The first genuine expression for the relationship to the absolute *telos* is a total renunciation."[12] Before there can be any question of whether the absolute relationship has been existentially established, the individual must be absolutely certain that he has surrendered all attempts to absolutize the finite. The self-relating act, then, is here a negative act in that its authenticity is expressed in the total renunciation of all relative ends and relations. To choose oneself as absolute means to renounce as absolute everything which is not taken up into the choice. In the choice, the individual chooses himself as absolute, and in resignation he establishes an absolute relation to himself by renouncing as absolute the relative matrix of relations and ends in which he lives out his daily existence. To choose oneself as absolute involves, then, this deeper and negative existential expression of spirit.

Now this language has an ascetic tone, but this is not Kierkegaard's intention. We must keep in mind that resignation heightens the consciousness of oneself as a task. In resignation, the worldly matrix of the choice is not abandoned but, on the contrary, remains central to this heightened consciousness. To be a "stranger in the world" who has "renounced all relative ends" means to negate the absolute claims of the relative and to express the absolute in the world of relativities.

> In the great moment of resignation he had no thought of mediation, but committed himself by a choice, and it is now similarly his task to acquire the requisite facility in the renewal of this choice, and in giving it existential expression. The individual does indeed remain in the finite, where he confronts the difficulty of maintaining himself in the absolute choice while still living in the finite. . . .[13]

12 *Ibid.*, p. 362.   13 *Ibid.*, p. 367.

The formula does not mean that the individual is to abandon the finite but that every finite relation, end, purpose, and task must come under the sanction of the absolute end. The relation to an absolute *telos* requires its existential expression in and through the finite and not in the abandonment of the finite. Kierkegaard continually criticizes the Middle Ages for seeking to express abstractly this task by abandoning the world for the cloister.

> In so far as, after having acquired the absolute direction toward the absolute *telos*, the individual does not pass out of the world . . . what then? Aye, then it is his task to express existentially that he constantly maintain the absolute direction toward the absolute *telos*, i.e., the absolute respect (*respicere*). He must express it existentially for the pathos of words is aesthetic pathos. He must express it existentially, and yet there must be no distinctive outwardness as its direct expression, for then we have either the cloister or mediation.[14]

One's absolute relation to his absolute *telos* is not held apart or separated from his finite relations but, on the contrary, penetrates the entire network of his finite relations, thereby bringing them to their full potential and meaning for him as an existing individual. The individual who relates himself to himself, does not abandon his finitude in order to express respect for himself as infinite, but, on the contrary, expresses himself as infinite in and through his finitude. Kierkegaard says that "the relative relationship belongs to the world, the absolute relationship to the individual himself. . . ."[15] Now to choose oneself as absolute means that one's relations to everything and everyone else is relative to one's absolute relationship to oneself. It is not as though one's relative relations bore no relation to one's absolute relation. It is the renunciation of all relative relations and ends which

14 *Ibid.*, p. 364.   15 *Ibid.*, p. 365.

establishes the absolute relation to the absolute. And it is one's absolute relation which ennobles and fulfills every relative relation.

This is the only way in which an individual who is conscious of himself as a self can be related to a relative relation, for as we have seen, to will absolutely a relative relation is a contradiction. Once the individual in the choice becomes conscious of himself as an absolute, an absolute relationship to anything or anyone else becomes unacceptable. The only way in which the existing individual can now be authentically in the world is through himself. That is to say, the only way that an individual can authentically be in the world is as a free man. And the recognition of oneself as absolute is the recognition of oneself as freedom. To absolutize any relative relation or end immediately subverts the self as freedom by situating him absolutely among relative ends and relations. As we have seen, freedom is possible only when the individual is conscious of the infinite as his task. Therefore, absorption in the finite results in the negation of absolute freedom. The finite, then, must be taken up into freedom if the individual as free is to maintain a relation with the finite. This is what Kierkegaard means when he says that the aesthetic is transformed by the ethical.

Such an individual's life "has, like that of other human beings, the various predicates of human existence, but he is in them as one who is in the borrowed garments of a stranger."[16] The difference between one who is resigned and one who is not is one of consciousness. The resigned individual is conscious of himself as having the task of reconstructing his very mode of existing.[17] Resignation is an

[16] *Ibid.*, p. 367.

[17] Reconstruction is an important term. Existence is not being abandoned. The journey of spirit is not a vertical spiral away from existence toward a mystical union with God. The reconstruction or transformation of the self is that movement through which the individual strives to become existentially what he already is as a self. That is to say, reconstruction is the striving to transform oneself as an immediate unity of finitude and infinitude into an existential unity of

act in which the individual attempts simultaneously to maintain an absolute relation to himself and a relative relationship to everything else. This expression of freedom more concretely establishes the self as a relation which is existentially actual. The existing individual is now conscious of himself as having an absolute responsibility for himself as an absolute. He understands his freedom as being absolutely bound to and by his task. The individual as freedom now more concretely and clearly comprehends that the only thing which absolutely claims him is himself. Moreover, there is no external distinction between the resigned individual and any other; the inward life of freedom which strives to be absolutely related to the absolute in the midst of a world of relative ends is an invisible, yet the most radical distinction possible.

We have already seen how self-understanding is grounded in action. The individual can in advance of the actualization of his *telos* know nothing about it except that it exists for him as a possibility.

> And therefore the resolved individual does not wish to know anything more about his *telos* than that it exists, for as soon as he acquires some knowledge about it he already begins to be retarded in his striving.[18]

There can be no objective, public knowledge about my *telos*, because it is my own particular and unique *telos*, and it cannot belong to anyone else. If the individual attempts to acquire information about himself, his attention is diverted from himself and the possibility of knowing himself as his

---

necessity and possibility. And this striving requires the move of resignation. "But how to strive to become what one already is: who would take the pain to waste his time on such a task, involving the greatest imaginable degree of resignation?" *CUP*, p. 116. Resignation is a step in the reconstruction of the self. It is not the abandonment or cancellation of oneself and existence, but a new way of understanding oneself in existence. And this new understanding constitutes a new way of being in existence.

18 *CUP*, p. 353.

possibility. Information about one's possibility gets confused with knowledge of it. It is wasted energy to attempt to define or prove one's *telos* apart from its actualization, says Kierkegaard, "since the existence of the absolute ethical good can be proved only by the individual himself expressing it existentially in existence."[19] The individual does not know himself by acquiring information from sources external to himself. It is no use inquiring objectively about who he is. The existing individual gains knowledge of himself only in his attempt to relate himself to himself in existence.

Now the reality of time is not negated once consciousness is deepened as resignation. Kierkegaard writes that

> just as he deprived the finite of its unchecked validity in the moment of resignation, *so it remains his task to reinstate repeatedly the determination by which this was first accomplished.*[20]

The event which makes resignation possible, choice, must be repeatedly accomplished if resignation itself is to be continually expressed. That is to say, the absolute must continually come into existence through choice before there can be an absolute relation to the absolute. And each reinstatement of the choice requires a concomitant reinstatement of resignation itself.[21] Nothing may enter the relative matrix of the individual's existence which does not undergo the inspection of resignation. Each new event, relation, and idea which enters the matrix of the individual's existence must be relegated to the status of relativity by resignation so that it cannot get an absolute hold upon him, thereby upsetting the delicate relation by which the individual remains absolutely related to the absolute. Time is constantly altering and adding to the existential matrix of each individual's existence, thereby demanding the constant vigilance of res-

19 *Ibid.*, p. 379. 20 *Ibid.*, p. 368. Italics mine.
21 *Ibid.*, pp. 354-355.

ignation. Time, then, continues to present itself as a great threat to the task of relating oneself to oneself.[22]

In conclusion, then, we can say that in the choice the absolute is established, and in resignation, the absolute relation to the absolute is established. Now Kierkegaard attempts to strengthen the absolute quality of the existing individual's relation to his absolute, i.e., to himself, through the introduction of the God-relationship into the development of spirit. We shall now turn to a discussion of that relationship, and the two questions which will guide our discussion are: How is the God-relationship introduced into the dialectical development of spirit without overstepping the bounds of the individual's being which was established in the choice? And in what manner does the God-relationship serve to strengthen the individual's absolute relation to himself?

THE GOD-RELATIONSHIP

The religious dimension in Kierkegaard's thought emerges in what he calls the God-relationship. Now this move is difficult to follow for two reasons. First, there is the technical difficulty of uncovering the precise point where the notion of the God-relationship enters into the dialectical development of spirit. Kierkegaard himself is very unclear about this. And, second, there is a personal difficulty. We are all moderns. We cannot escape our modernity. And, consequently, many know both personally, as a matter of faith, and intellectually, as a matter of doing theology and

---

[22] "And since an eternal happiness is a *telos* for existing individuals, these two (the absolute end and the existing individual) cannot be conceived as realizing a union in existence in terms of rest. This means that an eternal happiness cannot be possessed in time. . . ." *CUP*, p. 355. In Chapter VI we shall see what Kierkegaard means when he says that an external happiness does not occur in time but only in the Christian existence.

philosophy, the difficulties involved in maintaining the "god hypothesis." With respect to Kierkegaard, there is considerably less difficulty in following and accepting his underlying ontological self-structure and the choice through which the individual becomes conscious of and takes full responsibility for himself as an existing spirit. But now the God-relationship emerges. It is difficult not to ask the question, Why? Is it necessary? What does it add? It is not difficult to see why philosophers like Sartre and Heidegger and existentially oriented psychologists accept only the non-religious aspects of Kierkegaard's thought. Heidegger and existential psychology draw heavily on Kierkegaard's concept of dread. And Heidegger and Sartre both develop their notions of the resolve from Kierkegaard's notion of the choice. In both cases, however, a god concept is omitted. Neither found Kierkegaard's qualification of his ontology with a God-relationship compelling enough to include it in their own thought.[23]

But Kierkegaard himself unequivocably insists upon the presence of the God-relationship as necessary for the further development of spirit beyond the initial choice. We must, therefore, press forward in an attempt to see why the God-relationship is incorporated and how it contributes to the continuation and, ultimately, to the realization of the dialectical development of spirit.

Now God is initially disclosed as internal to the unfolding of spirit. Here God is "neither a something (He being all and infinitely all), nor is He outside the individual, since edification consists precisely in the fact that He is in the in-

---

[23] It is ironic that a theologian like Karl Barth found the notion of God in Kierkegaard the most important aspect of his thought and in so doing seriously neglected what philosophers like Sartre and Heidegger considered central to his thought. Kierkegaard, himself, I think, would disown both tendencies for failing to grasp what he himself appears to have considered central, viz., the dialectical tension between God and man apart from which knowledge of neither is possible.

dividual."[24] God's presence "is woven into and works through the slightest movement of my consciousness in its solitary communion with itself . . ."[25] Indeed, God is the very foundation of the self, and thus the denial of God eventuates not in the destruction of God but, according to Kierkegaard, in self-destruction.[26]

Kierkegaard accepted the Socratic principle that self-knowledge is knowledge of God.[27] God does not reveal himself in the objective world but rather in the subjective as the foundation of the self. He writes in *The Concept of Dread* that the religious genius is one who turns toward himself and in so doing "turns *eo ipso* towards God."[28] The dialectical penetration of one's own consciousness is simultaneously an illumination of one's God-relationship.

> God is at one and the same time infinitely close to man and infinitely far away. To come into relation to God is a voyage of discovery somewhat comparable to an expedition to the North Pole, so rarely does a man ever actually press forward on this way, to the discovery. But to fancy having done it—that almost everyone and every century have done this. *But if this journey of discovery of God is an "inland journey," the main point of it is specifically to preserve one's individuality and then inwardly simply to remove the obstructions, push them aside.*[29]

[24] *CUP*, p. 498.

[25] *Ibid.*, p. 163. Cf. "If a desert Arab suddenly discovered a spring in his tent, so that he would always have spring water in abundance— how fortunate he would consider himself! It is the same with a man who as physical being is always turned outward, thinking that his happiness lies outside himself. Finally he is turned inward and discovers that the springs lie within him, to say nothing of discovering the spring which is the God-relationship." *SKJP*, II, 1395. Cf. "What refreshment do we get from all their busy bustle in comparison with the delicious quickening of that lonely wellspring which exists in every man, that wellspring in which the Deity dwells in the profound stillness where everything is silent." *CUP*, p. 163.

[26] *SKJP*, II, 1349.   [27] *PF*, p. 14.   [28] *CD*, p. 96.

[29] *SKJP*, II, 1451. Italics mine.

155

The individual does not abandon himself in the establishment of his God-relationship. He must maintain himself and, indeed, only in so preserving himself absolutely can he discover his God-relationship. Conversely, only by discovering his God-relationship can he discover himself absolutely. Kierkegaard complicates the issue by dialectically posing it. The individual knows God when he knows himself, and he knows himself when he knows God. In inwardness, one discovers his God-relationship and, thereby, himself. But this raises questions concerning his ontology. If God is internal to the self, how is He to be conceived in relation to the self-structure? How do we introduce the notion of God without distorting the self-structure, as we have come to understand it, beyond recognition? Indeed, how can we even conceive of God now without overstepping the structural bounds laid down in Kierkegaard's ontology? Moreover, how is it possible for the individual to continue to be himself, and simultaneously, to establish a God-relationship which, presumably, would in some sense take him out of himself? Does Kierkegaard not have to abandon his self-structure in order to talk about the God-relationship and, in so doing, does he not project us into an altogether different conceptual sphere? All of these questions cannot immediately be answered. In the course of the further discussion of the development of spirit, we shall see how and why the notion of God comes into play and the nature of the relationship it maintains with the ontological self-structure.

The first point to be made is that the notion of God does not originate from outside the self-structure itself. That is to say, the notion of God is not derived apart from the dynamic structure of the self, and then imposed in some way upon it. More specifically, it does not originate metaphysically as a necessary being or first cause whose being reason rationally proves. It does not originate theologically as creator. Nor does it mystically originate as the "wholly other" whom the individual intuitively apprehends. We cannot, in incorporating the notion of God, exceed the bounds of the absolute established by the choice and, as we have seen, the further dialectical development of spirit is worked out within the limits established by the choice. Therefore, to exceed the limits of the absolute in the establishment of the notion of God would seriously, if not irreparably, damage this course of action.

The only alternative, therefore, is to grasp the notion as somehow inherent in the choice itself. And this is precisely the course which Kierkegaard follows.

> In fables and stories of adventure there is mention made of a lamp, called the wonderful; when it is rubbed, a spirit appears. Jest! But freedom is the true wonderful lamp; when a man rubs it with ethical passion, God comes into being for him.[30]

This passage states simply that God comes into being for an existing individual when he is ethically related to himself as freedom. The passage does not tell us much. All that it states is that God comes into being through the individual's struggle with himself as freedom. Kierkegaard expresses this idea in *Either/Or* when he says that to choose oneself as absolute is to choose God.[31] But, as we have seen from our investigation of the initial choice, only the self's triadic structure is brought to consciousness in the choice. Nothing is said about God. Now if the choice of oneself is somehow identical with the choice of God, we must expect an encounter with the notion of God in the further elucidation of the choice.

This is precisely where one encounters God. To stop with the choice of oneself as an absolute is to fail to establish a God-relationship. But to attempt to relate oneself absolutely to the subject of one's absolute choice, i.e., to one's absolute *telos*, is the action by which the God-relationship comes into existence.

[30] *CUP*, p. 124.   [31] *E/O*, II, 244-245.

One who distinguishes absolutely has a relationship to the absolute *telos*, and *ipso facto* also a relationship to God.[32]

Kierkegaard here contends that the God-relationship emerges with resignation. In the instant that the individual attempts to relate himself to himself absolutely as an absolute he relates himself to God. The following long passage explains the nature of this relation.

> Real self-reduplication without a third factor, which is outside and compels one, is an impossibility and makes any such existence into an illusion or an experiment. Kant held that man was his own law (autonomy), i.e., bound himself under the law which he gave himself. In a deeper sense that means to say: lawlessness or experimentation. It is no harder than the thwacks (sic.) which Sancho Panza applied to his own bottom. I can no more be really stricter in A than I am, or than I wish myself to be in B. There must be some compulsion, if it is to be a serious matter. If I am not bound by anything higher than myself, and if I am to bind myself, where am I to acquire the severity as A by which, as B, I am to be bound, so long as A and B are the same?[33]

One cannot be absolutely related to himself as an absolute apart from the notion of God as a binding authority. Free-

---

[32] *CUP*, p. 369.

[33] *SKJ*, #1041. Dupre more concisely translates the major sentence in this passage as "law, by its very essence, must be given and enforced by a higher authority." Louis Dupre, *Kierkegaard as Theologian: The Dialectic of Existence* (New York: Sheed and Ward, 1963), p. 75. And he correctly points out that Kierkegaard's conception of law here is not a strictly Biblical conception. "That Kierkegaard's ethical stage cannot be simply equated with the Old Law appears from the outset. As early as 1836, Kierkegaard cites with approval Hamann's parallel between law and intellect; what is true for the one is also true for the other (I A 237). This would be difficult to understand if it were meant to refer to a merely Biblical idea of law. By the word 'law' in that first moment, therefore, is to be understood any ethics before the religious stage proper." Dupre, p. 74n.

dom demands the concept of God if it is to be absolutely related to anything. The notion of duty which emerges with the choice as self-imposed is not negated but religiously, absolutely, accentuated. Freedom can be held on course only by reference to a theonomous authority[34] which accentuates the already existing bent of freedom toward the requirement.[35]

[34] Tillich's argument that theonomy cannot be understood apart from autonomy is helpful here. Autonomy is derived from the Greek words *autos*, meaning self, and *nomos*, meaning law. Autonomy means being a law to oneself. "This law is not outside of us, but inside as our true being." Autonomy, says Tillich is not "lawless subjectivity." On the contrary, it expresses the law implicit in man's structure. And any deviation from this law "hurts the essential nature of the will itself." Theonomy implies the "personal experience of the divine spirit within us. . . ." And, says Tillich, "autonomy which is aware of its divine ground is theonomy; but without the theonomous dimension, it degenerates into mere humanism." Heteronomy stands in opposition to this relation between autonomy and theonomy. It comes from the Greek words *heteros*, meaning strange or foreign, and *nomos*, meaning law. And it undermines the possibility of discovering the divine ground of the law which is implicit in the self by representing the law as alien and external to the self. (Paul Tillich, *Perspectives on 19th and 20th Century Protestant Theology*, ed. and with an introduction by Carl E. Braaten, New York: Harper and Row, Publishers, 1967, pp. 26-27.) This, it seems to me, is very much the way in which Kierkegaard understands the God-relationship. The dialectical penetration of the self-structure eventually discloses the divine ground of ethical existence. And the further development of the self proceeds not toward a heteronomous authority which is external to the self but toward the existential understanding of oneself as theonomously grounded in the divine.

[35] The notion of duty tends to be replaced by the notion of obedience once the ethico-religious stage is reached. Obedience is the hallmark of the God-relationship. "It is easy enough to see that only one thing remains which can interest him for whom everything is equally significant and insignificant—obedience. This is the absolute majesty." *SKJP*, II, 1436. And it is through obedience to the command of God that freedom is held on its course of absolutely relating the self to itself as absolute.

Kierkegaard concretely brings this notion into the dialectical development of spirit with the category of the God-relationship. This relationship is one in which the individual absolutely relates himself to himself before God.

> It is obvious that the New Testament (especially the Gospels) contains only the requirement of ideality and in an absolute sense. . . . Everyone has to be related to the requirement of ideality . . . and the apostolic approach is not to be related to the requirement of ideality but to the command of God. Everyone has to measure himself before God according to the requirement of ideality.[36]

The individual is now to relate to his ideality, i.e., to himself, not as a self-imposed requirement but as a requirement imposed by God. It is also significant that Kierkegaard here distinguishes between the requirement of ideality, on the one hand, and absolutely relating to it by virtue of divine authority, on the other. The requirement of ideality emerges with the choice and constitutes the ethical stage of existence. The dialectical development of spirit need not advance beyond that point, but to qualify this task by viewing it as a divinely and absolutely required task advances spirit beyond the strictly ethical stage into the ethico-religious stage of existence.

The individual's ideality, however, remains the same. It is always a matter of becoming oneself, as ideal, and this requirement of ideality, while it is accentuated by the notion of God, remains a purely secular task. That is to say, the individual's ideal is neither inherently divine nor divinely disclosed. The individual's ideality is a matter which he himself discovers and presents, as it were, to God as his understanding of who he is and what he ought to do.

> God does not immediately or directly tell me what I am supposed to do. I do it; according to my best deliberation I regard it as the best, and I present it now to God, hum-

36 *SKP*, X³ A 268.

bling myself and my resolution, my plan, my action, under God.[37]

God, says Kierkegaard, is not interested in man's attempting to understand Him. God is interested exclusively in each individual's becoming and understanding himself.

> The fact of the matter is that we are unable to form properly for ourselves an idea of God's sublimity. We always bog down in our aesthetic quantifying: the amazing, the tremendous, the very influential, etc. Whereas God is so infinitely elevated that the only thing he considers is the ethical.[38]

The God-relationship, then, is the expression for facing one's ethical task as a divine imperative. And, in Kierkegaard's view, such a position furthers the dialectical development of spirit by bringing the individual to a still higher understanding of himself as freedom. The existing individual cannot accomplish his task of relating himself absolutely to himself as an absolute without being bound to his task by divine authority. Moreover, divine authority does not relieve the individual of his responsibility, but, on the contrary, accentuates the individual's responsibility by holding him to his task in a way that he could never hold himself.[39]

---

[37] *SKJP*, II, 1373. Cf. "The relationship between God and man is quite simply this. The man does not dare demand that God give him revelations, signs, and the like. No, the man must have the bold confidence to be himself, and if he cannot, then he must begin by praying for this confidence, which is not a commentary on his own importance but on God's love being so infinite. . . ." *SKJP*, II, 1372.

[38] *SKJP*, I, 981.

[39] That the God-relationship does not relieve the individual of his responsibility for himself is illustrated by the fact that man continues to be responsible for his failures. "This implies that God desires not a contractual relationship but one of unconditional obedience. If a man fails, he accepts guilt and does not fault God." *SKP*, IX A 347. In my discussion of guilt, we shall see how the unconditional obedience required by the God-relationship makes man responsible for his absolute guilt.

161

It should also be pointed out that while the God-relationship accentuates the difficulty of the task, it is also the promise of its fulfillment.

> This is the way I think of it. When a man (the single individual) is related to God, he must readily grasp that God has the absolute right, the unlimited absolute right to require everything of him, and yet on the other hand, that the God-relationship itself is an absolute blessedness, is the absolutely unlimited depth of happiness.[40]

Through the God-relationship, freedom is empowered to realize its task of relating the ideal self to the real self, thereby actualizing a real and concrete unity in existence. Therein lies the happiness which each individual seeks. To relate oneself absolutely to oneself through freedom and before God is, in Kierkegaard's view, the only source of true happiness. Happiness is the enactment of one's own existence as an absolute requirement before God. More precisely, happiness is being obedient.

Kierkegaard is arguing, then, that the more seriously the individual takes his ideal, i.e., himself, the more he realizes that it must be authorized by God. Unless he comprehends his ideal task as a divine command, freedom will falter. Without its divine authorization, freedom will not find the strength to accomplish its task. Kierkegaard implies that the ideal will lack seriousness unless freedom is bound to it by a third factor, which he calls God.

The God-relationship, then, appears to function in two very closely related ways. The first reason is grounded in the dependent nature of freedom. As we have seen, Kierkegaard does not believe that freedom can fulfill its task unless it is empowered to do so by a God-relationship. He argues that in the attempt to actualize one's absolute *telos*, the God-relationship emerges. This seems to imply that in the attempt to relate the individual to his *telos*, freedom experiences its own dependence on God.

[40] *SKJP*, II, 1350.

> For God is spirit; he does not find additional pleasure in men's hymn singing any more than in the smell of incense. What is most pleasing to him is that a human being genuinely needs him, essentially feels that he needs him.[41]

And religious pathos is grounded in the struggle to exist. That is to say, the need of God emerges with freedom's struggle to relate the individual to his absolute *telos*.

> If the religious is in truth the religious, if it has submitted itself to the discipline of the ethical and preserves it within itself, it cannot forget that religious pathos does not consist in singing and hymning and composing verses, but in existing.[42]

The God-relationship is situated in the struggle to exist. And apart from the concrete experience of this struggle, there can be no such relationship. The God-relationship emerges, then, in the individual's consciousness of his need of God if freedom is to maintain its direction toward the actualization of the absolute *telos*. It should be noted, however, that while freedom in experience becomes conscious of its need for divine help, the power of the divine at this point in the development of spirit is limited to the power of the ethical, i.e., to the power of freedom itself.

The second reason is related to Kierkegaard's understanding of the ideal itself. The appearance of an absolute relation to an absolute *telos* in the choice and in renunciation of the relative as absolute requires a ground for the absolute ideal itself. If there is an absolute ideal to which the individual is bound, does this not imply a binding authority or power? Would not ethics lack seriousness apart from the divine imperative? In *Fear and Trembling*, Kierkegaard says that the ethical is divine. Every duty refers to God.[43] The ideality of the ethical must have its ground in a divine command if it is to be taken absolutely as an ideal.[44] Only

[41] *Ibid.*, II, 1414.   [42] *CUP*, p. 348.   [43] *FT*, p. 78.

[44] Croxall makes this point when he says that "if there is an 'ought,' i.e., a command, does this not imply a commander?" T. H. Croxall,

if the ideal is posited as a divine command can it resist qualification, experimentation, or abandonment. More specifically, the individual cannot have absolute significance for himself unless his ideality has a divine ground. Here, then, the relation to oneself as an absolute entails a relation to one's divine ground.

In both cases, however, the God-relationship comes to consciousness within the dialectical development of spirit. In the self-relating process through which the individual comes to understand himself, the notion of God comes into existence as part of that process. Moreover, the notion of God as the ground of ideality and freedom cannot exist in the individual's self-understanding apart from the choice and its deepening in resignation. The ethical stage of existence is essential to the emergence of the God-relationship.

> Here as everywhere the different spheres must be kept clearly distinct, and the qualitative dialectic, with its decisive mutation that changes everything so that what was highest in one sphere is rendered in another sphere absolutely inadmissible, must be respected. *As for the religious, it is an essential requirement that it should have passed through the ethical.*[45]

In the ethical stage, the absolute character of the aesthetic is replaced by the absolute character of the self; and in the ethico-religious stage, the absolute independence of freedom is replaced by a consciousness of its dependence on God. Ethico-religious consciousness must have passed through ethical understanding so that the notion of duty to the absolute could come to consciousness, thereby getting

---

Kierkegaard Studies (London: Lutterworth Press, 1948), p. 24. And Fahrenbach expresses the same thought when he writes that the individual in relating himself to a command relates himself to a commanding absolute. Helmut Fahrenbach, *Kierkegaards Ethik* (Frankfurt: V. Klostermann, 1968), p. 122.

[45] *CUP*, p. 347.

itself in position to be religiously accentuated. "Duty is absolute," says Kierkegaard.[46] It is not abandoned with the emergence of ethico-religious consciousness but divinely accentuated as obedience. The ethical remains within the religious as the task, the human obligation and responsibility. It does not lose its orientation as a factor in religious consciousness but is accentuated by the encounter with the divine imperative.

The choice, then, is not complete until the individual has chosen himself before God. The infinitely concrete self which is chosen as an absolute is not fully absolute until the individual has simultaneously renounced as absolute the relative matrix of relations and ends in which he exists and relates to his *telos* as a divine imperative. Only when the individual exists before God is he absolutely related to himself. Only when the individual is before God is he capable of fully becoming himself in existence. Kierkegaard writes that

> the self is potentiated in the ratio of the measure proposed for the self, and infinitely potentiated when God is the measure. The more conception of God, the more the self; the more the self the more conception of God. Only when the self as this definite individual is conscious of existing before God, only then is it the infinite self; and then this self sins—before God.[47]

The last stages of the dialectical development of spirit are characterized by this dialectical relation between self-knowledge and one's conception of God. With the introduction of the God-relationship, the development of spirit is taken up into the ethico-religious stage of existence. The task of self-relating by which the individual gains self-understanding is now to be worked out before God. Only in this awareness is the individual fully capable of choosing

46 *Ibid.*, p. 239.   47 *SUD*, p. 211; cf. *ibid.*, p. 210.

and understanding himself in existence. And, conversely, the struggle to choose oneself before God enhances one's conception of God, or, in the language of *Concluding Unscientific Postscript*, enhances one's God-relationship.

It is through the introduction of the notion of God that Kierkegaard's ontology is ultimately determined as divided against itself. If he had stopped with the first choice of oneself, he could have veered off into a pure and non-religiously qualified humanism. But, with the introduction of the God-relationship, the division which characterizes the self is not merely an illustration of the self's imperfection in the sense of having constantly to strive for oneself as possibility. On the contrary, the division comes to be regarded as guilt and sin, and the individual's *telos* or goal then becomes an impossibility. In the God-relationship, the individual is conscious of himself as existing under a divine imperative: "You shall attain immediacy." "You shall be perfect." We shall see how this religious qualification of the development of spirit constitutes two major problems. First, with the consciousness of the divine imperative, the division is no longer regarded as an imperfection which the individual is constantly attempting to overcome but as a permanent division which the individual is powerless to overcome. Hence, the individual's task or possibility of uniting itself as a synthesis of the finite and the infinite in existence becomes an impossibility. And, second, Kierkegaard argues that because the individual is absolutely responsible for himself, he must bear the full responsibility for the failure to fulfill the task.[48]

Having now established that the individual's absolute relation to himself as an absolute is grounded in the divine, we can now turn to an examination of the existential consequences of having so related to oneself before God.

[48] These problems are to be discussed below in the remaining sections of this chapter and in Chapter VI where the God-relationship receives its specific Christian qualification.

166

SUFFERING

To strive to relate oneself absolutely to one's absolute *telos* is to involve oneself in suffering. Suffering is the consequence of the failure to extricate oneself from an absolute relation to relative ends. The individual quickly discovers that in spite of his intentions to relate absolutely to his absolute *telos*, he is inextricably bound to relative ends. Kierkegaard writes that the individual who attempts to relate absolutely to his *telos* soon discovers "that there is not only no reward to expect, but suffering to bear."[49] Suffering is the expression for the attempt to actualize one's ideal task as posited by resignation. The ideal is trapped in a matrix of relative relations and ends to which the individual is not just relatively related.[50] Even though the individual is conscious of himself as ideal, he is at the same time in this matrix and is incapable of completely abandoning the absolute significance which it has for him.

Now suffering is a more concrete expression of spirit, but until it is brought to consciousness and existentially appropriated it persists as an unconscious reality resulting from the attempt to actualize one's absolute *telos*. Once the individual understands himself to be required by God to relate himself absolutely to himself, he is immediately confronted with the more strenuous task of penetrating that existential understanding reflectively in order to determine its content. To relate oneself absolutely to one's absolute *telos* necessarily involves the individual in suffering. Now the existing

[49] *CUP*, p. 360. "When an aesthetic sufferer bemoans his fate and seeks solace in the ethical, the ethical really has solace for him, but first it makes him suffer more than he did before. When this consideration is omitted the ethical makes everything too comfortable and easy; but in that case the ethical has also been taken in vain. If an aesthetic sufferer feels his pain ever so keenly, he may very well come to suffer more; when he sends for the ethical it first helps him from the frying pan into the fire, so that he gets something to complain about in real earnest—and then only does it give him help." *CUP*, p. 384.

[50] *SKJP*, II, 1788; cf. *ibid.*, II, 1825.

individual must bring to consciousness the reality of his own suffering and then once again attempt to relate himself to himself in order to exist actively in suffering.

Kierkegaard writes that now the task is "to comprehend the suffering and to remain in it, so that reflection is directed 'upon' the suffering and not 'away' from it."[51] The consciousness of suffering may more likely be the occasion for abandoning existence at this point in the development of spirit, as is illustrated by the following passage:

> The existing poet who suffers in his existence does not really comprehend his suffering, he does not penetrate more and more deeply into it, but in his suffering he seeks a way from the suffering and finds ease in poetic production, in the poetic anticipation of a more perfect, i.e., a happier, order of things.[52]

The artist may abandon the task of becoming who he is by fleeing into the imagination rather than existentially appropriating his suffering as an expression of what is involved in becoming and knowing himself. Rather than accepting his suffering as an expression of what it means to be a relation of possibility and necessity, he uses it as an occasion for artistic creation which removes him entirely from an understanding of what it is to suffer.

Self-consciousness is, as we have seen, only potentially existentially actual. The move from consciousness to actuality requires an act of freedom, for only in freedom is the content of consciousness existentially appropriated. The consciousness of oneself as suffering is, according to Kierkegaard, not the equivalent of actually choosing oneself as a sufferer. It is only in the actual choice that the individual understands himself as suffering. The task of reconstructing one's existence in action is achieved only through and in the

---

[51] *CUP*, p. 397.

[52] *Ibid.* Cf. "The introduction of the ideal is to him the greatest agony; of course, if it is introduced very poetically as fascinating make-believe, well this he accepts with pleasure." *SKJP*, II, 1823.

act of freedom made possible by consciousness. Now the existential expression of suffering is a still more concrete realization of what is involved in choosing oneself and in reconstructing one's self in existence through the choice. In the choice of himself, the individual must not only renounce the matrix of relative ends and relations in which he lives but also accept suffering as the necessary accompaniment of choosing one's absolute *telos*. That is to say, to exist actively as a sufferer is a deeper and more concrete existential understanding of what it means to be fully responsible for absolutely relating to one's absolute *telos* and relatively related to relative ends. In suffering, the individual as freedom more clearly and correctly understands himself.

But, for Kierkegaard, this knowledge is negative in character. The individual understands himself through understanding that he is not actually what he is potentially. As we have seen, self-knowledge or understanding is constituted by existential actualization. The existing individual knows only that which he has fully appropriated in existence. It follows from this that the individual does not have this kind of positive knowledge of himself as a unity of necessity and possibility constituted by freedom until freedom has actualized that unity. One's absolute *telos* cannot be known apart from its existential actualization, and there is no happiness apart from this achievement. Consequently, prior to the actualization of his *telos*, the individual does not have positive knowledge of his absolute *telos*, i.e., of himself. Knowledge of one's *telos* is, therefore, indirect or negative. "Suffering," writes Kierkegaard, "is rooted in the fact that he is separated from his happiness [*telos*], but also signifies that he has a relationship to this happiness."[53] Knowledge of one-

---

[53] *CUP*, p. 406. "For to be in existence is always a somewhat embarrassing situation, and the question is whether this again is not one of the pressures exerted by existence, namely, that the existing individual cannot effect the dialectical change which turns suffering into joy. In the eternal happiness itself there is no suffering, but when an existing individual establishes a relationship thereto, this relationship is quite rightly expressed through suffering." *Ibid.*, pp. 404-405.

self as a unity, i.e., knowledge of one's *telos*, is at this point a negative knowledge which is grounded in the understanding that the individual is not this unity because he has not actualized his *telos*.

To understand oneself as a sufferer is now the criterion by which the individual knows that he has an absolute relation to an absolute *telos*.

> Just as resignation looks to see that the individual has an absolute direction toward the absolute *telos*, so does the persistence of suffering guarantee that the individual remains in the correct position and preserves himself in it.[54]

The initial guarantee that the individual is related to his *telos* is the renunciation of relative ends and relations as having absolute significance. Now the criterion continues to be a negative one in the sense that the relationship is now essentially guaranteed through suffering as the understanding of the difficulty and pain involved in the initial movement of renunciation.

Kierkegaard refers to the existential appropriation of suffering as a religious act. "In suffering, religiosity begins to breathe."[55] And "to be without suffering means to be without religion."[56] Religiosity begins with the inward understanding of the individual's failure to relate himself absolutely to his *telos*.

> The much revered orator forgets that religiosity is inwardness, that inwardness is the relationship of the individual to himself before God, his reflection into himself, and that it is precisely from this that the suffering derives, this being also the ground of its essential pertinence to the religious life, so that the absence of it signifies the absence of religiosity.[57]

[54] *Ibid.*, pp. 396-397.
[56] *Ibid.*, p. 406.
[55] *Ibid.*, p. 390.
[57] *Ibid.*, p. 391.

Moreover, the persistence of religious understanding depends upon the persistence of suffering.

> The reality of suffering thus means its essential persistence as essential to the religious life, while aesthetically viewed, suffering stands in an accidental relation to existence, it may indeed be there but it may also cease, while viewed religiously the cessation of suffering is also the cessation of the religious life.[58]

The only way in which the individual can be guaranteed that he is sustaining an absolute relation to an absolute *telos* is through suffering. Therefore, when there is a cessation of suffering, the individual has ceased to maintain an absolute relation to his absolute *telos* and with that the possibility of the religious life is itself lost.

> The religious individual sustains a relationship to an eternal happiness and the sign of the relationship is suffering, and suffering is its [religion's] essential expression —for an existing individual.[59]

The religious life is grounded in the maintenance of a certain level of spiritual understanding. There can be no religion apart from the spiritual striving to maintain an absolute relation to an absolute *telos*. Religion is, according to Kierkegaard, the inward appropriation of what it means to be a relation which is required by God to be related absolutely to itself. Suffering, writes Kierkegaard, "is precisely the expression for the God-relationship. . . ."[60] Where there is no suffering, there is no absolute relationship to an absolute *telos*; and where there is no such relation, there is no God-relationship and, hence, no religious understanding.

Religion begins, then, with the inward understanding that the individual is not what he is. The difficulty involved in self-relating constitutes a religious problem, because the

[58] *Ibid.*, p. 400.   [59] *Ibid.*, p. 407.   [60] *Ibid.*, p. 405.

171

individual now views his task as a divine imperative. The knowledge of oneself as a sufferer is religious knowledge because the individual ultimately chooses himself as a task before God. If the choice of oneself were not divinely accentuated, the gap could still be inwardly understood as suffering, but suffering would then not be religiously construed. But Kierkegaard insists that the choice is not a serious one unless it ultimately is viewed as a divine imperative, and it is precisely for this reason that self-understanding now becomes at one and the same time religious knowledge. Self-understanding constitutes the knowledge of what is meant by having a relation to God. Such knowledge is neither speculative nor dogmatic, for it can only be meaningfully appropriated through existing. By striving to exist, the individual initially discovers in suffering that he is as nothing before God.

> This suffering has its ground in the fact that the individual is in his immediacy absolutely committed to relative ends; its significance lies in the transposition of the relationship, the dying away from immediacy, or in the expression existentially of the principle that the individual can do absolutely nothing of himself, but is as nothing before God. . . .[61]

The inward understanding of oneself as a sufferer means that the existing individual maintains his God-relationship through the awareness of the difficulty involved in absolutely relating to one's absolute *telos*.

Knowledge of God, then, is itself a negative knowledge. Kierkegaard writes that "here again the negative is the mark by which the God-relationship is recognized."[62] Posi-

---

[61] *Ibid.*, p. 412. Cf. "Religiously, it is the task of the individual to understand that he is nothing before God, or to become wholly nothing and to exist thus before God; this consciousness of impotence he requires constantly to have before him, and when it vanishes the religiosity also vanishes." *Ibid.*

[62] *Ibid.*

tive knowledge of what it means to be in a relationship with God is grounded in the positive knowledge of one's absolute *telos*. That is to say, a positive God-relationship is contingent upon the existential unification of one's necessity and possibility in an act of freedom. Prior to that instant, there can only be a negative knowledge which is grounded in the individual's understanding that he is not what God requires him to become.

We see how deeply rooted in the depths of self-consciousness the phenomenon of religion is. Religion is not an immediate phenomenon. That is to say, it cannot appear in the aesthetic stage of existence or in the initial stages of the development of spirit. Religion is, on the contrary, a highly reflective phenomenon in that it depends for its existence upon a highly advanced reflective, i.e., inward, penetration of human consciousness. "The religious individual," says Kierkegaard, "is reflected inward, is conscious of existentially being in the process of becoming, and yet maintaining a relationship to an eternal happiness."[63] I take him to mean here that religious understanding requires that degree of inward reflection which makes the choice possible. It requires the awareness of oneself as an existential task which engages the individual in a process of becoming. Prior to this level of self-understanding, there is no possibility whatsoever of having a genuine religious outlook on existence.

Rather than appearing in the aesthetic as an immediate phenomenon which is mediated by the development of spirit, religion only appears late in spirit's development; and, from Kierkegaard's point of view, it essentially and decisively contributes to the actualization of the dialectical development of spirit. The development of spirit advances toward a religious self-understanding rather than away from it. The remainder of this analysis of the development of spirit will illustrate how religion increasingly comes forward as the final index of the development of human self-understanding.

[63] *Ibid.*, p. 406.

GUILT

The reflective penetration of existential suffering gives rise to guilt-consciousness. The existing individual continues the regressive penetration of himself by reflecting upon the existential state of suffering and brings to consciousness a still deeper and more concrete level of existence. In suffering, the existing individual becomes conscious of a contradiction between himself and his absolute *telos*, but he understands the contradiction simply as the difficulty involved in relating himself to his absolute *telos*. In suffering, the contradiction comes to consciousness only by being naively understood as a difficulty involved in absolutely relating to one's absolute *telos*. The existing individual has not yet succeeded in reflectively penetrating and understanding his relationship to the contradiction which he expresses in suffering.

Guilt-consciousness is a deeper and more concrete consciousness of the relation of the individual to this contradiction in himself. In suffering the contradiction comes into existence and now it is the individual's task to reflect the contradiction itself.

> In comparison with guilt-consciousness as the characteristic note, suffering might seem to be a direct relationship (of course not aesthetically direct: happiness recognizable by happiness). If one were to affirm this, then guilt-consciousness is the repellent relationship. However, it would be more correct to say that suffering is a direct reaction of a repellent relationship, guilt-consciousness a repellent reaction of a repellent relationship.[64]

In suffering, the existing individual does not understand that he is the contradiction. He merely expresses the contradiction in suffering as a difficulty involved in relating himself to his absolute *telos*. In guilt, the contradiction is appro-

[64] *CUP*, p. 474.

priated in the sense that an existing individual comes to understand that one's self is this contradiction. The contradiction is not accidentally related to the individual's existence as a temporary and impermanent expression of what the self is. On the contrary, the self is this contradiction, and it is existentially appropriated by the existing individual in his understanding of himself as guilty. Consequently, the existing individual is no longer simply related to a repellent relationship, but existentially he becomes this contradiction, and in so doing advances the dialectical development of spirit one step further.

With the understanding of guilt, a deeper penetration into existence has been achieved.

> So it is that things go backward: to suffer guiltily is a lower expression than to suffer innocently, and yet it is a higher expression because the negative is a mark of a higher positive. . . .[65]

To suffer innocently is to suffer in ignorance. To understand oneself as a sufferer is an advance in understanding beyond the ignorance of not knowing the implications of the choice and resignation. In the choice, the existing individual comes to an understanding of the triadic structure of the self, and in resignation he comes to understand the way in which he is to relate to himself. The self's *Was-Sein* and the task of freedom are now understood by the existing individual. But suffering brings into question the naive expectations of the ethical individual with respect to the power of freedom to accomplish the task. Yet suffering is ignorant of its own meaning, and this ignorance is penetrated by the deeper step into guilt. The guilty sufferer understands that there is not merely a difficulty involved in relating oneself to oneself but, on the one hand, that he is divided against himself and, on the other hand, that the breach must not be understood as a difficulty but as a contradiction which expresses his very self. The suffering individual is still external to him-

[65] *Ibid.*, p. 475; cf. *ibid.*, pp. 494-495.

self in innocent suffering in the sense that he remains outside of himself. To maintain oneself in innocent suffering is,
for all its existential pathos, to be external to oneself. Only
by becoming the contradiction which suffering expresses is
it possible for the individual to penetrate into the core of
the self. In guilt-understanding, the individual has more
deeply penetrated into himself, and he thereby understands
himself more concretely. Consequently, he is more concretely, albeit more negatively, related to his absolute *telos*.

The pattern of the relationship between existential understanding and the absolute *telos* remains the same. On the
one hand, self-understanding depends upon maintaining a
relationship with oneself as an absolute *telos*; and, on the
other hand, it is an expression of the fact that one is related
to oneself as an absolute *telos*. As we have seen, the individual who understands himself as suffering must be related
to himself as an absolute *telos*, and it is suffering which
guarantees that there is such a relation. With the advance
in self-understanding, we now see that "as soon as one
leaves out the eternal happiness, the consciousness of guilt
also drops out essentially."[66] And the consciousness of guilt
is an expression for the relation to an absolute *telos*.

> So the existential consciousness of guilt is the first deep
> plunge into existence, and at the same time it is the ex-
> pression for the fact that an exister is related to an eternal
> happiness. . . . It is the expression for the relationship by
> reason of the fact that it expresses the incompatibility of
> the relationship.[67]

Kierkegaard's notion of guilt-understanding as the first deep
plunge into existence and as the expression of an incompatibility suggests that we have reached an important point in
the development of spirit. He is suggesting that in guilt-

[66] *CUP*, p. 474. Cf. "But still he is related to an eternal happiness,
and the consciousness of guilt is a higher expression of this than is
suffering." *Ibid.*, p. 475.
[67] *Ibid.*, p. 473.

understanding the individual has made a significant step in understanding the meaning of being a relation which relates itself to itself. This significance is brought out in the notion of totality.

For Kierkegaard man is *totally* guilty. He argues that this "is not to be determined empirically, is no *summa summarum*; for no determination of totality ever results from numerical computation."[68] It is perhaps unfortunate that Kierkegaard selects a term which usually expresses a quantitative determination to express a qualitative one. Guilt is not quantitatively determined. Kierkegaard says that "to have made oneself guilty fourteen times is child's play in comparison with this."[69] To determine guilt quantitatively expresses a reliance upon criteria which are external to the self.[70] To compare oneself with external criteria and to compute one's guilt quantitatively in relation to the number of times that one violates this external standard makes the individual undialectical in himself. This aesthetic view of guilt, which relies on a dialectical relation with the world rather than with oneself, assumes that the individual is not guilty unless he violates some social or legal standard and that the individual can avoid guilt by remaining within the bounds of legally and socially acceptable behavior.[71] Moreover, it assumes that the individual can himself overcome his guilt by publicly paying for it in the form of fine or punishment. According to Kierkegaard, this view of guilt is "childish and comparative" because it does not recognize "the requirement of existence: to put things together."[72] The requirement of existence is to put oneself in relationship not

[68] *Ibid.*, p. 471.

[69] *Ibid.*, p. 477. Cf. "The root of the matter is, however, that it is precisely unethical to have one's life in the comparative, the relative, the outward, and to have the police—justice, the court of conciliation, a newspaper, or some of Copenhagen's notables, or the rabble of the Capital, as the court of last resort in relation with oneself." *Ibid.*, p. 472.

[70] *Ibid.*, p. 472.   [71] *Ibid.*   [72] *Ibid.*, p. 473.

177

with the relative world but with one's absolute *telos*, in which case guilt is not relative and finite but absolute and total.

Now, as we have seen, Kierkegaard maintains that the attempt to relate oneself absolutely to one's absolute *telos* projects the existing individual into the ethico-religious stage of existence. To be dialectically related to oneself before God fixes the individual in an absolute relation to himself as an absolute. Kierkegaard writes that

> the concept of guilt, defined as a totality, belongs essentially to the religious sphere. As soon as the aesthetical essays to deal with it, the concept becomes dialectical like fortune and misfortune, and thereby everything is brought to confusion.[73]

The passage states that the notion of totality, as a qualitative determination, can be comprehended only on the plane of absolute distinctions and values. Aesthetic consciousness does not contain an awareness of the absolute and, therefore, cannot comprehend the qualitative distinctions of totality. Aesthetic consciousness says, "Now you are guilty; now you are not." The individual who understands himself in terms of the matrix of relations and ends determines his guilt accordingly, i.e., relatively.

> [But] the totality of guilt comes into being for the individual when he puts his guilt together with the relation to an eternal happiness. . . . He who has no relation to this never gets to the point of conceiving himself as totally or essentially guilty.[74]

The individual, then, can be totally guilty only when he is related to himself as an absolute. Every conception of guilt which does not put guilt together with the notion of being absolutely related to an absolute *telos* is a lower, i.e., quantitative and relative, determination of guilt.[75]

[73] *Ibid.*, p. 478.   [74] *Ibid.*, p. 471.   [75] *Ibid.*, p. 481.

Guilt is not an emotion or the voice of a judging and accusing conscience. If these notions exhausted its meaning, guilt would be neutralized by acts of compensation. Guilt, as we have seen, insinuates itself into a much deeper level of human reality than the emotions and conscience. Guilt, on the contrary, is the expression for a division within the structure of the self itself. The existing individual strives for himself, and in the process he becomes increasingly aware that however hard he strives he never succeeds in unifying himself as a synthesis of necessity and possibility. His ideal possibility, i.e., his *telos*, recedes deeper into the future and now begins to take on the character of an impossibility. The religious individual understands this distance between himself and his *telos* as an expression of a permanent rupture which characterizes his very existence and which he has come to understand through his striving to be obedient to the command of God to actualize his *telos*. He now understands this distance as reflective, not of a difficulty, but of a division in himself which freedom seems powerless to close.

But we still have not confronted the question concerning how guilt comes about. The following passages help us to begin to penetrate this problem.

What is my guilt? That I have ventured upon an undertaking I could not achieve.[76]

The deformed man has after all only to bear the pain of being deformed, but how dreadful if being deformed made him guilty.[77]

[76] *SLW*, p. 359. In the following passage Kierkegaard is very explicit about the undertaking which he cannot achieve: "Only when a life-view is no longer a thought-experiment among other thought-experiments, but rather an outlook which precisely by being this has a 'drive' (an inner, immanental power) requiring actualization and because of this posits itself at every moment, only then does true cleavage in man appear." *SKJP*, I, 868.

[77] *SLW*, pp. 356-357.

What does the "could not" mean in the initial passage? Does it suggest an impossibility, moral culpability, or both? Does the "could not" refer to the logical impossibility of achieving the task because of a basic structural division in the self which the existing individual may discover but does not create? If this is the case, it seems hardly just to regard the existing individual as culpable when his guilt is ontologically and not morally grounded. Or does the "could not" refer to a combination of these two possibilities?

In the second passage, Kierkegaard seems to suggest that the third alternative is the correct one for understanding guilt. When applied to the existential situation, this passage seems to be saying that it is understandable that a man should have to bear suffering which stems from being in contradiction to himself, but that it is more difficult to accept with any understanding the notion that he is responsible for a contradiction which characterizes the fundamental structure of his self.

This is one of the most difficult and knotty problems in all of Kierkegaard's thought. How can an existing individual be responsible for his failure to relate absolutely to his absolute *telos* when the failure seems to be ontologically grounded in the very structure of the self?[78] Now there appear to be two explanations for this apparent paradox. The first explanation is related to the question of time. The second explanation is concerned with freedom's culpability and with the way in which the relation between the existing individual and the universal self-structure is mediated in action, which leads to understanding. The principle passage on the relation of time and guilt appears in *Concluding Unscientific Postscript*.

[78] I stated in Chapter I that Kierkegaard's concept of the self constitutes an ontology but that Kierkegaard is more concerned with the existing individual's relation to his being (self) than with a theoretical elaboration of it. This ethico-ontological emphasis comes sharply into focus in our discussion of guilt and will continue to be the main emphasis throughout the remainder of the essay.

In existence the individual is a concretion, time is concrete, and even while the individual deliberates he is ethically responsible for the use of time. Existence is not an abstract spurt but steady striving and a continuous meanwhile; even at the instant when the task is clearly set there has been some waste, for meanwhile time has passed, and the beginning was not made at once. Thus things go backward: the task is presented to the individual in existence, and just as he is ready to cut at once a fine figure . . . and wants to begin, it is discovered that a new beginning is necessary, the beginning upon the immense detour of dying from immediacy, and just when the beginning is about to be made at this point, it is discovered that there, since time has meanwhile been passing, an ill beginning is made, and that the beginning must be made by becoming guilty and from that moment increasing the total capital guilt by a new guilt at a usurious rate of interest. The task appeared so lofty, and one thought "like for like; as the task is, so surely must he be who is to realize it." But then came existence with one "but" after another, then came suffering as a more precise determinant, and one thought, "Oh, yes, a poor exister must put up with that, since he is in existence." But then came guilt as the decisive determinant—and now the exister is in thorough distress, i.e., now he is in the medium of existence.[79]

We have, since the second chapter, seen how the existing individual's presence in time complicates his task, making it much more difficult than it would have been were it not for the fact that the existing individual is constantly being swept along in time. The fact that time is constantly adding to the self's necessity requires that the choice constantly be repeated, and now this fact has come to the center of the network of problems confronting the existing individual who is striving to realize his ethical task.

[79] *CUP*, p. 469.

The issue is now not how to repeat the choice but how to make the choice at all. In the initial choice, the existing individual's triadic structure comes to consciousness, and he becomes aware of himself as an absolute which he alone is responsible for actualizing in existence. The original choice, as we have already seen, is the choice to choose. The individual is now ready to make the second choice, i.e., to choose himself as his absolute *telos*. But resignation and suffering are costly causes of delay. He does not make the choice at once but first has to understand that the relative matrix of his life must itself be renounced. He further must understand the difficulty involved in this renunciation. And in this deliberation or this "continuous meanwhile" time has elapsed, and it is no longer possible to make the choice. The time which has passed is outside of the initial choice and, hence, cannot be part of his *telos*; therefore, he cannot at this point choose his *telos*, i.e., himself, without first making the initial choice again. A new beginning must be made. The *telos* must be posited again in the choice; the deliberative process must follow, and once again this choice will not have been made. It is at this point that the individual recognizes the impossibility and becomes guilty.[80]

But Kierkegaard does not allow the blame for guilt to fall upon the structure of the self. The existing individual, he insists, is responsible. Kierkegaard seems to understand the individual's responsibility for his guilt in terms of both freedom's culpability and the necessity of existentially appropriating, i.e., understanding oneself as guilty. First, Kierkegaard definitely insists that freedom must itself bear the responsibility for the failure. Having recognized that existence is essentially suffering, it seems that the individual

[80] "Thus it is the task appears to the exister; for an instant it deludes him with the notion that it is the whole thing, with the notion that he is now ready . . . but then existence comes in between, and the more deeply he is engaged with the task . . . the further he is from the task in which he is engaged." *CUP*, p. 470.

would be excused by blaming existence itself.[81] But Kierkegaard insists that he must go one step further and understand that because "he does not express the relationship properly he is responsible and guilty."[82] Guilt cannot be attributed simply to the fact that the medium of existence itself offers resistance to the demands of the ideal, for "it is due to the wrong decision in responsibility."[83] But the question remains as to how freedom fails and becomes culpable.

The answer seems to lie in freedom's resistance to its own realization. The initial choice of oneself is wrong because it is not at once absolute. There is a reluctance to abandon the absolute significance which the relative matrix of relations and ends has for the existing individual, and this reluctance is such a drag on the choice that it prevents it from ever being absolute. The absolute task is posited and simultaneously a conditional sub-task of dying away from immediacy is required so that the absolute task can be realized. But this sub-task is time consuming. Freedom's "grasping at finiteness to sustain itself"[84] in the face of its possibility in the instant in which it is absolutely to choose throttles the choice just long enough so that the choice cannot be made at all. The time required as preparation for the choice becomes decisive time in the sense that the time which passes cannot be redeemed into the absolute relationship. There is, consequently, no longer a possibility of establishing an absolute relation since the self's facticity (necessity), which is grounded in time, is no longer contained, or brought to consciousness in the initial choice. Herein lies the fatal discrepancy. In the initial choice, the infinitely concrete self enters consciousness as an absolute. But before the absolute can be absolutely chosen in existence, time has passed and the authenticity of the initial choice is negated,

[81] *Ibid.*
[82] Martin J. Heinecken, *The Moment Before God* (Philadelphia: Muhlenberg Press, 1956), p. 335.
[83] *Ibid.*   [84] *CD*, p. 55.

183

thereby making impossible the second and absolute choice of oneself as an absolute. Because of the on-goingness of time, freedom's reluctance, its obstinacy, to choose and to become itself is paid for with guilt. It is in this way that guilt is to be attributed to both the individual's self-structure and to the culpability of freedom.[85]

Kierkegaard pushes the matter of being responsible for one's guilt one step further. We have already seen that the individual is responsible because he does not absolutely choose when he becomes conscious that he is responsible for choosing himself. Consciousness of this failure follows the understanding of oneself as suffering, but there remains the responsibility of understanding oneself as guilty. The individual is now aware of himself as guilty and now he must choose himself as such. Kierkegaard expresses this distinction in *The Concept of Dread* when he writes that "when freedom then fears guilt, it is not that it fears to recognize itself as guilty, if it is guilty, but it fears to become guilty. . . ."[86] Until this movement is effected, the individual has not really become guilty.

[85] Price points out, and correctly so, that the "deeply chosen premise" that one is responsible for oneself has as its consequence the fact that the individual is responsible for his failure. George Price, *The Narrow Pass* (New York: McGraw-Hill, 1963), p. 180. To deny that the individual is responsible at the point of guilt would radically negate the enduring significance of the choice itself. To regard guilt solely as the inevitable consequence of being human would quickly lead the individual to the notion that he can do nothing for himself and that his life is entirely in the hands of God irrespective of his own freedom. Kierkegaard attributes the Calvinist notion of predestination to the loss of the vision of man as freedom. He argues that it is precisely in assuming responsibility for one's own failures that the notion of predestination has its rightful ground. The triumph of predestination and the loss of the dialectical tension between divine providence and human freedom reduces the notion of providence to divine necessity and the notion of freedom to an heretical illusion.

[86] *CD*, p. 97. Cf. "But when freedom is thus with all its wishful passion staring at itself, and would keep guilt at a distance so that not

Kierkegaard is here making a sharp distinction between the concrete act and consciousness of the act itself. In the act, the individual is, as it were, unconscious. The individual then reflectively turns back to the act and in so doing becomes conscious of himself in the act. Consciousness is, as we have seen, reflexive. Reflection turns back on what is already the case and brings it to consciousness. Reflection turns back on the act of renunciation and brings suffering to consciousness as the content of renunciation. The individual appropriates suffering existentially. This act of accepting the contradiction between oneself and one's *telos* is then reflected upon, and guilt is brought to consciousness as the content of suffering. The possibility of guilt is implicitly present in the existential appropriation of suffering. The existing individual must be aware of the contradiction before he can become it. The reflective penetration of suffering, then, brings guilt-consciousness into being, and the individual is, then, faced with the task of existentially appropriating guilt which is reflexively brought to consciousness. The appropriating event is itself an act of freedom.[87] And it is in this act that freedom comes to understand itself as guilty. Kierkegaard writes that "only by itself can freedom learn to know whether it is freedom or guilt which is

---

a jot of it might be found in freedom, it is not able to refrain from staring at guilt, and this staring is the ambiguity of dread. . . ." *CD*, pp. 97-98. Spirit as self-consciousness is ambiguously related to itself. For consciousness contains both spirit's awareness of its possibility and an uneasiness concerning this "unknown." This ambiguity is the source of dread. Kierkegaard speaks of dread as being sympathetic antipathy and antipathetic sympathy. *CD*, p. 38. Here freedom comprehends its possibility as guilt, and it is at once fascinated and repulsed by this awareness, hence freedom's dreadful relation to guilt.

[87] "No, the opposite of freedom is guilt, and it is the supreme glory of freedom that it has only with itself to do, that it projects guilt in its possibility and also posits it by itself, and if guilt is posited actually, freedom still posits it by itself." *CD*, p. 97.

posited."[88] That is to say, only by becoming guilty can freedom know itself as guilty, and conversely, only by becoming freedom can freedom know itself as such. In the existential actualization of itself as a contradiction, freedom knows itself as guilty, and conversely, in the existential actualization of unity, freedom knows itself as freedom. In the former, freedom knows what it is not; and in the latter, freedom knows what it is.[89]

The second way, then, in which the existing individual is held responsible for his guilt is in his being responsible for coming to know himself through existentially, i.e., freely, becoming what the self is. To internalize the contradiction and then to deny that the individual is responsible for it would be self-contradictory. For the contradiction cannot be existentially appropriated without being chosen, and only in choosing himself as a contradiction can the individual understand that that is what the self is. What could it possibly mean to say that the individual has chosen himself as a contradiction, i.e., as guilty, but is at the same time not responsible for having become guilty? To choose oneself is a free act. And it would be self-contradictory to say that the individual is not responsible for the self which he has freely chosen. To be responsible for oneself as guilty means that one has freely chosen oneself as guilty. The individual is responsible for what he becomes, because he freely chooses himself in becoming. Not to take responsibility for oneself as guilty, then, is to fail to become oneself. The issue

> is a question of one's essential relation to existence. But to will essentially to throw off guilt from oneself, i.e., guilt as the total determinant, in order thereby to become innocent, is a contradiction, since this procedure is precisely self-denunciation.[90]

[88] *Ibid.*

[89] In the final chapter we shall see why it is first necessary for freedom to know itself as guilty before it can know itself as freedom.

[90] *CUP*, p. 471.

The strongest assertion of existence is self-negation, i.e., guilt,[91] and the failure to denounce oneself is itself self-denunciation.[92]

The choice is now complete for, says Kierkegaard, "only when I choose myself as guilty do I choose myself absolutely."[93] The absolute relation to the absolute *telos* has now been established, but the quality of the relation is the exact converse of what the ethical individual originally and naively expected. The absolute relation has been established as an absolute non-relation. In guilt-understanding, the individual has actualized an absolute non-relation to himself.

Now the existing individual's absolute non-relation must be understood in terms of the underlying self-structure. Kierkegaard writes that

> though the consciousness [understanding] be ever so decisive; it is nevertheless the relationship which always sustains the disrelationship, only the exister cannot get a grip on the relationship because the disrelationship is

91 *Ibid.*, p. 470.

92 Kierkegaard is now willing to speak of the loss of innocence. "But only by guilt is innocence lost. . . ." *CD*, p. 33. Innocence here refers to both the unitary structure of the self and ignorance. Ignorance of oneself as a unity is dialectically diminished with respect to the progressive participation existentially in the self-structure itself. Aesthetic ignorance is overcome in the choice. Ethical ignorance is constituted not by ignorance of oneself as triadic in structure but by the naive confidence that freedom is autonomous and capable of holding the synthesis, which comes to consciousness in the choice, together in existence. Ethical ignorance is overcome in the ethico-religious stage, whereby the existing individual comes to understand the powerlessness of autonomous freedom and the division in the fabric of existence which develops as a consequence. Now Kierkegaard warns us that "innocence is not a perfection one ought to wish to recover. . . ." *CD*, p. 34. Innocence here refers to unity, and Kierkegaard warns that neither wishful thinking nor wishful passion is capable of restoring unity on the level of understanding. Freedom alone is responsible, and we shall see in the final chapter how Kierkegaard conceives of faith, the highest passion of freedom, as ultimately constitutive of the lost unity of innocence.

93 *E/O*, II, 221.

187

constantly placing itself between as the expression for the relationship.[94]

The disrelationship, guilt, is grounded in the relationship. Guilt-understanding is sustained by the maintenance of the relationship to one's *telos*.[95] But guilt is not attributable simply to the fact that the individual is always ahead of himself as possibility. Guilt is not only the expression for an incompatibility but also for an opposition. Guilt is the opposite of innocence. That is to say, guilt is the existential opposition of the underlying unitary nature of the self-structure, a unity which expresses what the individual should be in his fundamental being as a self. The reality of the underlying unitary self-structure sustains guilt, for guilt is a negative term whose meaning dialectically depends upon his opposite, viz., unity. The existential condition of guilt presupposes the prior and innocent relation of the individual to himself as a unity. The individual is, indeed, guilty because he is ahead of himself as possibility. But this understanding of guilt has its deeper explanation in the fact that he is a task which consists in the requirement to overcome this distinction between himself and his possibility through the existential actualization of the individual's fundamentally unitary being as a self.

Moreover, as guilty, the individual does not abandon his responsibility for relating himself to himself. For Kierkegaard says that

the eternal happiness and the exister do not so repel one another that it comes to an absolute breach; on the contrary, it is only by holding together that the disproportion repeats itself as the decisive consciousness [understanding] of guilt, not of this or the other guilt.[96]

There is no absolute breach, because the individual maintains himself in the relation, albeit, negatively. Guilt-understanding is the

[94] *CUP*, p. 473.   [95] *Ibid.*, p. 425.   [96] *Ibid.*, pp. 473-474.

decisive expression for the pathetic relationship to an eternal happiness, and this in such a way that every exister who has not this consciousness [understanding] is *eo ipso* not related to his eternal happiness.[97]

Kierkegaard insists that "he is as remote as possible, but nevertheless is related to it."[98] It would seem more obvious to assume that the more remote one is from something, the less concrete is his relationship to it. But Kierkegaard asserts the opposite.

The solution to this paradox lies in Kierkegaard's understanding of what constitutes an authentic relationship. Such a relationship is fundamentally, for Kierkegaard, concrete and not abstract.

> The more abstract the individual is, the less he is related to an eternal happiness, and the more remote he is from guilt; for abstraction assumes the indifference of existence, but guilt is the expression for the strongest self-assertion of existence, and after all it is an "exister" who is to relate himself to an eternal happiness.[99]

Kierkegaard adds that the guilty individual is denied a positive relation with his *telos* and has a relation with it "only as an annulled (*ophaevet*, German *aufgehoben*) possibility —not in such a way as the concrete is annulled so as to find the abstract, but as one annuls the abstract by being in the concrete."[100] The annullment of the abstract, i.e., non-existential, character of oneself as a relation is grounded in the existential actualization of that relation. As an abstraction, the relation does not exist. When the possibility is actualized, the existing individual understands it, i.e., himself, negatively, as guilty. The actualization of oneself as a relation in terms of both one's personal history and its cultural and social context is the condition of its concretion, and this is negatively understood as guilt. And, as we have seen,

97 *Ibid.*, p. 470.   98 *Ibid.*, p. 477.   99 *Ibid.*, p. 470.
100 *Ibid.*, p. 474.

189

maintaining oneself in the disrelationship of guilt-understanding does not create an absolute breach in the relation
because "man holds on to the happiness, suspended as it
were by the finest thread, by the aid of possibility which is
constantly being annulled. . . ."[101] The existing individual
exists, then, negatively by virtue of the power of himself as
freedom.

Now guilt-understanding is the highest expression for the
religion of hidden inwardness. Kierkegaard now defines
religiousness as "the totality[102] of guilt-consciousness [under-
standing] in the particular individual before God in relation to an eternal happiness. . . ."[103] Since religious knowl-

[101] *Ibid.*, p. 477.

[102] We would do well once again to note that self-understanding
depends upon total and not relative determinants. Kierkegaard is saying
that self-understanding in terms of the relative matrix of relations and
ends in which he lives is not self-understanding at all. The existing
individual truly understands himself only when he is driven inward
in order to understand himself in terms of the self-structure which
underlies and is constitutive of his existence. Moreover, only if he
understands himself as existing before God is it possible for total
(qualitative) determinations like suffering and guilt to qualify his
understanding of himself. Only if the individual understands his
possibility as absolutely required by God is it possible for guilt to
come into existence. Only God can absolutely require, and only God
can absolutely condemn. "The concept of guilt, defined as a totality,"
says Kierkegaard, "belongs essentially to the religious sphere." *CUP*,
p. 478. He more accurately expresses this point when he writes that
"the total determinant is the religious characteristic. . . ." *CUP*, p. 479.
That is to say, the concept of totality brings religious understanding as
a mode of existence into being, and the notion of totality itself comes
into being only when the individual understands himself as existing
before God. In relation to possibility, there is a standard which "transforms even the greatest effort into an insignificance, transforms the
continual struggle of year after year into a cockstride. . . ." *CUP*, p. 488.
The standard, of course, is the awareness of being responsible for
oneself before God. And apart from this standard, the ontological
self-structure veers toward a purely humanistic interpretation in which,
Kierkegaard implies, total determinants are completely lacking.

[103] *CUP*, p. 492.

edge is tantamount to self-understanding, guilt-understanding expresses the nature of the God-relationship.

> But to dwell upon thine own guilt . . . to fear for thine own guilt, is not egoism, for precisely thereby is man in a God-relationship.[104]

Since the God-relationship depends exclusively upon the power of the ethical for its actualization, it terminates, like the self-relation, in a negation. The existing individual maintains a negative relationship through understanding his guilt as the consequence of being absolutely related to his *telos* before God.

The first *deep plunge* into existence, then, is grounded in the existing individual's understanding that there is a division in his being which constitutes his separation from himself, i.e., his absolute *telos*, and, consequently, from God. But in spite of this recognition, the individual persists in maintaining the relationship as a non-relationship. Existing as a non-relation itself is an act of freedom, and what is now required is freedom's willful annihilation of itself so that even the non-relation is no longer maintained. This requirement is realized through the elevation of the totality of guilt to the level of consciousness so that it can be existentially appropriated. This particular relation between consciousness and act is played out in the relation between humor and repentance.

REPENTANCE

The next step in the development of spirit occurs through the dialectical relation between humor and repentance. In this move freedom rejects itself as capable of uniting the self-structure in existence and of establishing the God-relationship exclusively through an inward relation with the self. Humor is a level of consciousness which rises out of

[104] *SLW*, p. 418.

guilt-understanding and which opens the way for the highest autonomous act of freedom, viz., repentance.

"Humor," writes Kierkegaard, "as the borderline for the religiousness of hidden inwardness comprehends guilt-consciousness as a totality."[105] And, he continues, "humor puts the eternal recollection of guilt together with everything, but does not by this recollection relate itself to an eternal happiness."[106] Kierkegaard means that if the existing individual is totally guilty, then all his actions, including the highest struggles of freedom to actualize its *telos*, are comical. When self-consciousness reaches the level of humor, the individual abandons the attempt to become happy, i.e., to become himself, through the power of freedom. All acting is destined to culminate, at best, in guilt—hence, all is comical. "The comic," then, "lies in the fact that the total guilt is the foundation which supports the whole comedy."[107] Humorous consciousness abandons even the thread of hope which may linger as a residue in guilt-understanding. What remains is for the individual existentially, i.e., freely, to abandon all hope of actualizing his *telos* through his own freedom alone. The hope and the optimism which are implicitly present in the ironic consciousness slowly diminishes in the dialectical development of spirit and is ultimately replaced with the total pessimism of humorous consciousness concerning the power of freedom to actualize its absolute *telos*.[108]

It is important to note that the ethical task itself is not abandoned. The individual does not abandon his responsi-

[105] *CUP*, p. 489.   [106] *Ibid.*, p. 492.   [107] *Ibid.*, p. 493.

[108] Kierkegaard clarifies his meaning of the comic in this illustration: "When men's busy activity in running around has as its reason a possibility of escaping danger, this activity is not comic; but in case, for example, it is on a ship which is sinking, there is something quite comic in all this running around, for the contradiction is that in spite of all this movement they do not move away from the place where the destruction is." *Ibid.*

192

bility for himself. As we have seen, to be responsible means to understand oneself, and in the act of repentance the individual comes to understand himself as nothing before God. But abandonment does not mean the replacement of oneself as a task in the world with any sort of religious other-worldliness. Neither the individual's concrete and specific *telos* nor his responsibility for its actualization are negated. What is annihilated is the individual's freedom understood as autonomous. As we have seen, the phenomenon of religion is linked with the life of freedom, the individual's *Wie-Sein*. Initially, the individual understands his freedom as subject to the command of God, and now he becomes conscious of his freedom as being annihilated by that command. The final act of freedom is the existential acceptance of its nothingness.

Humorous consciousness clears the way for the ultimate act of autonomous freedom in repentance. And repentance is, says Kierkegaard, the highest act of the ethical.

> The highest expression of an ethical view of life is repentance, and I must always repent—but precisely this is a self-contradiction of the ethical, whereby, the paradox of the religious breaks through. . . . Speaking purely ethically I must say that even the best I do is only sin; consequently I will repent of it, but then I cannot actually get around to acting, because I must repent.[109]

[109] *SKJP*, I, 902. We will do well to notice that in this passage the term sin has replaced the term guilt. This is made possible by the new self-understanding which comes into existence with one's becoming a Christian. We will explore the dynamics of this move in the final chapter. For now, it is important to note that repentance is the highest act of ethico-religious stage of existence. Cf. "Inasmuch as the ethical sphere is a transitional sphere (which however one does not pass through once and for all), and as repentance is its highest expression, repentance is also the most dialectic thing." *SLW*, p. 430. Cf. "Repentance belongs in the ethico-religious sphere, and is hence so placed as to have only one higher sphere above it, namely, the religious in the strictest sense [Christianity]." *CUP*, p. 463.

Ethically, it is self-contradictory, because in the act of repentance freedom negates itself. The repentant individual totally negates his freedom before God. Through repentance, the existing individual completely abandons the thought of actualizing himself through freedom. In Kierkegaard's language, the individual admits to the impossibility of acting. He expresses this point in *Fear and Trembling* when he writes that the individual possesses the strength to repent, "but for that he uses up absolutely all his strength and hence he cannot by his own strength return and grasp reality himself."[110] In short, if the act of unification is to occur, freedom must necessarily rely upon an existential act of the divine.

But repentance itself is not a positive appropriation of that reliance. That is to say, repentance is not a direct movement toward God but an inward movement toward oneself through which the individual understands completely the nature of his self. Repentance, as the most concrete act of autonomous freedom, represents its highest possibility.[111] Through repentance, the ethicist binds together

---

[110] *FT*, p. 109.

[111] In Tillich's discussion of conversion, he comes very close to the Kierkegaardian notion of repentance. Repentance, for Tillich, is the "negation of a preceding direction of thought and action" which makes way for faith, "the affirmation of the opposite direction." Repentance is the negation of existential estrangement and faith the affirmation of the "New Being" which is discovered within the act of negation itself. Paul Tillich, *Systematic Theology* (Chicago: The University of Chicago Press, 1963), III, 219. Tillich also is very close to Kierkegaard in his denial of the pietistic emphasis on "suddenness" as the criterion for the authenticity of religious conversion. Tillich insists that the conversion process, which involves "all the dimensions of human life," is "a long process which has been going on unconsciously long before it breaks into consciousness, giving the impression of a sudden, unexpected, and overwhelming crisis." It is for this reason that neither repentance nor faith are completely new. *Ibid.*, III, 219-220.

the whole movement of self-choosing,[112] because the individual's freedom in its greatest concreteness is disclosed and chosen.

As a religious movement, repentance is a negative movement. A man's highest inward act is to repent. But to repent is not a positive movement outward or in the direction of something, but a negative movement inward; not a "doing" but a letting something "be done" to oneself.[113]

This certainly accords with Kierkegaard's view that repentance as an act of self-annihilation has been prepared for by the long and arduous development of spirit up to the point of its negation in repentance.

[112] The dynamics in the relation of choice and repentance are already worked out in *E/O*. "He who chooses himself ethically has himself as his task, and not as a possibility merely, not as a toy to be played with arbitrarily. He can choose himself ethically only when he chooses himself in continuity and so he has himself as a task which is manifoldly defined . . . he repents himself tightly into it, because this manifoldness is himself and only by being repentantly absorbed in it can he come to himself, since he does not assume that the world begins with him or that he creates himself." *E/O*, II, 262. This sounds rather different from saying that in repentance the individual annihilates himself. But basically the same point is being made in both cases. To annihilate oneself is the condition of returning to oneself. Through self-annihilation, faith becomes a possibility through which the individual returns to himself. The passage in *E/O* expresses correctly the notion that abandonment and return are two parts of the same movement. But the major weakness in *E/O*'s discussion of repentance is its failure to grasp both the degree of difficulty involved in the movement and the fact that repentance, when properly executed, projects the individual toward the Christian religion, conceived as paradox, and not toward the watered-down version of Christianity which is represented in *E/O*.

[113] The passage is a translation of a passage from *SLW*. Gregor Malantschuk, *Kierkegaard's Way to Truth*, trans. Mary Michelsen (Minneapolis: Augsburg, 1963), p. 107n. "A man's highest inward action is repentance. But to repent is not a positive movement out to or on till (sic.) but a negative movement, not a doing but a letting something befall one." *SLW*, p. 430.

The principle of religious knowledge, viz., that the positive is known by the negative, is adhered to with the move toward the Christian religion.[114] But there will be a major difference between the religious knowledge of the religion of inwardness and the Christian religion. In both, the knowledge of God is grounded in self-knowledge. Knowledge of God in the religion of hidden inwardness is negative knowledge because self-knowledge is itself negative. But, as we shall see, the knowledge of God in the Christian religion will be positive because it is grounded in the knowledge of oneself as a unity. Self-knowledge, which is ultimately mediated by the Christian religion, dialectically depends upon the negative move of repentance, for it is in this movement that the individual becomes receptive to that power by which it is existentially unified.[115] And it is in this unification that the individual positively knows both himself and God.

Repentance, then, annihilates both the struggle of the individual to relate himself to himself through himself and the religion of hidden inwardness. The achievement of unity as the condition for positive knowledge of oneself and of God is grounded in freedom's repudiation of its autonomy. The existential appropriation of oneself as nothing before God is the event through which a positive (direct)

[114] "The negative [repentance] does not come upon the scene once and for all, later to be replaced by the positive; but the positive is constantly wrapped up in the negative, and the negative is its criterion . . ." Kierkegaard, *CUP*, p. 467.

[115] Dupre clearly expresses this point in the assertion that "the choice in repentance is an implicit assertion of the self's dependence. . . ." Louis Dupre, "The Constitution of the Self in Kierkegaard's Philosophy," *International Philosophical Quarterly*, III (1963), 506-526. Cf. "Repentance as a totality is the highest negative expression of the break with existence. Through it man moves into a relationship with the concrete transcendence which is revealed truth." Malantschuk, *Kierkegaard's Way to Truth*, p. 107. In repentance, the individual clears the way for an act of God by which the task is completed. But prior to the divine act, the individual has no knowledge of himself as dependent.

196

knowledge of both oneself and God is ultimately mediated. I shall conclude this section on repentance with two long passages which summarize the movement of spirit to this point in its development and which point in the direction of its final unfolding.

> The edifying element in the sphere of religiousness A is essentially that of immanence, it is the annihilation by which the individual puts himself out of the way in order to find God, since precisely the individual himself is the hindrance. Quite rightly the edifying is recognizable here also by the negative, by self-annihilation, which in itself finds the God-relationship, is based upon it, because God is the basis when every obstacle is cleared away, and first and foremost the individual himself in his finiteness, in his obstinacy against God. Aesthetically, the holy resting place of edification is outside the individual, who accordingly seeks the place; in the ethico-religious sphere the individual himself is the place, when he has annihilated himself.[116]

> Basically the situation is such that if a person does not first use all the power given him against himself, thereby destroying himself, he is either a dolt or a coward in spite of all his courage. The power which is given to a man (in possibility) is altogether dialectical, and the only true expression for a true understanding of himself in possibility is precisely that he has the power to destroy himself, because even though he be stronger than the entire world, he nevertheless is not stronger than himself. Once this has been learned, then we can make sufficient room for religiousness and then also for Christianity, for the most radical expression of this powerless is sin. For this reason only is Christianity the absolute religion, because it conceives of men as sinners, for no other distinction can in this way recognize man in his difference from God.[117]

[116] *CUP*, pp. 497-498.   [117] *SKJP*, I, 46.

CONCLUSION

We have seen in this chapter how the two levels of the individual's being begin to become concrete. The individual's *Was-Sein* is actualized in the existing individual's concrete identity, his public and vocational being. The individual's *Was-Sein* is expressed in the concrete and specific way in which the individual fits himself as an absolute into the relative matrix of relations and ends in which he has his life. The existing individual's vocational identity comes to consciousness with the choice in the ethical stage of existence and remains, in principle, unchanged throughout the dialectical development of spirit. As long as the individual is in time, however, it is possible for him to change vocationally. The constant expansion of his facticity by the on-goingness of time requires constant adjustment of the individual's ideal being. The difference between evolutionary adjustment and revolutionary alteration of the individual's ideality depends entirely upon the rate of change which he undergoes in time. As for the matter of self-understanding, we have seen that there is no positive knowledge of one's ideality apart from its existential actualization.

In the individual's *Wie-Sein*, the individual finds himself as fundamentally free and responsible for himself as an absolute. This awareness also comes to consciousness in the choice at the beginning of the ethical stage of existence, but it has an abstractness which is lacking with respect to the individual's relation to his ideality as possibility. That is to say, the individual's ideality is very clear from the outset of the ethical stage of existence and has, though unactualized, a concreteness which is lacking in the initial awareness of oneself as freedom. One's freedom is unactualized and, hence, also related to itself as possible. Schematically, then, we can project two levels of possibility corresponding to the two levels of being in Kierkegaard's analysis of the self. Freedom's possibility is mediated by its struggle to actualize the individual's ideality, and the ethico-religious stage

198

of existence is the one in which freedom dialectically unfolds. Freedom's possibles, however, are negative. Renunciation, suffering, guilt, and finally, repentance emerge out of freedom's concrete struggle to actualize the self's ideality. Freedom reflexively understands itself through its pathetic striving to actualize the ideal. And inasmuch as the ideal recedes further into the distance with each move of freedom, freedom must know or understand itself negatively. As we have seen, freedom knows itself as freedom only with the actualization of ideality, but at this point in the development of freedom, it has come to understand itself in repentance as completely incapable of the task for which it, nevertheless, remains fully responsible. We may, then, speak of the *Was-Sein* as absolute, the *Wie-Sein* as the absolute relating, and the two together as the absolute relation which is eternal happiness. What now can we say about the relation of this ontological structure and individual existence?

For Kierkegaard, the individual's being is his task; therefore, the individual relates to his being not aesthetically but ethically. The existing individual is responsible for understanding, through becoming, what he is. Kierkegaard's conjoining of understanding (knowing) and becoming (existing) radically separates him from the western philosophical tradition which has sought to understand the nature of man through rationalistic metaphysics. Kierkegaard's radical personalization of knowledge of the self cuts off the possibility of the traditionally rational approach to the knowledge of man. He does not, however, abandon this tradition's emphasis on the nature of man, and he would be radically opposed to Sartre's position that there is no such thing as human nature.[118] Kierkegaard does not, with Sartre, abandon the "essentialist" formula "essence preceded existence." If this formula expresses one of the main presuppositions of western philosophy, then Kierkegaard remains within

[118] Jean-Paul Sartre, "Existentialism is a Humanism," *Existentialism from Dostoevsky to Sartre*, ed. Walter Kaufman (New York: World, 1968), pp. 290-291.

this tradition to the extent of maintaining that man does have a nature in terms of which his concrete existence is to be understood.

But if this is the case, wherein lies Kierkegaard's dispute with the western tradition? Principally, it centers on the issue of epistemology. That is to say, the issue concerns the way in which the individual knows and is constituted by his being. Rational speculation, according to Kierkegaard, can never disclose to the existing individual his nature, for it must be discovered in existence. Only through existing can the individual gain knowledge of the fact that he is a synthesis of finitude and infinitude, and only in existence does he know the meaning of having such a nature. Man's essential being is reflected in each individual's potential being. That is to say, each individual is essentially a potential existential unity of finitude and infinitude which is grounded in freedom. The unfolding of this being, i.e., the dialectical development of spirit, is constitutive of existence. This process of unfolding or becoming is driven forward by the individual's interest in knowing himself, and existence is the creation of freedom's drive to know (actualize) itself through the existential unification of the dialectically opposing moments of the self's *Was-Sein*. *Existence is the life of freedom.* And to regard freedom rather than the intellect as the organ of knowing means that self-knowledge is grounded in the existential actualization of freedom rather than in rational speculation.[119] To exist is to know. And the increas-

---

[119] Even the original comprehension of one's nature, viz., the triadic structure of the self, is grounded in an act of freedom. Even the most abstract knowledge of one's nature cannot be rationally achieved. I suspect that Kierkegaard would argue that were one's basic nature rationally given, each individual could not know that this nature was his nature, which was being designated or named. Indeed, there would even be a question in the individual's mind as to whether he even had a nature. All knowledge, including the initial awareness of one's basic nature, then, is grounded in an act of freedom.

ingly negative quality of existence is verification of freedom's determination to know itself at any and all costs—
even at the cost of self-destruction.

We must not, then, think of Kierkegaard as an ontologist
in any traditional sense of the word. That is to say, the
search for the structures and principles of being—in Kierkegaard's case man's being—will never yield itself to theoretical evaluation or speculation. To be certain, the individual is driven by the desire and the interest to know. But the
search for self-knowledge is not grounded in man's
penchant for wonder or in an eternal inclination toward the
metaphysical enterprise. Kierkegaard admits with Kant that
man tends toward metaphysics, but he argues, also with
Kant, that the solution to the problem of self-knowledge is
solved not by metaphysics but by ethics. In opposition to
rationalism, Kierkegaard argues that the drive for knowledge is inextricably linked to the drive to become. Knowing,
for Kierkegaard, is not grounded in theoretical speculation
but in that action in which the individual drives toward the
realization of his being. The highest form of knowing is interested knowing which both precipitates and is grounded
in the act through which man drives toward the actualization of what he essentially is.

Now we have also seen that man's knowledge of God is
similarly dependent upon His existential actualization.
Apart from the consciousness of God as the ground of the
individual's existential unity, there can be no positive or direct understanding of God. We have already glimpsed the
dialectical relation between knowledge of the self and
knowledge of its ground. There is no self-knowledge apart
from the mediation of the self's unity by the ground of its
being, and there is no knowledge of the self's divine ground
apart from knowledge of the self's existential unity. It is for
this reason that one can say with equal validity that both
knowledge of oneself is knowledge of God and that knowledge of God is knowledge of oneself. The overweighting of

this delicate balance on either side of the dialectic has the inevitable consequence of destroying the possibility of any existential knowledge whatsoever.

Kierkegaard states in *Concluding Unscientific Postscript* that "it is then not so much that God is a postulate, as that the existing individual's postulation of God is a necessity."[120] We can understand this statement within the context of the way in which Kierkegaard links the postulate to the categories of freedom and ideality. One does not take his freedom seriously, Kierkegaard argues, unless one is willing to postulate a divine authority which will hold freedom on its course. And, similarly, the ideal cannot really be construed as absolute apart from the notion of its divine ground. So it is the consciousness of the divine which guarantees and sustains the absolute relating to the absolute. God's being, then, is grounded in the life of freedom as its supreme postulate. A direct God-relationship is, likewise, grounded in the existential actualization of freedom's task. In the existential life of freedom, the existing individual comes to know the meaning of existing in a God-relationship. Apart from existence, there is only the essential postulate of God as the ground of freedom. This postulate comes to life only in existing. Now, although the negation of the religion of inwardness destroys the hope of knowing God through the life of freedom understood as autonomous, both the notion of realizing an eternal happiness and the need for God in its actualization are not negated but carried over into the individual's turn toward the Christian religion in freedom's final negative act of repentance.

[120] *CUP*, p. 179n.

CHAPTER VI

The Religion of Faith

THE religious qualification of the dialectical development of spirit leads to an impasse in repentance. The individual understands himself as in need of a divine ground, and yet as incapable of actualizing that ground. In this chapter I shall show that this religious impasse in the development of spirit requires a religious solution which appears in what Kierkegaard calls Religiousness B (Christianity). Specifically, I shall examine Kierkegaard's re-definition of the nature of the eternal and his concept of faith as the two major aspects of this higher mode of religious self-understanding. The chapter is divided into five sections. The first section is concerned with the two definitions of the eternal as they appear in Religiousness A and Religiousness B. In the second section, there is a brief discussion concerning Religiousness A as the propaedeutic of faith. The third and fourth sections are devoted to an analysis of the content of faith, viz., the consciousness of sin and the consciousness of the forgiveness of sin. The conclusion of this chapter constitutes the fifth section, and here I summarize the arguments of the chapter and then argue that Kierkegaard's interpretation of Christianity is shaped by the way in which his ontology and his view of the task of existence are combined to constitute the dialectical development of spirit.

TWO DETERMINATIONS OF THE ETERNAL

The ethical requirement to actualize one's absolute *telos* remains central to Religiousness B. In both modes of religious understanding, the fulfillment of the ethical requirement is the condition for becoming eternal. To be eternal

203

is to become oneself through existing in the God-relation-ship.

Religiousness A, on the one hand, assumes that the individual is eternal. This assumption hinges on the notion that the self is divine. That is to say, it assumes that the self's ideality and freedom are already grounded in the divine and that the individual's realization of himself is, simultaneously, a realization of his essentially divine nature in the God-relationship. The individual presupposes the divine foundation of the self, and he strives to establish an existential God-relationship through the reflective penetration of himself. Religiousness B, on the other hand, assumes that the individual is not in possession of the eternal. This assumption hinges on the notion that the self is not primordially divine. The realization of the individual's self, then, requires that it become something which it is not, viz., divinely grounded. That is to say, the individual must presuppose that the divine foundation of the self cannot be acquired reflectively. The establishment of a God-relationship in existence, according to Religiousness B, requires that the individual establish a relation with an historical actuality, and in so doing, the individual becomes what essentially he is not.[1]

In my discussion of time, we discovered that the task of uniting the self as a synthesis in existence involves the unification of time and eternity. It became evident that the polarities of the self, when reflected, are grounded in the temporal dimensions of past and future (the incognito of the eternal), and that the unification of past and future in the instant constitutes the present. We also saw that the pres-

[1] "In Religiousness A there is no historical starting-point. The individual merely discovers in time that he must assume he is eternal. The moment in time is therefore *eo ipso* swallowed up by eternity. In time the individual recollects that he is eternal. This contradiction lies exclusively within immanence. It is another thing when the historical is outside and remains outside, and the individual who was not eternal now becomes such, and so does not recollect what he is but becomes what he was not. . . ." *CUP*, p. 508.

204

ent, according to Kierkegaard, is the eternal. The eternal, however, lies in the future prior to the actualization of the self's ideality. In the instant in which the self's ideality is actualized in existence, the self becomes eternal in the sense that past (necessity) and future (possibility) are unified in the present. In this instant, the existing individual is eternal. Kierkegaard tells us that the eternal "is the full." The eternal, as presence, is an instant which is full of the self as past (necessity) and future (possibility). The inflection of the eternal in time constitutes the present; it is an instant in which necessity (past), reflected as possibility (future), is actualized in the present by an act of freedom. In the instant, then, the individual becomes eternal, i.e., the individual unifies himself as past and future in the present, eternal, instant. To become eternal is, then, to become oneself.

In Religiousness A the future is the medium of the self as a reflected possibility. The future is the medium of the self as an ideal which is grounded in the divine, and, as reflected, both the ideal and the divine appear as possible. The actualization of the ideal is the actualization of the God-relationship, and the responsibility for the establishment of this eternal God-relationship falls upon the individual's freedom. This is what is meant by Kierkegaard's claim that in Religiousness A, the individual assumes that he is eternal, and through reflection seeks to transform his existence by virtue of this relationship to himself as eternal. The repossession of oneself as eternal in existence constitutes the unification of the self's past and future in the present, eternal, instant.

In Religiousness B, however, the content of past and future are radically altered. In this mode of religious understanding, reflection is abandoned, and Kierkegaard asserts that now the individual no longer assumes that he is in possession of the eternal, but instead assumes that the eternal has appeared in time. This means, most simply stated, that God is already in time by virtue of his own freedom. The implication of such a claim is that the individual is no longer responsible for realizing the divine foundation of the self. This does not mean, however, that the individual is released from the responsibility of fulfilling the ethical requirement; for in the Deity in time the individual discovers the personal embodiment of the divine imperative. The ethical requirement, then, remains central to the individual's consciousness of himself as an existing individual.

The major distinction between these two modes of understanding is to be seen in the content of the temporal dimensions of past and future. In Religiousness B, the individual comprehends, in the future, the eternal embodied as an actuality and not as a possibility as in Religiousness A. The eternal appears to the individual as the actual, real concrete embodiment of the ethical requirement. The Deity in time, according to Kierkegaard, is the one who "possesses the ideal perfectly, and therefore does the noblest thing freely."[2] In the past, the individual comprehends himself as sinner. The individual's self is no longer reflected, i.e., it no longer appears to itself as possible. The past contains the sinful individual, i.e., the individual's self as absolutely divided against itself. The synthesis, then, is now one of the individual's actual self as sinner with his actual, eternal ground. The instant is the moment in which actual sinner is grounded in the eternal, actual ideal, so that the individual's self becomes eternal, unified, in its divine ground. This move requires, according to Kierkegaard, an act of faith, which, in turn, requires as its condition, the abandonment of immanence, i.e., reflection.

> Actuality, i.e., the fact that this or that actually occurred, is the subject of faith, and this surely is not any thought of man or of mankind, for thought at its highest is possibility, but possibility as the medium of understanding is precisely the understanding whereby the backward step is taken of ceasing to believe. He who understands the paradox will in his misunderstanding forget that Chris-

[2] *SKJ*, #1049.

tianity is the absolute paradox . . . *precisely because it nullifies a possibility (the analogy of paganism, an eternal divine becoming) as an illusion and turns it into actuality, and precisely this is the paradox. . . .*[3]

The religion of immanence is an eternal divine becoming by virtue of the individual's reflection of himself as possible and the concomitant striving to realize that possibility as an ethical requirement which is sanctioned by the divine. In Religiousness B, the individual's possibility is negated as an impossibility (sin), and he is forced, in an act of faith, out of himself in the direction of his divine ground as already actualized in the Deity in time.

Kierkegaard asserts that

> if there is any vestige of immanence, an eternal determinant left in the exister—then it [Religiousness B] is not possible. The exister must have lost continuity with himself, must have become another (not different from himself within himself) and then, by receiving the condition from the Deity, he must have become a new creature.[4]

To become another does not mean the abandonment of one's self but the loss of continuity with it. That is to say, the individual who exists in this second mode of religious understanding, does not cease to exist within the dynamic self-structure which is his being. The task of existence continues to define the nature and responsibility of the existing individual. *The loss of continuity by which the individual becomes another means that the individual's consciousness of himself depends upon the reality of another.* Religiousness B is a continuation of the dialectical development of spirit in the sense that it seeks, like every preceding state of its development, to fulfill the ethical requirement of existence. The discontinuity, characterizing the move to Religiousness B, is situated in the fact that the eternal determinant of the

---

[3] *CUP*, p. 515. Italics mine.   [4] *Ibid.*, p. 510.

ethical requirement is an actuality external to the self and not a possibility internal to it.

As we have seen, these two modes of religious understanding begin with opposing assumptions, viz., that the self is and is not eternal. We must not suppose, however, that these assumptions are unrelated in the sense that they constitute the presuppositions of two opposing, and entirely unrelated, modes of religious self-understanding. Both assumptions appear within the broader spectrum of the development of spirit, and both are essential to its development. More precisely, the latter assumption depends upon the former in the sense that the latter cannot develop apart from the former. The negative assumption that the self is not eternal relies upon the positive one that it is. It is not possible for the individual to assume that he is not eternal until he has understood existentially the implications of the assumption that he is. As we shall see, the Christian mode of religious self-understanding cannot become a possibility for an existing individual until he is conscious of himself as not being eternal. One arrives at this point only by assuming the opposite, viz., that one's self is eternal, and by following this assumption through to its negative conclusion.

Indeed, it is precisely the religious accentuation of the ethical requirement in Religiousness A which gives rise to the possibility of Religiousness B as a mode of self-understanding. Apart from the religious interpretation of the ethical requirement, the Christian mode of self-understanding cannot be introduced into the dialectical development of spirit. In the following pages, we shall turn to an analysis of faith as an act of spirit by which this negative assumption comes to consciousness, on the one hand, and the completion of the development of spirit is affected, on the other.

The Propaedeutic of Faith

Faith is not in any sense a departure from existence. It is not intellectual assent to theological doctrines which defy rationality. That is to say, faith is not the suicide of rationality in which an irrational assent to theological doctrines is required. Faith is not an irrational expression of the will in which the individual is required to exist in categories which bear no understandable relation to the problem and meaning of existence as they have come to be understood prior to the act of faith. Faith is, on the contrary, the realization of the self in existence. That is to say, faith is an act in which the ethical requirement is fulfilled, and the self is unified in existence. It is an act in which the individual's self is fully actualized and understood in existence. It is, consequently, an act in which happiness is attained.

But the possibilities of understanding the content of faith and of actually existing in faith depend upon a prior existential situation. That is to say, it is impossible both to know the content of faith and to exist in faith apart from a preceding striving to exist.

> Usually it is presented in this way: first, one must have faith and then existing follows. This has contributed greatly to the confusion, as if it were possible to have faith without existing. . . . The matter is quite simple. In order to have faith, there must first be existence, an existential-qualification. This is what I am never sufficiently able to emphasize—that to have faith, before there can even be any question about having faith, there must be the "situation." And this situation must be brought about by an existential step on the part of an individual. We have completely done away with this propaedeutic element. . . . Take an example, the rich young ruler. What did Christ require as the preliminary act? He required action that would shoot the rich young ruler out into the infinite. The requirement is that you must venture out, out into water 70,000 fathoms deep. This is the situation. Now there can be a question of having faith, or of despairing. . . . Then there is another existing which follows faith. *But the first must never be forgotten—otherwise Christianity is completely displaced.*[5]

[5] *SKJP*, II, 1142. Italics mine.

The situation, as we have seen, is constituted by the individual's "pathetic" striving to realize the ethical requirement which culminates in the negative knowledge of oneself and of God, on the one hand, and the absence of an eternal happiness, on the other. But it is precisely this situation which is the condition for the possibility of faith. In his concrete discussions of the situation, Kierkegaard sometimes emphasizes the striving to fulfill the ethical requirement and, at other times, the striving for happiness. But, in either case, the message is the same: To exist as a Christian both requires and is determined by a prior ethico-religious mode of existence.

The individual's "pathetic" striving to fulfill the ethical requirement, or to be absolutely related to his absolute *telos*, i.e., himself, constitutes the situation whereby faith becomes a possibility.

> As the individual develops, God becomes for him more and more infinite, and he feels himself farther and farther from God. . . . The ideal becomes so infinitely elevated that all my striving transforms itself before my eyes into a distracted nothingness, if it is directed at resembling the ideal, or into a kind of devout jest, even though I am honestly striving. . . . The youth does not notice how enormous the task is; he starts out briskly and in the pious illusion that he will succeed. The adult comprehends with infinite depth the distance between himself and the ideal —and now "faith" must first of all intervene as that in which he actually rests; the faith that fulfillment has been made, the faith that I am saved by faith alone.[6]

In *Sickness Unto Death*, the same point is expressed, but here the emphasis is on the consciousness of oneself as an impossibility. Kierkegaard writes that

> the decisive thing is, that for God all things are possible. . . . This is commonly enough recognized . . . and . . . it is

[6] *SKJP*, II, 1135.

commonly affirmed; but the decisive affirmation comes only when a man is brought to the utmost extremity, so that humanly speaking no possibility exists. Then the question is whether he will believe that for God all things are possible—that is to say, whether he will believe.[7]

Together, these passages affirm that the recognition of oneself as an impossibility through striving with oneself as a possibility is the necessary condition for the emergence of faith.

When Kierkegaard emphasizes the pursuit of happiness, rather than the ethical requirement, the same point is asserted with respect to the possibility of faith.

Only when a person has become so unhappy or has penetrated the wretchedness of this existence so deeply that he must truly say: For me life has no value—only then can he make a bid for Christianity.[8]

Kierkegaard goes so far as to say that it is much more difficult to realize the existential propaedeutic of faith than it is to realize faith itself.

Actually, the difficulty is not, when feeling absolutely one's wretchedness, to grasp [in faith] the consolation of Christianity. . . . No, the difficulty is to become wretched in this way, to want to risk discovering one's wretchedness. To be made well with the aid of Christianity is not the difficulty; the difficulty is in becoming sick to some purpose. If you are sick in this way, Christianity comes with matchless ease, just as it is incomparably easy for the starving person to be interested in food.[9]

[7] *SUD*, p. 171. Cf. "To understand that humanly, it is his own destruction, and then nevertheless to believe in the possibility, is what is meant by faith." *Ibid.*, p. 172. "The believer possesses the eternally certain antidote to despair, viz., possibility: For with God all things are possible every instant. This is the sound health of faith which resolves all contradictions." *Ibid.*, p. 173.

[8] *SKJP*, II, 1152.   [9] *SKJP*, II, 1137.

This is a surprising passage, because it clearly contradicts his emphasis in major works like *Philosophical Fragments, Concluding Unscientific Postscript,* and *Sickness Unto Death* on the difficulty and pain involved in the movement of faith. It appears to be an overstatement when compared with the statements in these works concerning the paradoxical and absurd character of faith. But it is not for this reason to be dismissed. After all, in the privacy of his Journals, Kierkegaard removes himself from his public battle with the Danish Hegelians and is, for that reason, more likely to abandon the polemical stance which so frequently appears in the published works. Given this qualification that the passage overstates the simplicity of the movement of faith, it nevertheless illustrates Kierkegaard's conviction that the wretchedness of existence is not only the condition for grasping Christianity but also a very sound reason for doing so.

But what is faith? A discussion of the conditions of its possibility does not tell us what it is. Kierkegaard writes that

> one can discern that faith is a more concrete qualification than immediacy, because from a purely human point of view the secret of all knowledge is to concentrate upon what is given in immediacy; in faith we assume something which is not given and can never be deduced from the preceding consciousness—that is, the consciousness of sin and the assurance of the forgiveness of sin. . . .[10]

Faith is a free act[11] in which the preceding reflective development of consciousness is abrogated and a still higher level of consciousness, not deductible from the preceding levels of consciousness, is attained. All preceding acts of freedom

---

10 *SKJP*, ii, 1100; cf. *ibid.*, ii, 2274.

11 Kierkegaard makes this point elsewhere in the following assertions: "Faith certainly requires an expression of the will." *SKJP*, ii, 1094. "Faith is the highest passion in the sphere of human subjectivity." *CUP*, p. 118.

had the individual's self as its object, but "to ask with infinite interest about the reality which is not one's own is faith. . . ."[12] Kierkegaard states that

> the object of faith is hence the reality of the God-man in the sense of his existence. . . . The object of faith is thus God's reality in existence as a particular individual, the fact that God has existed as an individual human being.[13]

The object of faith is not the self but the Deity in time, and its content, viz., the consciousness of sin and the assurance of the forgiveness of sin, is not reflectively mediated but communicated by the existence of the Deity in time.

Because the act of faith is directed away from the self and toward the Deity in time, we are not to assume that the act of faith is an abandonment of the individual's task of realizing himself in existence. Indeed, it is through the dynamics of faith that his task is finally accomplished. Kierkegaard writes that faith is the "anticipation of the eternal which holds . . . together the discontinuities of existence."[14] That is to say, in faith, the division in the individual's self which he has been unable to bridge is healed. We shall now turn our attention to the consciousness of sin and the forgiveness of sin, the content of faith, in order to determine how the accentuation of guilt as sin and the eternal as the embodiment of the Ideal who forgives leads to the realization of the ethical requirement and the attainment of knowledge and happiness.

SIN-CONSCIOUSNESS

We have seen that repentance is a negative ethical movement. It is the existential expression of freedom's rejection of itself as capable of fulfilling the ethical requirement. The movement has no external referent. It is an exclusively self-consuming movement in which freedom rejects itself as cap-

---

[12] *CUP*, p. 288.   [13] *Ibid.*, p. 290.   [14] *SKJP*, II, 1347.

able of fulfilling the self-relating task imposed upon it as a divine imperative. Repentance is an act in which freedom understands its powerlessness, but, according to Kierkegaard, it is still not the most radical expression of freedom's powerlessness. He asserts that once an individual uses his power to destroy himself in repentance, he "can make sufficient room for religiousness and then also for Christianity, for the most radical expression of this powerlessness is sin."[15] The abandonment of ethical striving in repentance is freedom's acceptance of its powerlessness, but Kierkegaard insists that repentance only makes room for the consciousness of sin as a still more radical expression of this powerlessness. It is to this level of consciousness that we must now turn our attention.

Kierkegaard refers to sin as a mode of consciousness. In order to understand his conception of sin, then, we must place our analysis of it within the larger framework of our discussion of the dialectical development of spirit. Indeed, this is precisely the procedure which Kierkegaard himself follows.

> The gradations in the consciousness of the self with which we have hitherto been employed are within the definition of the human self, or the self whose measure is man. But this self acquires a new quality or qualification in the fact that it is the self directly in the sight of God. This self is no longer the merely human self but is what I would call, hoping not to be misunderstood, the theological self, the self directly in the sight of God.[16]

We have observed that up to this point in Kierkegaard's discussion of the development of the self, each level of exist-

---

[15] *SKJP*, I, 46. Cf. "Sin belongs to ethics only in so far as upon this concept [sin] it [ethics] founders by the aid of repentance." *CD*, p. 16.

[16] *SUD*, p. 210. Here the phrase "before God" refers to God as historically revealed as the Deity in time. It has a specifically Christian connotation which is lacking in its use in his discussion of Religiousness A. Cf. *Ibid.*, p. 214.

ence has implicitly within itself a higher level of consciousness. Resignation contains the deeper consciousness of suffering, suffering the deeper consciousness of guilt, and guilt the deeper consciousness of humor, Further, humor, as a mode of self-consciousness, makes way for the act of repentance. The next level of consciousness is the consciousness of sin. But sin-consciousness is not, according to Kierkegaard, implicit in guilt and repentance. That is to say, sin-consciousness is not a reflected level of consciousness. It cannot be derived by human reason from the preceding level of existence. Sin-consciousness, on the contrary, depends upon the historical revelation of the Deity in time.[17] To allow one's self-consciousness to be informed by such a revelation requires an act of faith.[18] In such an act, a break with immanent self-reflection is firmly established. This distinction between self-consciousness achieved within immanence and through a relation to an historical fact is made clear by Kierkegaard in his discussion of the relation of guilt-consciousness and sin-consciousness.

The issues in this important distinction are best expressed in the following passage.

> In the totality of guilt-consciousness, existence asserts itself as strongly as it can within immanence; but sin-consciousness is the breach with immanence; by coming into being the individual becomes another, or the instant he must come into being he becomes another, for otherwise the determinant sin is placed within immanence. . . .
>
> [The] consequence of the Deity's presence in time . . . prevents the individual from relating himself backwards to the eternal, since now he comes forwards into being in order to become eternal by relationship to the Deity in time. Hence the individual is unable to acquire Sin-Con-

---

[17] "For since the relation to that historical fact (the Deity in time) is the condition for sin-consciousness, sin-consciousness could not have been during all that time when the historical fact had not been." *CUP*, p. 517. Cf. *SUD*, pp. 220, 225-226 and *PF*, p. 59.

[18] *SKJP*, II, 1530; cf. *ibid.*, II, 1100.

sciousness by himself, as he can guilt-consciousness; for in guilt-consciousness the identity of the subject with himself is preserved, and guilt-consciousness is an alteration of the subject within the subject himself; sin-consciousness, on the other hand, is an alteration of the very subject himself, which shows that outside of the individual that power must be which makes clear to him the fact that in coming into life he has become another than that he was, has become a sinnner. This power is the Deity in time.[19]

In guilt-understanding, the self immanently asserts itself as strongly as it can in existence. Immanence means, for Kierkegaard, the inward reflection of one's self. Self-reflection is constitutive of existence. As we noted in Chapter Three, the individual goes forward in existence by penetrating backward into the self. To exist in guilt is constituted by the deepest backward penetration into the self within immanence. The attainment of guilt-understanding constitutes a transformation within the self, but not such a radical alteration that the self loses its identity with itself. Sin-consciousness, however, is a breach with immanence. According to Kierkegaard, this constitutes, not an alteration within the self, but an alteration of the self so that the self's identity with itself is destroyed. This can only mean that the individual abandons this process of inward self-reflection as the means of understanding and becoming himself. More explicitly, the existing individual negates the possibility of realizing the ethical requirement of relating absolutely to his absolute *telos* in existence through the power of his own freedom. The individual now relates to his *telos* as an absolute impossibility.

This is precisely what is meant by becoming another. Kierkegaard does not mean that there is an actual physical change or that there is a basic change in the individual's public and vocational being, i.e., his *Was-Sein*. Becoming

[19] *CUP*, p. 517.

216

another refers to a radical change in self-consciousness. In this sense, the existing individual becomes something other than what he was before. Prior to the consciousness of sin, the existing individual relates to himself as possibility. That is to say, prior to the consciousness of sin, the existing individual is conscious of himself as being in possession of the power to realize the ethical requirement in existence. But in the consciousness of sin, he becomes an impossibility or another. That is to say, in the consciousness of sin, there develops a radical change in self-consciousness. The existing individual now comprehends himself as other than the possibility of achieving the ethical requirement. In sin-consciousness, the existing individual becomes another in the sense that by virtue of a leap in self-consciousness, he projects himself into the "new existence medium"[20] of sin in which he recognizes himself as other than the ethical.

We are now ready to provide a definition of sin. Let us begin by repeating the assertion that, according to Kierkegaard, sin is a more radical interpretation of human guilt. In guilt-understanding, the existing individual discovers both a deep division within himself and a concomitant separation from God. Kierkegaard now asserts that in the confrontation with the Deity in time, guilt becomes sin.[21] The existing individual gets a more radical perspective (sin-consciousness) on the division with himself and the separation from God.

We have seen that sin is the abandonment of immanent self-reflection in the consciousness of one's self as an impossibility. Let us now say, more concretely, that sin is the "suspension of the ethical." Kierkegaard writes in *Concluding Unscientific Postscript* that

the terrible emancipation from the requirement of realizing the ethical, the heterogeneity of the individual with

20 *CUP*, p. 516.

21 *SUD*, p. 211. Cf. J. Sperna Weiland, *Philosophy of Existence and Christianity* (Gorcum and Co., 1951), pp. 118-119.

the ethical, this suspension from the ethical, is "Sin," considered as the state in which the human being is.[22]

In sin-consciousness, the individual recognizes that the division in himself, which is disclosed in guilt and accentuated as sin in faith, is not to be attributed to the failure of ethical striving[23] but is a state which characterizes the very

[22] *CUP*, p. 239. Here sin is referred to as a "state" which characterizes the individual's self, but elsewhere Kierkegaard refers to sin as an expression of the will. "What determinant is it then that Socrates lacks in determining what sin is? It is will, defiant will." *SUD*, p. 220; cf. *ibid.*, p. 224. In the former case, sin is consciousness of a state of the individual's self which is comprehended through an historical revelation, and, in the latter case, sin is an expression of the will. Torsten Bohlin finds these two conceptions contradictory and has argued that they are two completely different notions of sin, having nothing to do with each other. The notion of sin in *SUD*, Bohlin maintains, is grounded in Kierkegaard's personal religious experience, and in *CUP* and *PF*, sin is a state of the individual's being. But these two notions are not, it seems to me, contradictory as Bohlin argues. In *SUD*, Kierkegaard uses both notions of sin in order to give a full account of its reality. "After having been informed by a revelation from God what sin is, then before God in despair not to will to be oneself . . . is to sin. . . ." *SUD*, p. 232. This refusal to will to be oneself constitutes the "continuation in sin . . . which in turn becomes the potentiation of sin in itself, an abiding in the state of sin with the consciousness thereof. . . ." *SUD*, pp. 239-240. Kierkegaard describes this potentiation of sin as being "in despair at not willing to be oneself, or in despair at willing to be oneself. Thus sin is potentiated weakness or potentiated defiance. . . ." *SUD*, p. 208. Both potentiations are expressions of the will in response to the consciousness of being in the state of sin. Sin, as an expression of the will, then, depends upon a prior consciousness of sin which is disclosed by an historical revelation. But even the consciousness of sin, as a state of the self, is a "free act" (*SKJP*, II, 1100), and, consequently, the will is even involved in the existential appropriation of one's self as sinful. Bohlin, then, is mistaken in regarding these two descriptions of sin as contradictory rather than as two aspects of a single reality.

[23] "This impotence of the individual must not be understood as the imperfection of a persistent striving toward the attainment of an ideal: For in that case no suspension is posited; just as an official is not suspended from his office if he performs his duties only moderately well." *CUP*, p. 238.

being of the individual. The existing individual literally *is* heterogeneous with the ethical by virtue of the impotence of his freedom and his on-goingness in time which, together, constitute the division in his being. Sin, then, as a state, is not to be understood as the failure of ethical striving,[24] although ethical striving is responsible for the development of the consciousness of sin.

Sin, however, as a mode of self-consciousness, is dialectically conceived, because it cannot exist as a level of consciousness apart from the preceding consciousness of the ethical requirement. Hence, it is impossible to exist in sin unless the requirement is maintained.

The suspension of the ethical does not mean, however, that the ethical requirement itself is negated; for in the suspension, "the ethical will then be present every moment with its infinite requirement, but the individual is not capable of realizing this requirement."[25] To be heterogeneous with the ethical does not mean that the individual is absolved of the ethical requirement. On the contrary, it means that the individual finds himself completely incapable of realizing the task for which he continues to be responsible. The terrible nature of the suspension consists precisely in the fact that the individual remains responsible in the face of his heterogeneity with the ethical. The guilty individual remains within the ethical, because he is not conscious of himself as heterogeneous with it. He does not abandon ethical striving. As we have seen, the existing individual maintains himself in guilt only by continually striving to realize the ethical requirement. To become heterogeneous with the ethical means to abandon the striving in sin-consciousness. But this is a terrible emancipation because the requirement

24 Fahrenbach has accurately understood the nature of sin in Kierkegaard's thought and expresses this notion very succinctly: "The suspension means that man (in sin) is heterogeneous with the ethical, indeed finds himself in the opposite condition of what the ethical demands, and therefore is not capable of realizing the ethical requirement." Fahrenbach, *Kierkegaards Ethik*, p. 150.

25 *CUP*, p. 238.

remains a task for the individual, although he has abandoned all striving, whereby that requirement might be fulfilled in existence. The infinite requirement continues to exert its claim upon him and, "each moment it requires itself of the individual . . . each moment it thereby only more definitely determines the heterogeneity as heterogeneity."[26]

Kierkegaard writes in *Concluding Unscientific Postscript* that "in none of the pseudonymous books had sin been brought to the attention."[27] This is, of course, an overstatement since the concept is significantly treated in *The Concept of Dread* and *Philosophical Fragments*. Kierkegaard, no doubt, is thinking of *Either/Or* and *Fear and Trembling*. In *Concluding Unscientific Postscript*, he writes that in *Either/Or* repentance is the deepest level attained in the development of spirit, and as such, repentance is an "ethical category."[28] Even the "edifying reflection" at the conclusion of the book, which maintains "that over against God we are always in the wrong," is not a "determination of sin as a fundamental condition. . . ."[29]

In *Fear and Trembling*, "sin was used incidentally to illuminate the nature of Abraham's ethical suspension, but not further."[30] The definition of sin as a state of the individual's being is not present in *Fear and Trembling* because Abraham "was quite completely capable of realizing it [the ideal], but was prevented by something higher, which through accentuating itself absolutely transformed the voice of duty into a temptation."[31] Kierkegaard continues that "now the situation is different. Duty is the absolute, its requirement an absolute requirement, and yet the individual is prevented from realizing it."[32] Neither in *Either/Or* nor in *Fear and Trembling*, then, is sin understood as a condition in which the individual discovers himself as heterogeneous with the ethical.

In *The Concept of Dread*, however, we find agreement

---

[26] *Ibid.* [27] *CUP*, p. 239. [28] *Ibid.*
[29] *Ibid.* [30] *CUP*, p. 240. [31] *Ibid.*, p. 238.
[32] *Ibid.*, p. 239.

with *Concluding Unscientific Postscript* and *Philosophical Fragments* with respect to the notion of sin as a state, although the term heterogeneous is not used to describe the individual's sinful state in relation to the absolute ethical requirement.

> In the fight to realize the task of ethics sin shows itself not as something which only casually belongs to a casual individual but sin withdraws deeper and deeper as a deeper and deeper presupposition, as a presupposition which goes well beyond the individual. Now all is lost for ethics, and ethics has contributed to the loss of all.[33]

Ethics founders upon the reality of sin. The individual is prevented from realizing the absolute ethical requirement by virtue of sin, but in *The Concept of Dread,* Kierkegaard

[33] *CD*, p. 17. Kierkegaard here refers to sin not as a mode of consciousness, an act of the will, or a state of being, but as a presupposition. He does so because he is now discussing the relationship of the "sciences" of ethics and dogmatics and the nature of their starting points. The science of dogmatics, according to Kierkegaard, begins with the presupposition of sin. *CD*, p. 18. Just as existing as a Christian requires that the individual first exist as a sinner, so also the development of a Christian Dogmatics requires the presupposition of sin as its starting point. In both, sin is a postulate which is not logically necessary but an hypothesis on which the existing individual stakes his existence and with which the theologian begins his interpretation of the nature of man and his relation to God. "That I exist," writes Kierkegaard, "was the eternal presupposition of the ancient world; that I am a sinner is the new spontaneity of the Christian consciousness; the one can be demonstrated no more than the other." *SKJP*, I, 1032.

It is important to keep in mind that here in the discussion of sin as in the discussion of other religious notions like faith, repentance, and forgiveness, Kierkegaard is not working as a theologian. The task continues to be one of illuminating the ontological conditions making Christianity an existential possibility. Kierkegaard does at times in the pseudonyms lapse into theological discussions as, for example, in his discussion of original sin in *The Concept of Dread.* But the main thrust of the pseudonyms is the development of an ontology and a description of the modes of human existence, including Christianity, which that ontology makes possible.

also states that the individual must either remain imprisoned in ethical failure or discover the condition for its fulfillment beyond itself.

> Either the whole of existence is locked up in the requirement of ethics, or the condition for its fulfillment must be provided—and with that the whole of life and of existence begins afresh. . . .[34]

Ethics founders upon sin, but discovers in sin the condition for its fulfillment.

The consciousness of sin, writes Kierkegaard, "is the *conditio sine qua non* for all Christianity."[35] Sin is a "decisive expression for the religious mode of existence."[36] Kierkegaard means by this assertion that the way to an immanent God-relationship is lost because sin absolutely separates one from God. The individual is now other than the ethical presupposes. Religiousness A sought the God-relationship and an eternal happiness in spirit's striving to unify the self in existence. That striving, as we have seen, is negated by sin. This more radical consciousness recognizes that the existing individual is completely incapable of overcoming both the division within himself and the consequent separation from God. Sin is the condition for the emergence of the possibility of existing as a Christian, and it is in this stage of existence that one discovers the cure for sin. Kierkegaard writes that "only the agony of the consciousness of sin can explain the fact that a person will submit to this radical cure."[37] In sin, then, the existing individual is simultaneously suspended from the ethical and projected toward a reconciliation with it. By existing as a Christian, the division in one's self is healed and the ethical is fulfilled through the establishment of an existential God-relationship.

In the following section of this chapter, I shall argue that

[34] *CD*, p. 16n.
[35] *SKJP*, I, 452; cf. *SKJ*, #820 and *SUD*, pp. 251-252.
[36] *CUP*, p. 239; cf. *ibid.*, p. 240.
[37] *SKJP*, I, 496.

the two major presuppositions of Religiousness A are reversed in Religiousness B. First, the eternal toward which the existing individual strives is not beyond time, as is maintained by Religiousness A, but in time. Second, the power by which the eternal is actualized in individual existence is not the power of human freedom alone, as is maintained by Religiousness A, but the power of both human and divine freedom. It is of absolute importance to note, however, that even though the presuppositions of Religiousness A are reversed by Religiousness B, the goal of Religiousness A is carried over into Religiousness B and becomes its goal. First, the realization of the ethical requirement maintains its centrality for the existing individual. Second, the realization of this requirement requires the participation of the divine. Third, complete knowledge of one's self and God is contingent upon the fulfillment of this requirement. And, fourth, the condition for the attainment of happiness is the realization of the ethical requirement. In the following section on the forgiveness of sin, we shall see how Religiousness B is the fulfillment of the individual's task as it is ethically posed and striven for in Religiousness A.

THE FORGIVENESS OF SIN

To base one's self-consciousness on the word of another is the most radical expression possible of dependence upon another.[38] It involves the abandonment of self-reflection

[38] By using the term "dependence" to explain the nature of the relation between the existing individual and the Deity in time, I do not intend to align Kierkegaard with Schleiermacher's definition of faith as a pre-reflective sentiment. (*SKJP*, II, 1096.) He argues that Schleiermacher's definition of faith deprives it of its dialectical character and converts it into a static situation or a mere datum. *SKP*, X² A 417. This is quoted from Louis Dupre, *Kierkegaard as Theologian* (New York: Sheed and Ward, 1963), p. 118. We have seen that faith is post-reflective in Kierkegaard's thought. Faith is a post-reflective acknowledgment of the individual's dependence upon God for both self-consciousness and the enabling power to master the division which characterizes his

and, thus, the abandonment of one's freedom. Once internal self-reflection is abandoned, freedom is likewise abandoned since the exercise, indeed the reality, of one's freedom depends upon a prior self-consciousness which is mediated by reflection. To be informed by another about oneself, then, is tantamount to an admission of dependence upon the other for the fulfillment of the task of freely actualizing one's *telos*. To allow another to inform one's self-consciousness is also to find one's possibility in that other.

We have seen that the determination of spirit as consciousness is spirit's first move toward becoming itself. Consciousness is, as we have seen, reflexive, for in consciousness spirit becomes aware of what it already is. Spirit's reflection of itself as consciousness constitutes freedom's possibility of itself. That is to say, the possibility of freedom is derived from spirit's reflection of itself as consciousness. Now Kierkegaard tells us that sin-consciousness is also a determination of spirit, but it is not a reflective determination because the consciousness of sin is mediated by a divine revelation. In this move, then, spirit does not become what it is, but it becomes another. In the consciousness of sin, the individual becomes something other than himself. The dialectical relation between consciousness and freedom, however, is maintained. Once the individual becomes conscious of himself as sinful, he must still make the further move of existentially appropriating the content of consciousness in existence. That is to say, once the individual becomes conscious of sin, he still must choose himself as, or become, sinful. To become sinful is an act of faith because there is no rational justification for the move. Once the individual relies upon a divine revelation for the determination of a level of consciousness, he abandons ethical reflection, and in so doing,

---

being. Faith is not simply a spontaneous feeling of dependence but an act of the will in which the existing individual chooses himself as being dependent upon the Deity in time.

he abandons the possibility of determining himself as free. He is now dependent upon the source of his consciousness of sin for the actualization of his possibility. He is dependent, then, upon the Deity in time.

This, it seems, is the reason for the accentuation of guilt as sin. In guilt-understanding, it cannot occur to the existing individual to look to another for self-understanding. The guilty individual still may repent, and although it is an act in which the individual contradicts the assumption of the ethical striving, it is still an act of freedom in which the individual hopes to overcome his failure to realize the ethical requirement. The consciousness of oneself as absolutely other than the possibility of fulfilling the ethical requirement can never occur to the individual apart from a divine communication in which he is informed of precisely this fact. The existential expression of oneself as "heterogeneous" with the ethical requirement is the necessary condition for dependence upon another through whom one's freedom is realized.

We have seen that the ethical requirement of actualizing one's absolute *telos* is not negated in sin. Indeed, one persists in sin only so long as the relationship of obligation with the ethical requirement is maintained. In faith, then, the existing individual does not relinquish his responsibility for actualizing his ideal *telos*. Faith, however, is to be distinguished from the preceding ethical striving by virtue of its new starting point. Ethics begins with the "You Shall" and proceeds with the assumption that the existing individual possesses the power to actualize the ideal. Faith, however, begins with the presupposition of sin and proceeds with the assumption that divine intervention is necessary for the realization of the requirement. In both cases, however, actualization of the ideal in existence remains the task and the responsibility of the existing individual.

Now Kierkegaard writes that the New Testament informs us that God is interested in the ethical individual.

In the New Testament it is precisely ideality, the intensive, one who is driven to the highest, which interests God. . . .[39]

Conversely, the ethical individual, who is striving to actualize his ideal *telos*, himself becomes interested in the New Testament. The existing individual discovers in the New Testament the incarnation of the ethical requirement. The Deity in time appears to him as the embodiment of this requirement, the ideal, who reaffirms his ethical struggle to exist by demanding that the individual be like him.

In the New Testament the criterion for being human is this: the New Testament contains the requirement, the God-man as the prototype—and every man, unconditionally every man of these countless millions, falls quite simply under this requirement without any nonsense or middle terms.[40]

According to Kierkegaard, "Christ is essentially the model, and consequently we should be 'like' him and not merely make use of him."[41] The Deity in time is the model for the existing individual, because he, unlike the existing individual, "possesses the ideal perfectly, and therefore does the noblest thing freely."[42]

In Kierkegaard's view, we find in the New Testament a reaffirmation of the divine sanction of the "ought" characterizing the preceding ethico-religious stage of existence. The ethical requirement is not abandoned in Religiousness B but reaffirmed in the person of the Deity in time. The requirement, now, is no longer sanctioned by a divine "postulate" but by the personal embodiment of the ideal itself.

---

[39] *SKJP*, II, 1807.

[40] *SKJP*, II, 1802. Cf. "Christianity has made being a human being as significant as possible—that is, being in kinship with God and striving to be like God, imitation." *SKJP*, II, 1803.

[41] *SKJ*, #698.   [42] *SKJ*, #1049.

But the Deity in time is not simply the ideal man in whom we find our humanity through imitation, as he is for Kant. The Deity in time, to be certain, is the model, but he is, as the model, also the one who forgives sin.

> If I try without further ado to act from a purely ethical standpoint I am taking the model in vain. . . . The model itself must help the one who is to imitate. And in one respect no one can be like it, nor even think of wishing to imitate it (that would be blasphemy), in so far as the model is our savior and atoner.[43]

The model of ideality is also the savior and atoner. Kierkegaard asserts that the existing individual must have the "courage to believe existentially in the ideal."[44] The courage of faith in the ideal does not simply mean the recognition and acceptance of the model as the prototypical man whom we are to imitate. Belief certainly requires this, but it also requires the much more radical existential appropriation of oneself as sinful. Belief requires not only the conviction that the model is the prototypical man but also the acceptance of oneself as heterogeneous with the ethical and in need of divine forgiveness if the ethical requirement is to be fulfilled.

Kierkegaard insists that to exist in the existence-medium of sin is a matter of faith, and now he adds that the notion of forgiveness of sin is equally a matter of faith. Moreover, it is through belief in the forgiveness of sin that the existing individual becomes spirit.

> To believe the forgiveness of one's sin is the decisive crisis whereby a human being becomes spirit; he who does not believe this is not spirit. . . . The forgiveness of sins is not a matter of particulars—as if on the whole one were good . . . no, it is just the opposite—it pertains not so much to the particulars as to the totality; it pertains to

---

[43] *SKJ*, #887.   [44] *SKJP*, II, 1781.

one's whole self, which is sinful and corrupts everything as soon as it comes in slightest contact with it.[45]

To accept the model as judge and atoner is, according to Kierkegaard, a free act in which the existing individual is elevated into an existence medium which ethics cannot comprehend but which, nevertheless, fulfills the very task of ethics, viz., the realization of spirit in individual existence through the fulfillment of the ethical requirement. Belief in the forgiveness of sin is required if the individual is to be helped to imitate the model. Imitation of the model requires that the individual possess the ideal perfectly and do the noblest thing freely. To possess the ideal freely means to become spirit. The fulfillment of the ethical requirement signifies that the individual has actualized himself in existence and has, therefore, become himself.

Now Kierkegaard refers to the individual's actualization of spirit as repetition.

> In case repetition is not posited, ethics remains a binding power; presumably it is for this reason he [Constantine Constantius] says "it is the solution in every ethical view." . . . In the sphere of nature, repetition exists in its immovable necessity. In the sphere of spirit the problem is not to get change out of repetition and find oneself comfortable under repetition, as though spirit stood only in an external relation to the repetitions of spirit. . . . The problem is to transform repetition into something inward, into the proper task of freedom, into freedom's highest interest, as to whether, while everything changes, it can actually realize repetition.[46]

As we have seen, repetition operates on two interrelated levels. The first level of repetition is the individual's repetition of his reality as ideality. In this move, the individual becomes conscious of himself. The second level of repetition

[45] *SKJP*, I, 67.   [46] *CD*, pp. 16-17n.

is the individual's repetition of himself as possible (ideal) in actuality. In the act of repetition the individual becomes spirit through the actualization of himself in existence. Kierkegaard maintains that "what is repeated has been, otherwise it could not be repeated."[47] The existing individual, in the act of repetition, becomes what he is, i.e., becomes himself.

Kierkegaard attempts to explain this movement by contrasting it with the Greek notion of recollection.

> When the Greeks said that all knowledge is recollection they affirmed that all that is has been; when one says that life is a repetition one affirms that existence which has been now becomes.[48]

In these strange words, Kierkegaard tries to express what is most crucial and fundamental about his system—namely, that the self can be restored to its original, pristine condition in existence. The emphasis in recollection is on the *has been*, while the emphasis in repetition is on *now becomes*. Greek recollection returns to what is already the case. It is essentially a backward movement into the past. Repetition is concerned with what was the case, but is a forward movement, whereby what has been is reappropriated in existence. In contrast to recollection, repetition is fundamentally a forward movement, oriented exclusively toward the future.

We are also informed that true repetition is eternity. That is to say, in the instant of repetition, the existing individual becomes eternal by virtue of his choice of the Deity in time as his eternal, divine ground. In choosing the Deity in time, the gap between his sinful self (past) and his eternal, divine ground, the Deity in time (future), is bridged in the present instant in which the self is grounded in its eternal, divine ground and, thereby returns to itself.

We might speak of the sacralization of time as the funda-

[47] Kierkegaard, *Repetition*, trans. Walter Lowrie (London: Oxford University Press, 1941), p. 52.
[48] *Ibid.*

mental creation of repetition. As we have continually noted, the self is in time, and the task of existence is the reflection of the self in time as possibility so that it can be reappropriated consciously and freely. The on-goingness of time, however, constantly throttles the individual's striving to take hold of himself in an act of freedom. The infinite on-goingness of time renders impossible the individual's appropriation of himself and the establishment of his eternal, divine ground. The future forever eludes the existing individual so long as he remains in time. The on-goingness of time and the culpability of freedom render him guilty and sinful. The only conceivable alternative is for the eternal, divine ground of the self to constitute itself. Now, for the individual, existing in faith, the past is the sinful self, the future his eternal, divine ground already actualized as the Deity in time, and the present the instant of their unification. When time and eternity intersect in the present instant, the timely self is completely grounded in its eternal, divine ground, thereby restoring its original and pristine unity.

This is the move which the individual could not make in the ethical striving which constitutes the pathos of Religiousness A. Only in faith does repetition begin.[49] This means, concretely, that the existing individual, simultaneously, admits to the fallibility of his freedom and submits himself to the freedom of God in order to accomplish what he cannot do for himself.

> The most tremendous thing which has been granted to man is: the choice of freedom. And if you desire to save it and preserve it there is only one way: in the very same second unconditionally and in complete resignation to give it back to God, and yourself with it.[50]

[49] *CD*, p. 17n.

[50] *SKJ*, #1051. It is precisely at this point, according to Kierkegaard, that the notion of divine providence meaningfully enters into consideration. We must not, warns Kierkegaard, think of providence apart from the problem of human freedom. *SKJP*, II, 1230. It is only in holding human freedom and divine providence together that the former can be

This is precisely the movement of faith. The individual preserves and fulfills his freedom ultimately by relying upon the freedom of God as the power by which the ethical requirement is fulfilled. This is what is implied in the assertion that repetition is the solution "in every ethical view."[51]

It is the solution in every ethical view because repetition realizes the ethical task of existence. The self as a synthesis of finitude and infinitude is actualized in existence by a free act. Unity is the achievement of repetition. Freedom's highest act is the unification of the self in existence. Kierkegaard gives a vivid account of this achievement in *Repetition*.

> I am again myself. This self which another would not pick up from the road I possess again. The discord in my nature is resolved, I am again unified. The terrors which found support and nourishment in my pride no longer enter in to distract and separate.[52]

The unification of one's self in existence is the goal of the individual's striving. This goal determines, as we have seen, the movement of existence, giving it its continuity and meaning. The individual's only goal is the actualization of his own self in complete concreteness in existence, and this goal is ultimately achieved in faith.[53] We have a *reintegratio*

---

existentially realized and the latter meaningfully understood. "If we consider how the doctrine of predestination has arisen, it is clear that as long as there is no consideration of any freedom which plays a role in the world, it is impossible for the question of predestination to arise. Only when the conception of human freedom had developed and in reflection was coupled with God's governance of the world, only then could it arise, and it had to make its appearance as an attempt to solve the problem. But in this connection it is nevertheless curious that the intended solution of the problem now constitutes for us the problem, namely, how the two concepts are to be united." *SKJP*, II, 1231.

[51] *CD*, p. 17n.   [52] *R*, p. 125.

[53] "The Christian heroism (and perhaps it is rarely to be seen) is to venture wholly to be oneself, as an individual man, this definite individual man, alone before the face of God, alone in this tremendous exertion and this tremendous responsibility. . . ." *SUD*, p. 142.

in statum pristinum. We have a reintegration of the self, a return to the self's pristine unity but with the paramount differences that this unity is intentional rather than accidental, conscious rather than ignorant, and existential rather than immediate.

It is clear that self-understanding is inextricably linked with self-actualization and that positive knowledge of one's self is constituted by the unification of the self in existence. In the act of faith, the ethical failure to achieve this positive knowledge is radically accentuated through the individual's existential expression of himself as a sinner. But faith is also the belief in the forgiveness of sin. The second movement of faith is the belief that the "suspension of the ethical" is itself suspended. Faith is the belief that the self's lost unity is restored in existence through the atoning significance of the existence of the Deity in time. The act of faith, then, is the paradigmatic expression of the principle of religious knowledge, viz., by the negative you will know the positive.

The second move of faith is impossible apart from the first. That is to say, there can be no positive knowledge of one's self except by means of the negative. The entire development of spirit up to the achievement of guilt-understanding and repentance is one continually developing negative movement. The consciousness of sin is a continuation of this movement, because sin is a radical accentuation of the direction of this movement. To exist in faith is to believe that one is absolutely separated from one's self and God and absolutely incapable of restoring the self's lost unity in the divine ground. To come back to one's self through the help of another requires the negation of the notion that one can come back to one's self through one's own power. Faith, then, requires this double movement. First, the individual must abandon this notion that his own freedom can existentially unify himself, and second, the existential assertion of one's helplessness is the condition whereby the individual comes back to himself through the help of another. The positive, then, is known by the negative. The realization of one's self in the divine ground requires, first, a radical separation from one's self and God in the existential medium of sin.

We must not forget, however, that Kierkegaard is never more right than when he affirms that faith is a leap. It is literally just that, because there is neither rational justification for the move nor logical certainty that the move of faith will overcome the wretchedness of existence. There can be no logical demonstration of the unity of God and man. But neither is faith an irrational and totally discontinuous act. For what it presupposes and hopes for has already been clearly and firmly established. Faith presupposes a definition of the self and the notion that the task of existence is an ethical one in which the individual actualizes and understands himself in existence. Faith hopes for the realization of this task and the attainment of happiness through the establishment of a God-relationship. The act of faith, then, is deeply situated in a prior ethico-religious understanding of the nature and purpose of human existence. Sponheim has seen very clearly this relation between the act of faith and the preceding ethico-religious understanding of the nature and purpose of existence.

> But surely it seems more correct to see Kierkegaard's conception of the Christian's passion as the fulfillment rather than the repudiation of his understanding of the nature of the human spirit set in existence.[54]

[54] Paul Sponheim, *Kierkegaard on Christ and Christian Coherence* (New York: Harper and Row, 1968), p. 38. Cornelio Fabro sees Religiousness A as having a propaedeutic value. "For Kierkegaard, Religiousness A is true religiousness, and in the spiritual structure of man it has the same positive value that it had in the course of history. . . . It is first of all necessary to have authentic men ready to fulfill the duties that come from human nature as such. Religiousness A must already be present, therefore, before any attention can be given to the dialectic of the other. It is necessary that the individual be already in relation with the eternal beatitude, in the purest expression of any existential 'pathos,' as was the case with Socrates, before any question

In this sense, then, faith is an act which is explicitly and understandably continuous with the preceding development of spirit. Faith accepts the already established fact that the individual's self is a synthesis and that he has the ethical task of actualizing that synthesis as a relation (unity) in existence.

But the act of faith is also discontinuous. Its discontinuity is grounded in the individual's recognition of the failure of his freedom to fulfill the ethical task of existence. In the act of faith, a relationship of dependence is established in which the individual depends upon a divine communication for both his consciousness of himself as sinful and the power by which he overcomes his sinful condition and realizes himself as an existential unity. Such an act, according to Kierkegaard, is absurd for human reason but not so for one who is existentially engaged in the pursuit of himself.

> When the believer has Faith, the Absurd is not the Absurd—Faith transforms it; but in every weak moment it is again more or less absurd to him. The passion of faith is the only thing which masters the absurd—if not, then, faith is not faith in the strictest sense, but a kind of knowledge.[55]

For the existing individual, the object of faith is not fundamentally a challenge to objective reason or understanding. The Deity in time is, rather, a challenge to his existence as a whole. The issue is not how he, when confronted with the paradox of the Deity in time, is to resolve intellectually a paradox. The issue is, rather, whether the existing individual will accept the God-man as the resolution to the prob-

---

can arise of this dialectic raised to the second power which throws a man into the 'pathos' of the paradox." Cornelio Fabro, "Faith and Reason in Kierkegaard's Dialectic," trans. J. B. Mondin, *A Kierkegaard Critique*, ed. Niels Thulstrup and Howard Johnson (Chicago: Henry Regnery, Gateway Edition, 1962), p. 191. Cf. Weiland, *Philosophy and Christianity*, pp. 117-118.

55 *SKJP*, I, 10.

lem of his existence. The paradox is, indeed, absurd when the existing individual forgets himself and confronts the paradox objectively. In Michalson's words, "when Christianity announces the presence of God in Jesus of Nazareth, it offends anyone who relates himself to the world objectively. That is the intention of the paradox: to discourage efforts at appropriation which omit one's existence from the reality appropriated."[56] For faith, the paradox is not absurd; it is a challenge to the existing individual to risk dependence upon another as the way to the realization of the ethical requirement. Kierkegaard writes that to a third party

> the believer relates himself by virtue of the absurd; so must a third person judge, for a third person does not have the passion of faith. Johannes de silentio [the pseudonym for *Fear and Trembling*] has never claimed to be a believer; just the opposite, he has explained that he is not a believer—in order to illuminate faith negatively.[57]

The object of faith is absurd for the one who sees it from outside the struggle to exist as an ethical human being.

Thus, the primary concern of the Christian paradox of the God-man is the individual in existence. To become one's self in existence and to believe the paradox are not two different and unrelated tasks. The two tasks, in fact, are inseparably linked. It is impossible for the individual to become himself apart from belief in the paradox, and belief in the paradox is not possible apart from a preceding striving with the task to become one's self by fulfilling the ethical requirement. Existence and the paradox, then, are linked in the individual's striving to realize the ethical requirement in existence.[58]

[56] Carl Michalson, "Kierkegaard's Theology of Faith," *Religion in Life,* XXXII (Spring 1963), 235.

[57] *SKJP*, I, 10.

[58] Fabro correctly argues that "the object of faith is the absurd, the paradox, which is the inevitable cause of scandal, but only for whoever

In Kierkegaard's view, the Christian paradox is an advance on the Socratic paradox. According to Kierkegaard, Socrates maintains that for the existing individual the eternal can never be a static and secure possession. The individual is always striving to maintain the relationship. Moreover the relationship between the existing individual and the eternal is one of contradiction. The eternal itself, however, contains no contradiction and becomes so only in relation to an existing individual. The Socratic paradox consists in the fact that the eternal and the existing individual are related in existence. The difference between this paradox and the Christian paradox (*paradox sensu strictiori*) is expressed as follows:

> Forgiveness is a paradox in the Socratic sense, in so far as it involves a relationship between the eternal truth and an existing individual; it is a paradox *sensu strictiori*, because the existing individual is stamped as a sinner, by which existence is accentuated a second time, and because it purports to be an eternal decision in time with retroactive power to annul the past, and because it is linked with the existence of God in time.[59]

Kierkegaard's understanding of the absolute paradox entails the notions of sin, existence marked a second time, and the Deity in time. According to Kierkegaard, both notions defy logical demonstration or empirical verification and are, as such, matters for faith.

Traditionally the term paradox has been understood as

---

sees this object from the outside, i.e., for him who has no faith. . . .
For the believer, for the man of faith, this object is neither absurd
nor paradoxical: by virtue of faith his criterion is God, for whom all
things are possible; in the light of faith he sees that this absurd, far
from being a contradiction, is the one truth which saves. . . ." Fabro,
"Faith and Reason," p. 179.

[59] *CUP*, p. 201.

something which is either *contra rationem*[60] or *super rationem*.[61] In either case, the maintenance of the paradox signifies opposition to a rationalistic attitude. When the paradox is understood as being against reason, it will seek to defeat the rationalistic attitude with its own categories. Tertullian's *credo quia absurdum* is a clear example of this kind of paradoxical thinking. When the paradox is understood as being beyond reason, one leaves the rationalistic battle-field as quickly as possible. An attempt is made to transcend the categories of reason as a means of knowing a certain subject matter. Schleiermacher's characterization of religion as *weder ein Wissen noch ein Tun*, neither knowing nor acting, is a good example. Religious understanding is rooted in the awareness of absolute and unconditional dependence in immediate self-consciousness. Schleiermacher himself does not use the term paradox, but the sharp opposition between theoretical knowing and belief exemplifies the meaning of *super rationem*.

In both cases, paradoxical belief is always in conflict with and determined by reason itself. Either against or beyond reason means only that the object of belief is antirationalistic and involves the believer in a confrontation with reason. Now Kierkegaard speaks often enough in *Concluding Unscientific Postscript* of the necessity "to believe against the

[60] For a discussion of Kierkegaard's view of faith and the paradox as being "against" reason, see J. Weldon Smith, III, "Religion A and Religion B: A Kierkegaard Study," *Scottish Journal of Theology*, xv (March 1962), 245-265.

[61] The more popular position has been that Kierkegaard views the Christian religion as "beyond" reason. Emmanuel Hirsch, for example, argues that the paradox is not governed by dialectical or dogmatic concerns but that it intends to safeguard the purity of personal religious experience from intrusion by rationalistic factors. Emmanuel Hirsch, *Kierkegaard-Studien*, 2 vols. (Gutersloh: C. Bertelsmann, 1930-1933). This view of the paradox is also supported by N. H. Soe in "Kierkegaard's Doctrine of the Paradox," *A Kierkegaard Critique*, pp. 156-207.

understanding."[62] However, Lonning persuasively argues that the context of this terminology "indicates that 'reason' here is meant in a sense quite different from the one usual in philosophy as well as in every day conversation. 'Reason' stands for 'objectivity' which again is the non-existential attitude of self-objectification."[63] To approach the paradox objectively certainly requires belief against the understanding, but the mode of understanding, which we have come to know through our analysis of Kierkegaard's dialectical development of spirit, is not an objective mode of understanding but is, on the contrary, fundamentally and essentially subjective in nature. It is within this mode of understanding that the paradox is encountered, and it is this mode of understanding which gives rise to the paradox.

Kierkegaard writes in his journals that if understanding —here he means the subjective understanding—is to understand itself,

> it would simply have to posit the paradox. The paradox is not a concession but a category, an ontological definition which expresses the relation between an *existing cognitive spirit and eternal truth.*[64]

This assertion, it appears to me, forces us out of the traditional ways of understanding the meaning of paradox. The paradox is not simply a category of the objective understanding which signifies the relation between theoretical and objective understanding and belief; on the contrary, it is a category which signifies the relation of the whole person, the existing cognitive spirit, to the Deity in time. Lonning again correctly argues that the "primary concern of the paradox is not reason, but I, the existent I, the individual entirely separated from God and entirely loved by

[62] *CUP*, pp. 501, 502, 503, 504.

[63] Per Lonning, "Kierkegaard's 'Paradox,'" *Kierkegaard Symposion* (Copenhagen: Munksgaard, 1955), p. 163.

[64] *SKJ*, pp. 117-118.

God."[65] When approached from the standpoint of objective understanding, the battle over whether faith is either against or beyond reason is certainly relevant and to a point, and, in either case, faith will certainly appear to be absurd. But when the paradox is understood in relation to existence, these lines of debate fall away, and the issue becomes one of determining how existence and the Deity in time are in fact related.

In two passages from *Concluding Unscientific Postscript*, Kierkegaard asserts that the paradox and passion are a "mutual fit." Concerning the existentially conditioned nature of the paradox, Kierkegaard asserts that

the paradox is not a transitory form of the relation of the religious in its stricter sense to the existing subject; *but is essentially conditioned by the fact that a man is in existence*, so that the explanation which takes away the paradox fantastically transforms at the same time the exister into a fantastic something or another which belongs neither to time nor to eternity—but such a something or another is not a man.[66]

And concerning the mutuality of passion and paradox, Kierkegaard writes that

subjectivity culminates in passion, Christianity is the paradox, paradox and passion are a mutual fit, and the paradox is altogether suited to one whose situation is, to be in the extremity of existence.[67]

[65] Lonning, "Kierkegaard's 'Paradox,'" p. 164. Thomas comes very close to this position when he writes that "because this doctrine [of the paradox] is related to the person's mode of existence it cannot be something that demands simply an effort of understanding. Therefore once more the ethical or ethico-religious meaning of the Paradox becomes clear." J. Heywood Thomas, *Subjectivity and Paradox* (Oxford: Basil Blackwell, 1957), pp. 128-129.

[66] *CUP*, p. 162. Italics mine.   [67] *Ibid.*, p. 206.

To assert that existence conditions the paradox is not to imply that existence, in its most extreme passion, creates the paradox. There is, as we have seen, in Kierkegaard's thought the presence of a transcendent fact which is not the product of human reason. The absolute paradox is the free expression of God's love and concern for the individual exister. By arguing that existence conditions the paradox, Kierkegaard means to say that the two are dialectically dependent. Existence and the paradox are related in the way that sunrise and sunset are related. One cannot be understood or be complete without the other.

To reach the most remote extremity of existence is the condition for the existence of the paradox itself.

> In [Religiousness] A, the fact of existing, my existence, is a moment within my eternal consciousness . . . and is thus a lowlier thing which prevents me from being the infinitely higher thing I am. Conversely, in [Religiousness] B the fact of existing, although it is a still lowlier thing as it is paradoxically accentuated [as sin], is yet so much higher that only in existing do I become eternal, *and consequently the thing of existing gives rise to a determinant which is infinitely higher than existence.*[68]

The emergence of the paradox as an existential determinant is contingent upon the penetration of the extremity of existence. The existing individual discovers his transcendent ground only by penetrating the depths of himself, whereby he is cast upon the extremity of human existence. The paradox itself is an impotent and meaningless jumble of logical contradictions when approached from outside the extremity of the human situation. The dialectical dependence of these two phenomena is underlined in Kierkegaard's contention that the attempt to explain the paradox destroys both existence and the paradox. One can ask about the meaning of the paradox only from within the existential arena, and in such asking, the individual knows simultaneously both him-

[68] *Ibid.*, p. 508. Italics mine.

self and the paradox. To come to the paradox with the intention of demonstrating its logical necessity means that the individual has already ceased to exist in which case both existence and the paradox elude him. To inquire about the meaning of the paradox within the context of the prior question of one's own possibility is to discover that both the paradox and one's own possibility are understood exclusively within the union of one with the other. There is no knowledge of one's self apart from the paradox and no knowledge of the paradox apart from a knowledge of one's self.

Now Kierkegaard asserts that the paradox and passion are a mutual fit. That is to say, the paradox is altogether suited to the individual who finds himself in the extremity of existence. On the outer limits of existence, the individual discovers a deep and unbridgeable chasm within himself. He is tormented by guilt and despair over his failure to fulfill the ethical requirement. He has failed to obtain happiness and positive knowledge of himself and God by establishing an eternal God-relationship. The deep division within himself is unbridgeable, and yet, the individual knows that only by healing the breach can the requirement be fulfilled and happiness and self-knowledge obtained. The Deity in time then appears before the despairing individual. Before his despairing consciousness appears an incarnation of the ethical requirement, a paradoxical unity of the antinomies of his own self.[69] The individual is now confronted with the historical actuality of his divine ground. The eternal no longer eludes him. He is no longer responsible for actualizing the divine ground of his own being. It is

---

[69] David Roberts has offered the idea that Kierkegaard's "view of human nature as a synthesis of eternity and temporality, infinitude and finitude, freedom and necessity, coincides perfectly with his view of the God-man as a paradoxical union of these same antinomies." Roberts, unfortunately, leaves this fertile thought entirely undeveloped. David Roberts, *Existentialism and Religious Belief* (New York: Oxford University Press, 1957), p. 81.

already present in time, and all that is required of him is an act of faith in which he submits to his own powerlessness, on the one hand, and to the power of God, on the other. In this submission of total dependence, he grounds himself in the historical actuality of the divine, and the task of existence is accomplished. Passion and paradox are, indeed, a mutual fit.

Properly understood, then, faith is neither against nor beyond reason. If the paradox is conceived exclusively as a challenge to the objective mode of understanding and faith is regarded exclusively as believing against the understanding, then the move to Religiousness B must be construed as a move engaging certain aspects of the individual's nature, while disengaging others. Indeed, faith would have to be conceived as a blind, i.e., irrational, act of will, aided perhaps by some emotional experience. The rational aspects of one's nature would be operative in all areas of one's life excluding one's religion. Such a religion, ultimately, divides rather than heals, makes whole, an individual exister.

The understanding simply is not summarily abandoned with the move of faith. As we have seen, faith is explicitly continuous with the preceding development of spirit which has been mediated by the understanding. Faith's continuity with the preceding development of spirit is situated in its acknowledgment of the ethical task of existence as its own. The issue for faith is also the fulfillment of the ethical requirement. Faith, then, is explicitly continuous with the preceding levels of the ethico-religious stage of spirit's development. But faith is equally discontinuous. We have already noted that faith believes against the objective understanding because it rejects the self-objectifying requirement of objectivity as sufficient for the resolution of the problem of one's own existence. This does not constitute, however, the real discontinuity of faith and understanding, for faith is in a real sense discontinuous with subjective understanding as well. Faith is subjective understanding's paradoxical expression of its inability to realize its task by itself.[70] This constitutes the discontinuity of faith.

The move of faith involves the whole person in an affirmation of total dependence upon another for both self-understanding and self-actualization. Such dependence involves the individual reflectively, willfully, and emotionally. Nothing is excluded, and no particular faculty is more prominent in its dependence than any other. Reflection depends upon a divine communication concerning the sinful nature of the individual's self. The individual's freedom depends upon the freedom of God in order to overcome the sinful chasm in himself through the realization of the ethical requirement. Happiness depends upon the submission of reflection and will to the freedom of God in order to accomplish the ethical task which the individual discovers within himself. When the paradox and the act of faith are understood in this way, the whole argument over whether faith is either against or beyond reason loses its force and falls into insignificance.

Now it has already been made clear that self-understanding is inextricably linked with self-actualization and that positive knowledge of one's self is constituted by overcoming negative knowledge of one's self through the unification of the self in existence. In the realm of knowledge, according to Kierkegaard, spirit

is not to determine through an infinite development what it is to become, but it is to become through development

[70] Soe is very close to this point when he points out that it is the "heart" and not the "mind" which is offended in *PF*, p. 86. He writes that "here the offense caused by the paradox is not seen in relation to the mind but to the heart. Kierkegaard does not elaborate this further. That this remark should occur in this particular work is astonishing and therefore worthy of attention. It indicates, undoubtedly, that Kierkegaard's awareness of the fact that the Incarnation, as he understood it, does cause offense as it wounds self-confidence." Soe, "Kierkegaard's Doctrine of the Paradox," p. 216.

that which it is. . . . It is not to produce through development a new thing but it is to acquire through development what it has.[71]

This attained unity takes the concrete form of an ethical individual who, in an act of faith, has realized the ethical requirement to actualize his absolute *telos*. In the instant, the existing individual gains a concrete understanding of himself as an existential unity which is grounded in the divine. Kierkegaard expresses this achievement more clearly when he writes that the existing individual has become "contemporaneous" with and "transparent" to himself.

All men desire to be or to become "contemporary" with great men, great events, etc.—but only God knows how many men really live contemporaneously with themselves. To be contemporary with oneself (therefore neither in the future of fear or expectation nor in the past) is transparency in repose, and this is possible only in the God-relationship, or it is the God-relationship.[72]

To be contemporaneous with one's self is to transform one's reality or necessity into existence through its actualization as the ethical requirement. It is to possess one's facticity in existence through its realization as the absolute *telos*. To be contemporaneous with one's self is to exist in the instant, i.e., to synthesize one's past and future in the present. To gain contemporaneity with one's self is the achievement of faith. Kierkegaard writes that "by willing to be itself, the self is grounded transparently in the Power which constituted it. And this formula again, as has often been noted, is the definition of faith."[73] The achievement of this instant is the gaining of "transparency," for in this ethical achievement, the individual fully understands himself as a free being who has realized himself concretely in existence. It is an instant of spiritual transparency, for the individual's *Was-Sein* coheres perfectly and completely with its *Wie-Sein*.

[71] *SKJP*, II, 2274.   [72] *SKJP*, I, 1050.   [73] *SUD*, p. 262.

The duality of the individual's self is overcome and a perfect and harmonious unity is actualized in the existence of the single individual.

Self-knowledge is the God-relationship. To be contemporaneous with one's self is to be transparent to one's self, and this is possible, according to Kierkegaard, only in the God-relationship. Apart from a God-relationship, there can be no unity or self-knowledge.

> If a man did not have absolute need of God he could not (1) know himself—self knowledge, (2) be immortal [unified].[74]

Belief in the forgiveness of sin is an acceptance of the atoning significance of the existence of the Deity in time, and it is only in the moment in which the "suspension of the ethical" is itself suspended that unity is attained in individual existence. An act of faith, then, is the condition for the realization of unity and self-knowledge. Existential unification of the self is, then, grounded in the divine, or, in Kierkegaard's words, "it is the God-relationship." And in the God-relationship, the cycle of spirit's development is complete. The self has returned to itself, and the individual can say with Kierkegaard:

> I am again myself. The self which another would not pick up from the road I possess again. The discord in my nature is resolved, I am again unified.[75]

CONCLUSION

We have seen that spirit is the third element of the self. It is that element which actualizes the self, and in so doing, constitutes existence. *Existence is the outgrowth of the self*

---

[74] *SKJP*, I, 53.

[75] *R*, p. 125. Cf. "There are only three positions on the relation between faith and knowledge. (1) Paul: I know what I have believed. (2) *Credo ut intelligam*. (3) Faith is spontaneity. In all of them knowledge comes after faith." *SKJP*, II, 1111.

coming to a knowledge of itself. The dialectical development of spirit is, therefore, a transformation of the immediate self into a fully existential self. It is on this continuum of self-seeking and self-actualization that Christianity (Religiousness B), as an "existence-communication,"[76] makes its appearance. Kierkegaard never more accurately defines Christianity than when he defines it as an "existence-communication." Existence is, as we have seen, self-understanding mediated by freedom. Christianity is, according to Kierkegaard, the communication of true consciousness (sin-consciousness) and the power by which this alienation from one's self and God is overcome. To exist, then, as a Christian is simply to become and to understand one's self. Christianity is, in the strictest sense, the culmination of the development of spirit.

Kierkegaard has reversed the Hegelian relation of faith and reason. Faith is, according to the Hegelian dialectic, an immediacy which reason dialectically penetrates, thereby bringing its content to the level of knowledge. The only difference between the content of faith and the content of reason is that the former is brought to the level of consciousness by the latter. Kierkegaard reverses this relation by arguing that faith is a higher mode of consciousness by which the content of reason (Religiousness A) is brought to consciousness. Faith is a mode of understanding which understands perfectly what reflection, as a mode of knowing, understood only incompletely. Viewed in this light, one can say that in repentance, the highest act of reflective penetration of one's self, the individual remains unconscious of himself. But reflection is the necessary propaedeutic of faith. Faith requires reflection because without reflection there is nothing for faith to know. In order for the faithful individual to know both the self and its eternal ground as "paradoxically accentuated," he must first know reflectively, i.e., immanently, the self and its eternal ground. This latter level of knowing constitutes the achievement of the dia-

76 *CUP*, pp. 497, 501, 507.

lectic up to the point of faith and the emergence of Religiousness B.

Christianity, according to Kierkegaard, must then be understood in a strictly dialectical manner. That is to say, its existence can occur only at a certain point, the culminating point, in the dialectical development of spirit. The divine communication and the human response of faith constitute a continuation of the movement of spirit which is motivated originally by interested reflection. The individual's *Was-Sein*, i.e., his public and vocational being, is in no sense altered by his confrontation with the divine communication. The task of existence continues to be the realization of the ethical requirement to actualize one's absolute *telos* as a divine imperative. The task of existence, then, is not in any sense abrogated by the move to Christianity. Moreover, the fulfillment of the requirement continues to be the single condition for the attainment of happiness and self-understanding. The divine communication and the individual's response of faith do not escape, then, the ethico-ontological matrix of existence. Christianity clarifies one's understanding of what it means to be a self and enables the individual to become that self in existence.

We must conclude that the self is the Archimedean point in Kierkegaard's thought. The fact of its centrality allows for the continuity of spirit's development through all the stages of existence. The transition from Religiousness A to Religiousness B tends to become murky and opaque, even muddled, unless we keep this single point in view. In a passage from the center of *Concluding Unscientific Postscript*, Kierkegaard explicitly states that the self and the task of existence as self-understanding are central to an understanding of both modes of religious existence.

To understand oneself in existence is also the Christian principle, except that this "self" has received far richer and deeper determination [*sic*], still more difficult to understand, in conjunction with existence. . . . Here again the "self" is not humanity in general, or subjectivity in general, in which case everything becomes easy because the difficulty is removed, and the whole task transferred to the realm of abstract thought with its shadow-boxing. The difficulty is greater than it was for the Greek, because still greater contradictions are conjoined, existence being accentuated paradoxically as sin, and eternity accentuated paradoxically as God in time. The difficulty consists in existing in such categories, not in abstractly thinking oneself out of them; abstractly thinking, for example, about the eternal God-becoming and the like, all of which ideas emerge as soon as the difficulty is taken away.[77]

How are we to understand this enigmatic passage? It appears that its single dominating theme, viz., the independent and autonomous nature of the self, provides the key. The independence of the self implies that Kierkegaard formulates a definition of the self without metaphysical, theological, or religious presuppositions which are determinative of the definition as a whole. We have seen that the definition contains a religious dimension, *but this dimension is a constituent of and not a determination of the definition of the whole.* The autonomy of the self implies that it has its own teleology quite apart from any Christian interpretation of it. Indeed, we have seen that Christianity is interpreted by Kierkegaard in terms of the structure and teleology of the self. Furthermore, the passage states that both Socrates and Christianity are concerned with the same self and that for both the ethical task of existence is construed in terms of understanding or knowing that self in existence. The only difference between the two selves lies in the Christian "paradoxical accentuation" of the temporal and eternal poles of the self so that it becomes "still more difficult" to understand one's self in existence. Now, if the Christian self is an accentuation of the Socratic self, it follows that it is impossi-

[77] *CUP*, p. 316.

ble to exist as a Christian, i.e., to know one's self through the Christian categories of sin and the God in time, until one has first understood the meaning of existing as a self *qua* self.[78] How else would it be possible to accentuate the Socratic self?

The divine communication exhibits, then, a profound respect for the simple givenness of the self. Specifically, it presupposes an explicit and already established self which may be defined as a synthesis of opposing moments. It presupposes the notion that the task of existence is an ethical one in which the individual actualizes and understands himself. Moreover, to exist as a Christian means to hope for the realization of this task and the attainment of happiness and self-knowledge through the establishment of a God-relationship. In short, Kierkegaard's conception of Christianity is deeply situated in and influenced by a prior ethico-religious understanding (Religiousness A) of the nature and purpose of human existence.

I do not mean to imply that Kierkegaard's conception of Christianity can be reduced to ontology. As has been noted, there is the irrefutable presence in his thought of a divine act by which God freely enters into time. Kierkegaard undeniably affirms that the appearance of the Deity in time is demonstrative of a free act of a transcendent God. But Kierkegaard's interpretation of the Deity in time as a communication of divine knowledge and divine power in the person of the Deity in time, it seems to me, is precipitated and controlled by his prior understanding of the self, individual existence, and ethics as the triadic constituents of the nature, meaning, and purpose of human life, This triad determines not only Kierkegaard's conception of Christianity but also, along with his theory of knowledge, it determines his

[78] Kierkegaard will not have it any other way. The dialectical nature of Christianity simply must be maintained. "If we overleap the dialectical, Christianity as a whole becomes a comfortable delusion, a superstition, and a superstition of the most dangerous kind, because it is overbelief in the truth, if Christianity be the truth." *CUP*, p. 385.

view of the conditions under which Christianity becomes a possibility for an individual human being.

I have already noted that his epistemology requires that the individual discover his self-being in existence. The individual cannot have rationalistic access to his own being. If he is to know himself, he must know himself through choosing himself in existence. Now this process of self-knowing reaches a crucial stage with repentance because the act of repentance exhausts the power and range of reflection. If the task is still not complete, then the individual is forced to abandon the reflective process for another means of self-understanding and self-actualization. At this point, as we have seen, the dialectic turns toward an encounter with the Deity in time as the means by which the development of spirit is completed. But Kierkegaard's rigorous enslavement of knowledge to subjectivity is strictly adhered to with respect to one's knowledge of the being of God as well. The assertion that the eternal has come into time is an ontological assertion, because it is a proposition concerning the relation between two modes of being. But the existing individual, stranded as he is in the act of repentance, cannot suddenly abandon existence in order to engage theoretically this event of the Deity in time as an ontological problem. To do so would entail nothing less than the complete abandonment of existence. No, the only alternative open to the individual is the choice of the Deity in time. Just as the individual discovered his own being in the choice of himself, so he discovers the healing reality of the being of God through the choice of the Deity in time. In both instances, the knowledge of being is understood in existence by virtue of its actualization through freedom.

Since the individual does not have rationalistic access to his being, he knows himself only in the choice of himself, in the existential action of his freedom. Deprived, then, of all access to his own self except through existence, it is equally impossible for him to have any access, except existential access, to the resolution of the breach which he discovers in his own self. He cannot resort to any form of theism, to rationalistic metaphysics, or to mysticism at this point without denying the epistemological principle to which he has fully committed himself. There can be no turning back to any sort of reflection without at the same time sacrificing all the ground that one has gained. Either there is an existential solution to the problem of the individual's being or there is no solution at all. One must make either the choice of the Deity in time or the choice of one's self as permanently divided.

To become one's self requires, then, the existential choice of the Deity in time. Such a choice enables the individual to become and to understand himself through the realization of the ethical requirement. This is the task of existence. The divine grounding of the self, then, must be construed in terms of the divine's contribution to the realization of the ethical requirement. To understand one's relation to the divine in any other way than in terms of the ethical requirement and the quest for self-knowledge would involve either an alteration of one's understanding of the task of existence or a dismissal of Christianity as irrelevant to the real issue of one's existence. That is to say, to interpret one's relation to the divine apart from the ethical task of existence would require either the abandonment of the task itself or the rejection of Christianity. Kierkegaard does not require either alternative. Religion, then, according to Kierkegaard, inevitably derives its importance from its relation to the ethical task of existence.

The postulary nature of the divine in Religiousness A certainly accentuates the ethical requirement to the point that duty comes to be understood as obedience. The transformation occurring in the existence of one who relates to his absolute *telos* out of a sense of obedience certainly attests to the power of the postulate. But the ultimate mediation of the division which develops in the individual's self requires more than a postulary Deity. What is in fact required is a Deity who can communicate knowledge to the

251

individual exister concerning the nature of the division in the self. Only the Deity who possesses the power to communicate the truth to the existing individual has the power to heal the breach in the individual's self. The divine postulate of Religiousness A is powerless precisely because it is powerless to communicate any knowledge to the individual concerning the nature of his being. The only Deity who has power to heal the breach in the individual's self is the Deity who communicates the true nature of the breach itself. Such a communication requires a divine act, and this divine intervention occurs in the appearance of the Deity in time. By appearing in time, the Deity communicates to the individual the knowledge that the eternal grounding of the self depends upon the action of the eternal rather than upon the action of the individual's freedom alone. The Deity's existence in time is knowledge, i.e., the knowledge that the individual is eternally separated from his eternal ground and, thus, from himself. And the shift of the source of self-knowledge from the individual to the divine signals the shift of power from the individual to the divine. "You shall know the truth, and the truth will make you free."[79] Kierkegaard, to my knowledge, does not ever use this Biblical passage, but it precisely expresses his understanding of the kerygma. Divine power to make the individual free is present in the divine truth that the individual is a sinner and that only the Deity in time can mediate the division in his being.

Christianity, then, is a divine communication of knowledge and enabling power. Christianity is saving knowledge and power. Christianity affirms that God knows man better than he knows himself. This is why man, ultimately, must view himself through the eyes of God. In so doing, man sees more clearly, more correctly, more truthfully what he has already seen before. To know one's self, then, by means of a divine communication is to exist in the God-relationship and, thus, to become one's self in existence.

[79] John 8:32.

Conclusion

A Christian Philosophy of Spirit

I have attempted to understand the self as the organizing principle in Kierkegaard's pseudonymous works and am now in a position to venture some concluding remarks concerning this interpretation itself. The following thoughts are not intended as a final and definitive interpretation of Kierkegaard's pseudonymous corpus. They are not offered in a dogmatically conclusive spirit. They serve only to reflect a light in which this interpretation of Kierkegaard can be summarily expressed and understood.

I have attempted to steer an even course between those existentialist interpretations of Kierkegaard's thought which wanted to remove "the sting of one's life before God and eternity,"[1] and Neo-orthodox theology which saw in his thought only its religious dimension. I have avoided picking and choosing those aspects of his thought which support either of these positions and have, on the contrary, attempted to demonstrate the coherence of these two dimensions of his thought in the pseudonymous works.

To this end, I have argued for the following major points: (1) There is in Kierkegaard's pseudonymous thought an ontology which is present in his concept of the self. (2) This self is autonomous and absolute. (3) This dialectically structured self gives rise to the reality of ethics, which establishes the task of existence as the striving of the individual to realize and understand himself through the fulfillment of the ethical requirement to actualize one's absolute *telos*.

[1] James Collins, *The Mind of Kierkegaard* (Chicago: Henry Regnery, 1953), p. 243.

i.e., one's self. (4) I have argued that the striving to achieve this goal involves, preliminarily, the affirmation of divinity as immanent in ethical acting and knowing, and ultimately, the affirmation of the Deity in time as the divine manifestation of one's task as already accomplished. (5) I have maintained that the affirmation of the autonomy of the self need not be regarded as a challenge to religious truth, but, on the contrary, that the autonomous self in its development in the individual exister refers to the religious, in its second and stricter sense, as its truth. Religious faith, rather than contravening the autonomy of the self, is its highest and most concrete assertion. Kierkegaard is attempting to reconcile subjective reflection and religious faith.

We saw that religious faith, when encountered, does not deny that the self is a process but, on the contrary, affirms this self-development and self-understanding by bringing it to its conclusion. The self-active nature of the self is not contravened by the faithful affirmation of the Deity in time but is intensified to its highest level of self-actualization by it. We saw that the Deity in time is not simply "wholly other" than the human. Such a Deity would simply destroy the individual and his selfhood, and this is not a real or genuine religious possibility. Self-destruction is not the consequence of religious faith. It is certainly true that in the encounter with the divine other the self is dissolved in the individual's expression of final dependence upon the other for self-knowledge and enabling power. But the individual recognizes this, and it is precisely this recognition and acceptance of dependence which constitutes the relationship. The individual recognizes himself as dependent and the divine other as that upon which he is dependent. This recognition is a free act of surrender, and in this acceptance of dependence the self is, as it were, dissolved. But it is precisely in this self-dissolution that the individual gains himself.

Were it the case that the self is either completely obliterated or radically redefined with respect to its nature and purpose, we could speak of two radically different and totally unrelated levels of truth, viz., the truth of the self before and of the self after its encounter with the Deity in time. But this is not the case, for we discover in religious faith an explicit reaffirmation of the nature and purpose of the self as it is ethically understood. Therefore, we must think of these two levels of consciousness as a unity, a totality. The Christian communication has been inextricably linked with the nature and destiny of the autonomous and absolute self. *The ethical self's conflict between reality (necessity) and ideality (possibility) and its drive for reconciliation with itself in individual existence becomes the reality in which the Christian communication is situated and understood.* The notion of the self as a conflict between reality and ideality, which is to be explained by a prior unity which the individual is striving to reinstate, is the matrix in which Kierkegaard's understanding of religious faith is situated.

Kierkegaard accepts the modern notion[2] that the ethical pursuit of one's self as an ideal is unsurpassable, and that the pursuit—however inadequately achieved by the ethical self—is the unrevokable requirement of existence. The tension within the self is never reconciled by the ethical individual. The drive to return to oneself can never be satisfied by the ethical individual. The division within the self is

2 By the modern notion of the self, we mean the concept of the moral self running through the philosophies of Kant, Fichte, Schelling, and Hegel. The self is conceived as a process of moral activity which requires the recognition and production of its own freedom. The acknowledgment of its freedom constitutes a moral process in which a conflict arises between what the particular and real self is and what, as universal and ideal, it ought to be. This self is forever striving to unify this split in its being. As an example, Schelling refers to Fichte's moral philosophy as an "idealism of the finite self." He means that Fichte's self is a finite self in the sense that it takes infinity as an ideal which it forever aims at but never attains. It is this gulf between a finite self and its infinite ideal which Schelling and then Hegel attempt to bridge. And it is this modern notion of the self which is at the roots of Kierkegaard's own understanding of the human self.

overcome only because the individual recognizes that what ethical striving seeks to produce, viz., unity, already *is* a reality and because, by recognizing and accepting what already *is*, the ethical individual in faith reattains his lost unity. In the instant in which the individual consciously appropriates this unity, he transcends the state of reflection, which is merely conscious of a reality forever yet to be appropriated, and finds himself in this unity. *The certainty of self-seeking is transformed into the truth of possession in religious faith.*

We have already observed that the Christian communication of sin and the forgiveness of sin concludes the dialectical development of spirit. We may conclude from this observation that Christianity is, in Kierkegaard's view, reconciled with the modern notion of the unsurpassability of the self. To argue that the modern notion of the self and Christianity are reconciled does not mean that an agreeable stalemate has been worked out between two fundamentally irreconcilable views of reality and truth. On the contrary, their reconciliation means that the two are sublimated in a single and unified higher Christian Philosophy of Spirit. An understanding of the modern individual's pursuit of himself can no longer be confined to the province of moral philosophy, and an understanding of the doctrines of the Incarnation and Atonement can no longer be confined to the special province of theology.[3] Christianity is no longer exclusively the subject matter of theology. By this we mean that Kierkegaard's Christology is not a compartmentalized subject matter for a special intellectual discipline but becomes part of a total definition of the self. The wide distinction between moral philosophy and Christology is collapsed in the unification of the subject matter of both in a higher Christian Philosophy of Spirit.

[3] Kierkegaard's Christian communication is comprised of these two doctrines. The Incarnation communicates the consciousness of sin and the Atonement the awareness of the forgiveness of sin. Together they constitute Kierkegaard's Christology.

We have seen that the ethical requirement cannot be and is not revoked by religious faith. We have also seen that the content of Christianity, according to Kierkegaard, is the communication of sin and the forgiveness of sin and, further, that this communication serves the purpose of completing the development of spirit. What else can we conclude but that these two realities are reconciled in a Christian Philosophy of Spirit? Neither the self nor Christianity can exist apart from the other. Kierkegaard insists over and over that the two must be maintained in a dialectical union which authenticates, i.e., realizes, both. Apart from Christianity, the self remains divided against itself. And apart from ethical striving, Christianity becomes a "superstition of the most dangerous kind."[4] Only as a unity can the two exist. Ethical striving for the unification of selfhood points to a religious truth, viz., the unification of the self as accomplishable in the Deity in time. The object of ethical striving, then, becomes the truth of ethico-religious (Christian) self-understanding.

But what precisely is meant by a higher Christian Philosophy of Spirit? I mean simply that neither the modern notion of the self nor the Christian communication realizes its full reality, i.e., comes into existence, until the two are synthesized in this dialectical union of ethical striving and divine grace. The realization of the existential self requires the divine communication, on the one hand, and God exists only for faith, on the other. In Michalson's words, "faith is the appearance of God in existence, in subjectivity."[5] I refer to this synthesis as *philosophical* in nature because the dialectical development of selfhood, as it has come to be understood in modern philosophy, constitutes the framework within which the nature and purpose of human life and its religious dimension are worked out. It is a *Christian Philosophy*, not because the Christian faith dictates an under-

4 *CUP*, p. 385.

5 Carl Michalson, "Kierkegaard's Theology of Faith," *Religion in Life*, XXXII (Spring 1963), 234.

standing of the nature and purpose of the self, but because the development of the self culminates in the affirmation of the Christian communication as its truth. And I refer to it as a *higher* Christian Philosophy because the striving to overcome the alienation of God and man requires the mutual participation of both in a process which culminates in the moment of religious faith in which both come into existence. The self and God require each other in order to exist. Apart from the existential synthesis achieved in faith, both the self and God remain existentially unrealized. Moral philosophy is as incapable of realizing and understanding the self as theology is incapable of understanding Christ when the two are isolated from each other. Only when moral philosophy's exclusive concern with the self and theology's exclusive concern with Christ *qua* Christ are transcended by Kierkegaard's Christian Philosophy of Spirit's concern with both do they achieve their existential fulfillment.

The use of the term Christian Philosophy immediately raises difficulties and, in Kierkegaard's case, doubly so. In the first place, Kierkegaard never refers to his thought as a philosophy. For that matter, he never refers to it as a theology either. His strong reaction to both academic philosophy and theology propelled him out of academia and into *living* itself, and Kierkegaard seems content simply to describe what he finds, on the one hand, and to throw down a challenge to the individual to follow him in his own way, on the other. Perhaps we should be willing to settle for this and not insist on labeling his thought when he himself refused to do so. But the price of such an option is high, for it requires nothing less than the abandonment of the effort to understand Kierkegaard's *understanding*. And it does not seem to me that we should apologize either to Kierkegaard or to any radical Kierkegaardian for attempting to understand what he is saying.

I have described his pseudonymous thought as philosophical for three reasons. The first reason has already been mentioned. The notion of the self in modern philosophy is the controlling principle in Kierkegaard's pseudonymous thought. He does not merely use the concept in the interest of another theological idea or position because he actually accepts modern philosophy's contention of the unsurpassability of the self. The second reason for considering this position as philosophical is Kierkegaard's adoption of the reflexive method of the analysis of consciousness as his own. And the third reason is that if we define theology as "participation in and reflection upon religious faith," there can be no theological reflection apart from participation in faith. Existence in faith provides the individual for the first time with the experience necessary for Christian theological reflection. Kierkegaard's reflexive analysis of consciousness is barren of religious faith up to the point of its affirmation of the Christian communication as its truth.

Now I have called his philosophy a Christian Philosophy. What justification can there be for combining two terms which Kierkegaard seems so intent on holding apart? By this term I simply mean that Kierkegaard has transcended the distinction between philosophy, which has as its subject matter the purely human self, and theology, which has as part of its subject matter the nature of Christ. Kierkegaard is arguing that neither the self nor Christ is properly understandable apart from the other. He then combines the subject matter of these two disciplines in the description of what it means to become a self and in so doing transcends the gap separating these two disciplines of thought. I do not mean to imply, however, that his Christian Philosophy can be abstracted from existence and promulgated as the truth apart from the reality of the existing individual. Kierkegaard maintains a strict and undeviating commitment to the existential nature of truth. Therefore, this Christian Philosophy is true for the individual only insofar as it is the concrete and realized mode of self-understanding of an existing individual.

Bibliography

PRIMARY SOURCES

Extensive quoting from *E/O*, *CD*, and *SUD* is made possible by the permission of Princeton University Press, from *CUP* by Princeton University Press and The American-Scandinavian Foundation, from *SKJP* by Indiana University Press, and from *SKJ* by Alexander Dru.

Kierkegaard, Søren. *Concluding Unscientific Postscript.* Translated by David Swenson and Walter Lowrie. Princeton: Princeton University Press, 1941.

———. *De Omnibus Dubitandum Est.* Translated with an assessment by T. H. Croxall. Stanford: Stanford University Press, 1958.

———. *Edifying Discourses,* 4 vols. Translated by David Swenson and Lillian Swenson. Minneapolis: Augsburg Publishing House, 1943-1962.

———. *Either/Or.* Vol. I translated by David F. Swenson and Lillian M. Swenson. Vol. II translated by Walter Lowrie. Princeton: Princeton University Press, 1959.

———. *Fear and Trembling.* Translated with an introduction and notes by Walter Lowrie. Princeton: Princeton University Press, 1954.

———. *Papirer.* Edited by P. A. Heiberg, V. Kuhr, and E. Torsting. 20 vols. Copenhagen: Gyldendal, 1909-1948.

———. *Philosophical Fragments.* David Swenson translation revised and Niels Thulstrup commentary and notes translated by Howard V. Hong. 2nd ed. rev. Princeton: Princeton University Press, 1962.

————. *Repetition.* Translated with an introduction and notes by Walter Lowrie. London: Oxford University Press, 1941.

————. *Samlede Vaerker.* Edited by A. B. Drachmann, J. L. Heiberg, and H. O. Lange. 3rd ed. 20 vols. Copenhagen: Gyldendal, 1962-1964.

————. *Søren Kierkegaard's Journals and Papers.* Translated and edited by Howard V. Hong and Edna H. Hong. 2 vols. Bloomington: Indiana University Press, 1967-1970.

————. *Stages on Life's Way.* Translated with an introduction by Walter Lowrie. Princeton: Princeton University Press, 1940.

————. *The Concept of Dread.* Translated with an introduction and notes by Walter Lowrie. Princeton: Princeton University Press, 1957.

————. *The Journals of Søren Kierkegaard.* Translated and edited by Alexander Dru. New York: Oxford University Press, 1938.

————. *The Sickness Unto Death.* Translated with an introduction and notes by Walter Lowrie. Princeton: Princeton University Press, 1954.

SECONDARY SOURCES

Allison, Henry E. "Kierkegaard's Dialectic of Religious Consciousness." *Union Seminary Quarterly Review.* XX (March, 1965), 225-233.

Anz, Wilhelm. *Kierkegaard und der deutsche Idealismus.* Tübingen: Mohr, 1956.

Arbaugh, George E. and George B. *Kierkegaard's Authorship.* London: George Allen and Unwin, 1968.

Blass, Josef L. *Die Krise der Freiheit im Denken Søren Kierkegaard.* Duesseldorf: A. Henn, 1968.

Bohlin, Torsten. *Kierkegaards dogmatische Anschauung in ihren geschichtlichen Zusammenhange.* Aus dem

Schwedischen von Ilse Meyer-Lune. Gutersloh: C. Bertelsmann, 1927.

Brookfield, Christopher M. "What Was Kierkegaard's Task? A Frontier To Be Explored." *Union Seminary Quarterly Review.* XVIII, no. 1 (1961), 18-23.

Collins, James. *The Mind of Kierkegaard.* Chicago: Henry Regnery Company, 1953.

Copp, John D. "The Concept of Soul in Kierkegaard and Freud." Unpublished Ph.D. dissertation, Boston University, 1953.

Crites, Stephen D. *In the Twilight of Christendom.* Chambersburg, Pennsylvania: American Academy of Religion, 1972.

———. "The Author and the Authorship: Recent Kierkegaard Literature." *Journal of the American Academy of Religion,* XXXVIII (1970), 37-54.

Croxall, T. H. *Kierkegaard Commentary.* London: J. Nisbet, 1956.

———. *Kierkegaard Studies.* London: Lutterworth Press, 1948.

Cumming, Robert. "Existence and Communication." *International Journal of Ethics,* LXV, no. 1 (1954-1955), 79-98.

Dewey, Bradley R. *The New Obedience: Kierkegaard on Imitating Christ.* Washington: Corpus Books, 1968.

Diamond, Malcolm L. "Faith and Its Tensions: A Criticism of Religious Existentialism." *Judaism,* XIII, no. 3 (Summer, 1964), 317-327.

Diem, Hermann. *Kierkegaard: An Introduction.* Translated by David Green. Richmond: John Knox Press, 1966.

———. *Kierkegaard's Dialectic of Existence.* Translated by Harold Knight. Edinburgh: Oliver and Boyd, 1959.

Dupre, Louis K. *Kierkegaard as Theologian: The Dialectic of Christian Existence.* New York: Sheed and Ward, 1963.

————. "The Constitution of the Self in Kierkegaard's Philosophy." *International Philosophical Quarterly*, III (1963), 506-526.

Edwards, C. N. "Guilt in the Thought of Søren Kierkegaard." *Encounter*, XXVII (Spring, 1966), 141-157.

Fahrenbach, Helmut. *Die Gegenwartige Kierkegaard-Auslegung in der deutschsprachigen Literature von 1948 bis 1962*. Tübingen: J. C. B. Mohr, 1962.

————. *Kierkegaards existenzdialektische Ethik*. Frankfurt: V. Klostermann, 1968.

Findlay, J. N. *The Philosophy of Hegel*. New York: Collier Books, 1966.

Fremond, Hans. *Existenz in Liebe nach Søren Kierkegaard*. Munchen: Anton Pustet, 1965.

Garelick, Herbert. *The Anti-Christianity of Kierkegaard*. The Hague: Martinus Nijhoff, 1965.

Geismar, Eduard O. *Lectures on the Religious Thought of Søren Kierkegaard*. Introduction by David Swenson. Minneapolis: Augsburg Publishing House, 1937.

Gill, Jerry H., ed. *Essays on Kierkegaard*, Minneapolis: Burgess Publishing Company, 1969.

Grene, Marjorie. *Dreadful Freedom: A Critique of Existentialism*. Chicago: University of Chicago Press, 1948.

Haecker, Theodore. *Kierkegaard the Cripple*. Translated by C. Van O. Bruyn with an introduction by Alexander Dru. New York: Philosophical Library, 1950.

————. *Søren Kierkegaard*. Translated by Alexander Dru. London: Oxford University Press, 1937.

Halevi, J. L. "Kierkegaard's Teleological Suspension of the Ethical: Is It Jewish?" *Judaism*, VIII, no. 4 (Fall, 1959), 291-302.

Hamilton, Kenneth. *The Promise of Kierkegaard*. Philadelphia: Lippincott, 1969.

Hartt, J. N. "Christian Freedom Reconsidered: The Case of Kierkegaard." *Harvard Theological Review*, LX, no. 2 (April, 1967), 133-144.

Hegel, G. F. W. *The Logic.* Translated with an introduction by William Wallace. 2nd ed. rev. New York: Oxford University Press, 1965.

————. *The Phenomenology of Mind.* Translated by John B. Bailey. New York: Harper and Row, Publishers, 1967.

Heidegger, Martin. *Being and Time.* Translated by John Macquarrie and Edward Robinson. New York: Harper and Row, Publishers, 1962.

————. "The Onto-Theo-Logical Constitution of Metaphysics." *Identity and Difference.* Translated with an introduction by Joan Stambaugh. New York: Harper and Row, Publishers, 1969.

Heinecken, Martin J. *The Moment Before God.* Philadelphia: Muhlenberg Press, 1956.

Henriksen, Aage. *Methods and Results of Kierkegaard Studies in Scandinavia: A Historical and Critical Survey.* Copenhagen: E. Munksgaard, 1951.

Himmelstrup, Jens. *Søren Kierkegaard: International Bibliography.* Copenhagen: Nyt Nordisk Forlag, 1962.

Hirsch, Emmanuel. *Kierkegaard-Studien.* 2 vols. Gutersloh: C. Bertelsmann, 1930-1933.

Holm, Søren. *Søren Kierkegaards Geschichtsphilosophie.* Stuttgart: W. Kohlhammer, 1956.

Holmer, Paul. "Kierkegaard and Religious Propositions." *Journal of Religion,* XXXV, no. 3 (July, 1955), 135-146.

————. "Kierkegaard and Theology." *Union Seminary Quarterly Review.* (March, 1957), 23-31.

Horn, Robert L. "On Understanding Kierkegaard's Understanding." *Union Seminary Quarterly Review,* XX, no. 3 (March, 1966), 341-345.

————. "Positivity and Dialectic: A Study of the Theological Method of Hans Lassen Martensen." Unpublished Th.D. dissertation, Union Theological Seminary in New York, 1969.

Jaspers, Karl. *Reason and Existence*. Translated with an introduction by William Earle. New York: Noonday Press, 1955.

Johnson, Howard A., and Thulstrup, Niels, eds. *A Kierkegaard Critique*. (Gateway Edition) Chicago: Henry Regnery Company, 1967.

Johnson, Ralph Henry. *The Concept of Existence in "Concluding Unscientific Postscript."* The Hague: Martinus Nijhoff, 1972.

Jolivet, Regis. *Introduction to Kierkegaard*. Translated by W. H. Barber. London: Frederick Muller, 1950.

Kaufmann, Walter. *Hegel*. New York: Doubleday, 1965.

Kierkegaardiana. Copenhagen: Munksgaard, 1955.

Kierkegaard Symposion. Copenhagen: Munksgaard, 1955.

Loning, Per. "Kierkegaard's 'Paradox.'" *Kierkegaardiana*. Copenhagen: Munksgaard, 1955.

Lowrie, Walter. *Kierkegaard*. London: Oxford University Press, 1938.

Mackey, Louis. *Kierkegaard: A Kind of Poet*. Philadelphia, Pennsylvania: University of Pennsylvania Press, 1972.

Malantschuk, Gregor. *Kierkegaard's Way to Truth*. Translated by Mary Michelsen. Minneapolis: Augsburg Publishing House, 1963.

———. *Kierkegaard's Thought*. Edited and translated by Howard V. Hong and Edna H. Hong. Princeton, New Jersey: Princeton University Press, 1971.

Martin, Harold V. *The Wings of Faith*. New York: Philosophical Library, 1951.

Michalson, Carl. "Kierkegaard's Theology of Faith." *Religion in Life*, XXXII (Spring, 1963), 225-237.

Miller, Libuse. *In Search of the Self*. Philadelphia: Muhlenberg Press, 1961.

Novak, Michael. *The Experience of Nothingness*. New York: Harper and Row, Publishers, 1970.

Perkins, Robert L. *Søren Kierkegaard*. Richmond: John Knox Press, 1969.

Price, George. *The Narrow Pass*. New York: McGraw-Hill, 1963.

Rehm, Walther. *Kierkegaard und der Verfuhrer*. Munchen: H. Rinn, 1949.

Rhode, Peter P. *Søren Kierkegaard*. Translated with a foreword by Alan Moray Williams. New York: Humanities Press, 1963.

Roberts, David. *Existentialism and Religious Belief*. New York: Oxford University Press, 1957.

————. "Faith and Freedom in Existentialism: A Study of Kierkegaard and Sartre." *Theology Today*. (January, 1952), 469-482.

————. "Kierkegaard on Truth and Subjectivity." *Journal of Religious Thought*, XVIII, no. 1 (1961), 41-56.

Ruggiero, Guido de. *Existentialism: Disintegration of Man's Soul*. New York: Social Science Publishers, 1948.

Sartre, Jean-Paul. "Existentialism Is a Humanism." *Existentialism from Dostoevsky to Sartre*. Edited by Walter Kaufmann. (Meridian Books) New York: The World Publishing Company, 1968.

Schaefer, Klaus. *Hermeneutische Ontologie in den Climacus-Schriften Søren Kierkegaards*. Munchen: Kosel-Verlag, 1968.

Schrag, Calvin. *Kierkegaard and Heidegger: The Ontology of Human Finitude*. Chicago: Northwestern University Press, 1961.

Schulz, Walter. *Die Vollendung des deutschen Idealismus in der Spatphilosophie Schellings*. Stuttgart: W. Kohlhammer, 1955.

————. "Existenz und System bei Søren Kierkegaard." Hrsq. von Klaus Ziegler. *Wesen und Wirklichkeit des Menschen*. Göttingen: Vandenhoeck und Ruprecht, 1957, pp. 107-128.

Shestov, Lev. *Kierkegaard and the Existentialist Philosophy*. Translated by Elinor Hewitt. Athens: Ohio University Press, 1969.

Shmueli, Adi. *Kierkegaard and Consciousness.* Translated by Naomi Handelman. Princeton, New Jersey: Princeton University Press, 1971.

Sløk, Johannes. "Das existenzphilosophische Motiv im Denken von Kierkegaard." *Studia Theologica,* IX (1956), 116-130.

————. *Die Anthropologie Kierkegaards.* Copenhagen: Gyldendal, 1954.

Smit, Harvey. *Kierkegaard's Pilgrimmage of Man.* Grand Rapids: William B. Eerdmans Publishing Company, 1965.

Smith, J. Weldon, III. "Religion A and Religion B: A Kierkegaard Study." *Scottish Journal of Theology,* XV (March, 1962), 245-265.

Sponheim, Paul R. *Kierkegaard on Christ and Christian Coherence.* New York: Harper and Row, Publishers, 1968.

Thomas, John H. *Subjectivity and Paradox.* Oxford: B. Blackwell, 1957.

Thompson, Josiah. *Kierkegaard.* New York: Alfred J. Knopf, 1973.

————. *Kierkegaard: A Collection of Critical Essays.* (Anchor Book Edition) Garden City, New York: Doubleday, 1972.

————. *The Lonely Labyrinth: Kierkegaard's Pseudonymous Works.* Foreword by George K. Plochmann. Carbondale: Southern Illinois Press, 1967.

Thomte, Reider. *Kierkegaard's Philosophy of Religion.* Princeton: Princeton University Press, 1948.

Thulstrup, Niels. *Kierkegaards Forhold til Hegel og til den spekulative Idealisme indtil 1846.* Copenhagen: Gyldendal, 1967.

Tillich, Paul. *Systematic Theology,* 3 vols. Chicago: The University of Chicago Press, 1951-1963.

Tweedie, Donald. "The Concept of Anxiety in Kierkegaard and Heidegger." Unpublished Ph.D. dissertation, Boston University Press, 1957.

Ussher, Arland. *Journey Through Dread: A Study of Kierkegaard, Heidegger, and Sartre.* New York: Biblo and Tannes, 1968.

Wahl, Jean. A. *Études Kierkegaardiennes.* 2nd ed. Paris: J. Vrin, 1949.

————. "Freedom and Existence in Some Recent Philosophies." *Philosophy and Phenomenological Research,* VIII, no. 4 (June, 1948), 538-557.

Warnock, Mary. *Existentialist Ethics.* London: Macmillan, 1967.

Weiland, J. Sperna. *Philosophy of Existence and Christianity.* Gorcum and Co., 1951.

Widenman, Robert. "Kierkegaard's Terminology—and English." *Kierkegaardiana,* VII. Copenhagen: Munksgaard, 1968, pp. 113-130.

Wild, John D. "Kierkegaard and Contemporary Existentialist Philosophy." *Anglican Theological Review.* (January, 1956), 15-32.

Wyschogrod, Michael. *Kierkegaard and Heidegger: The Ontology of Existence.* New York: Humanities Press, 1954.

Index

action, 78n, 105
actuality, 62, 69
Aristotle, 89n
Augustine, St., 5
authority, 158, 160, 162, 163

Barth, Karl, 154n
body, 37

choice, 126, 131-40, 144f, 148, 169,
    181f, 183f, 186f, 195n, 198,
    250f; and God, 157-59, 165
consciousness, 76n, 80-82, 95, 97,
    142n, 185, 224; and time, 67;
    Hegel, 44f; humorous, 193;
    Kierkegaard, 47, 49-53; of guilt,
    178; of sin, 224; of suffering,
    167f
conversion, 194n

Deity in time, 226f
Descartes, René, 79n
despair, 57, 59, 84, 85n, 97n, 98,
    127-29, 135n
dread, 84, 85n, 97n
duty, 57, 117f, 159n, 163, 164f,
    220

epistemology, 200
eternal, 66, 67-69, 203-08
ethical task, 161, 206, 210f, 219,
    223, 225, 241, 242, 251
ethics, 24-25, 57f, 69, 117, 121f,
    201, 221; and ontology, 118f,
    125; suspension of, 217-19, 222,

232, 245; two definitions of,
    114, 122n, 124f
existence, 20-22, 55, 98, 200, 240f,
    245; aesthetic stage of, 127-31;
    and self, 111-13; Christian, 222;
    ethical stage of, 198f; ethico-
    religious stage of, 124n, 142;
    stages of, 3-5, 93f, 111

facticity, 33f, 48, 55, 68, 120, 121,
    131, 139, 183, 198, 244
Fahrenbach, Helmut, 6, 27, 112n,
    219n
faith, 206, 208-13, 223n, 225, 231-
    35, 242f, 244, 254-56; and rea-
    son, 246
Fichte, Johann Gottlieb, 49, 79n,
    255n
finite, 33, 145, 146f
freedom, 59-63, 74-76, 92n, 183f,
    186, 191, 193f, 198, 200, 224; and
    choice, 133-34; and time, 67
future, 67, 206

God, 70n, 153-66; and self, 156f;
    and self-knowledge, 156
guilt, 58, 82, 166, 174-91, 192, 199,
    215, 217, 225

happiness, 144n, 162, 169f, 192,
    209, 211, 223, 241, 243
Hegel, G.W.F., 43-45, 49, 70n,
    89n
Heidegger, Martin, 61, 70n, 154
humanism, 166
humor, 191f, 193, 215

spirit, 30f, 39, 41-43, 72f, 77, 82,
106, 147, 228, 245; as consciousness, 40f, 49f, 53, 60; as eternal,
66; as freedom, 42, 54, 60; development of, 93, 94-98, 126,
160, 164, 165f, 173, 191, 200, 203,
207, 214f, 232, 242, 246f
subjectivity, 99
suffering, 58, 81, 167-73, 185, 199,
215

temporality, 65, 93

Tertullian, 237
time, 65-69, 93, 104, 128, 137-39,
152f, 181f, 183, 198, 204, 229f,
242
transcendence, 63

understanding, 77n, 78f
unity, 85-89, 91f, 99-107, 188, 200,
201, 231f, 255f

will, 80-82
Wyschogrod, Michael, 7f

Library of Congress Cataloging in Publication Data

Elrod, John W   1940-
    Being and existence in Kierkegaard's pseudonymous
works.

    Bibliography: p.
    Includes index.
    1. Kierkegaard, Søren Aabye, 1813-1855—Ontology.
I. Title.
B4378.O5E44   111   74-25615
ISBN 0-691-07204-3